Brick by Brick

Democratising Local Governance in Kerala
Insights from the People's Planning Campaign

Brick by Brick

Democratising Local Governance in Kerala

Insights from the People's Planning Campaign

Manjula Bharathy

Published on behalf of

KILA

GIFT GULATI INSTITUTE OF FINANCE AND TAXATION

Concept Since 1974

Series Editors

K.N. Harilal, K.J. Joseph and Joy Elamon

Book Design
Godfrey's Graphics

ISBN: 978-93-5439-780-6

First Published 2022

Published and Printed by

Concept Since 1974

Concept Publishing Company Pvt. Ltd.
A/15-16, Commercial Block, Mohan Garden,
New Delhi-110059 (INDIA)
T: +91 11 41101460
E: publishing@conceptpub.com; *W*: www.conceptpub.com

Cataloging in Publication Data--Courtesy: D.K. Agencies (P) Ltd. <docinfo@dkagencies.com>

Bharathy, Manjula, author.
Brick by brick : democratising local governance in Kerala : insights from the people's planning campaign/ Manjula Bharathy.
pages cm
Includes bibliographical references and index.
ISBN 9789354397806

1. Decentralization in government--India--Kerala. 2. Local government--India--Kerala. 3. Kerala (India)--Politics and government. I. Kerala Institute of Local Administration, issuing body. II. Gulati Institute of Finance and Taxation (Trivandrum, India), issuing body. III. Title.

LCC JS7025.K43B43 2022 | DDC 320.8095483 23

Dedicated to

The Love within & with me

That holds me

Anchors me

Breathes life into me

To make this Life just ordinarily beautiful

Foreword by
TM Thomas Isaac

Democratic decentralization is to widen and deepen the democratic system which is confined to the central and state levels to the grassroot level; to go beyond representation towards direct participation of people. It requires that message and awareness go beyond the administrative structures to reach the ordinary citizens. Politics of production, distribution, and circulation of information impact the process of participation, an important condition for the success of any form of decentralization of power – de-concentration, delegation, or devolution. In democratic decentralization, ordinary citizens are expected to actively participate in the devolution process.

The communication programme of PPC had three components: Training, environment creation and review. The training component has been largely top-down in nature with cascading level of training of around 500 key resource persons at state level, 10000 district resource persons and 100000 local resource persons. Every phase of PPC was preceded by around of training, six in all. Participatory methods were consciously incorporated to the extent possible and there were also fully participatory peer group training by local governments with best practices. This training program was largely successful in that the thousand and more local governments in Kerala have been preparing their own local plans, whatever be their limitations, with visible successful outcomes. The PPC is definitely the largest non-formal education campaign, perhaps in the country itself.

The reviews were bottom-up process based upon its feedback programmes and orders were modified. This iterative and learning by doing process was a very important aspect of PPC. Besides in the two-way vertical communication process in both training and review processes PPC also had two-way horizontal communication in the local level grama sabhas, development seminars and other fora of PPC.

Through linking decentralised planning with budgeting to eradicate poverty, mitigate inequalities, and empower the historically disadvantaged citizens, the People's Planning Campaign (PPC) sought to capitalize on local knowledge while using participatory decision-making as a means to change attitudes and behaviors associated with sexist, class-based, caste and ethnic prejudices that impede the egalitarian civic culture in Kerala. At the outset, tensions existed between respect for local knowledge and efforts to transform beliefs that sustain gender, class, caste, and ethnic hierarchies.

In this volume Manjula Bharathy has taken up two programmes, Women Component Plan (WCP) and Tribal Sub plan (TSP), and critically analyses the reasons for their poor performances in the initial years of PPC and traces the interventions made to address the inadequacies. All local governments were supposed to earmark ten percent of the plan funds for WCP and to include the gender impact statement in all the project proposals, but very few did. Even the projects that included the WCP, in effect, turned out to be general projects with little consideration for the strategic gender needs of women empowerment. However, interventions of agencies like elected women representatives and women neighbourhood groups under Kudumbashree made significant improvement in the gender programme of PPC.

In contrast, though PPC attempted to modify the design of TSP by insisting on decision-making through village assemblies and introduced social animators from among the tribal population, there was no visible change in the implementation of programmes under TSP. It was expected that the participation of the tribal people in the planning process would enable to break the vicious circle of underdevelopment among tribal population. But the tribal animators got fascinated by bureaucracy and the local governments failed to give sufficient attention to the community needs. The projects were stereotyped; many of them were not implemented resulting in the lapse of funds. Attempts to rectify the situation failed. Prof. Bharathy in this book succinctly documents the relative success of WCP and the failure of TSP with case studies of two panchayats—Ulloor and Panamaram.

The contrasting experience of the two sectors is the result of a complex set of factors related to history, sociology, attitudes of hegemonic groups and, the communication strategy. On the basis of review of the first year's experience, special decentralised sectoral training programmes were adopted. For gender, it included continuous and participatory training of women elected representatives, participatory review of WCP, and extensive horizontal and vertical dialogues within the women neighbourhood groups resulting in better outcomes.

The tribal representatives were a small minority, except in a few panchayats, to give effective voice to the tribal needs. Special review meetings and orientation programmes for social animators and department officials failed to produce the desired results, partly due to the dysfunctional nature of the training programmes. However, the most important factor was the failure to reach out the tribal collectives and generate a new consciousness. Unfortunately, the tribal population by and large remained alienated from the planning process.

The above situation brings us to a major weakness of the decentralised communication strategy of PPC with respect to the 'environment creation'. The very attempt to organize the technical process of planning as a social mobilization process was precisely to take the message to people and create the right environment for a break from the past. The role of media in decentralised planning is to function as a facilitating force for dialogic participation by providing a meeting ground for information exchange, public awareness, and stakeholder dialogues. The extent to which people participate in activities around them depends upon their knowledge of the issues at stake and an understanding of how these issues affect their lives and livelihoods. Media was expected to conscientise people through information dissemination, create an environment for the new development culture, relate with people to help them plan and organise the developmental activities of PPC, and capacitate people through forward and backward communication linkages.

But in PPC, the key failure was the absence of a clear media strategy. The folk media was effectively used but its reach was limited. But for certain initiatives in Doordarshan and videos produced by C-DIT for training purposes, PPC neglected the electronic media. The focus was on print media, which after initial support, adopted an adversarial role. The media generated so much background noise in the later years that the message of the Campaign was lost. Prof. Bharathy in this book has gone into a detailed content analysis of major newspapers to document the shift in the media stance towards PPC. It is an important argument of the book that the absence of a focused and clear media strategy was a factor that limited the participation, the essence of democratic decentralization.

This is indeed an important insight gained because declining participation continues to be a major weakness of the democratic decentralization experiment. Many urge a new campaign—similar to PPC, conducted 25 years ago— focusing on watershed based planning and disaster management is the need of the hour. But the media situation in Kerala has become even more commercialised and manipulative. At the same time social media has rapidly expanded. The challenges to draw a media strategy have grown manifold, the book underlines that this is a challenge that has got to be faced for going forward.

Foreword by
Series Editors

We are in the Silver Jubilee year of the People's Campaign for Participatory Planning in Kerala. It is now widely recognized as the most enduring as well as one of the most successful experiments of its kind in the world. Even the much-celebrated governance experiments in different parts of the world, like the famous Participatory Budgeting (PB) of Brazil in Porto Alegre, have dried out or discontinued. Scholars identify multiple reasons for the success of the Kerala experiment, including the legacy of the larger democratic movement in the state, which the people's campaign had sought to take forward. In our opinion the single most reason for the success of the people's planning in the state has been the commitment to democracy not only for its intrinsic value but also for its obvious instrumental importance. The people's plan, no doubt had several other important goals, such as development of local infrastructure, enhancing efficiency in service delivery, improving local production and distribution, ensuring environmental harmony, extending social justice, augmenting welfare, and many more. But the over-arching goal has been deepening democracy. People's planning widened the scope for collective action. It is this extensive scope for citizen's participation and collective action, which worked as an inbuilt mechanism of self-learning and rectification from within, that made the Kerala experiment successful as well as enduring.

The epochal intervention would not have been possible without the inspiring guidance of E M S Namboodiripad. The programme took off at the instance of Chief Minister, E K Nayanar and the Minister for Local Administration Paloli Mohammed Kutty with the active involvement of Kerala State Planning Board led by I. S. Gulati. It was declared that 35 to 40 percent of the ninth plan would be devolved to the local plans prepared and implemented from below. However, the key constraint was the widely prevalent capacity deficit for designing and implementing development projects/programmes at the local level. The answer to the issue, which made decentralized development in Kerala a unique experience, was the People's Planning Campaign (PPC) spearheaded by the Members of the State Planning Board T M Thomas Isaac and E M Sreedharan. The campaign aimed at a reorientation towards decentralized development along with the building of needed capacity to design and implement such a development strategy. This has been accomplished by harnessing the capabilities of different stakeholders that include but not limited to scholars of eminence, the elected representatives, officials in the various departments and the expertise of the non-officials and mass organizations.

People's planning generates informed deliberations involving people at all levels. Moreover, it has attracted large number of scholars from within as well as outside the state undertaking insightful studies on various aspects. This incessant process of learning from the experience of doing, especially self-critiquing, helped correcting the mistakes and strengthening the virtues. Undoubtedly the people and the local governments have evolved many successful development models. It is important to follow up such good work by undertaking research so that the lessons to be learnt are picked up and added to the body of existing knowledge in the relevant discipline. It is highly encouraging to note there has been a number of Ph D dissertations that analysed the Keralas People's Planning Campaign as well as the decentralization process and its outcome. This book series, jointly published by KILA and GIFT, as part of the 25th year celebration of People's Planning Campaign aims at highlighting the achievements and limitation of Kerala's decentralized development strategy. The series comprises mostly of Ph D dissertations that analysed the decentralized development. Our aim is to ensure that the continuity of 'doing and learning and doing' is sustained well.

This volume by Professor Manjula Bharathy presents a detailed analysis of women component plan, tribal sub plan, and media plan and highlights their achievements and limits. The focus on women and adivasi or scheduled tribes enable Professor Manjula to address the developmental issues of certain sections of Kerala society that remained as the out layers of development process. Especially commendable has been the analysis of the process of information dissemination to varied and heterogenous stake holders that include but not limited to elected representatives, bureaucrats, policymakers, and citizens engaged in the People's Plan Campaign. The scholarly analysis of these important issues makes this volume a must read for not only for the planners and policy makers but the academia and public at large.

K N Harilal, K J Joseph, Joy Elamon

Preface

Nothing is static. Everything changes, even the status of subordination, is what we would like to think and believe. But the tragedy of subordination in the time of neoliberal governance is it goes deeper and deeper into its inner spaces where it exists as a non-entity; appears as the invisible; heard as the inaudible; portrayed as an illusion; debated as a non-issue, and thought of as oblivion. However, the developmental turn in political governance has introduced a suite of new perspectives, theoretical approaches, and analytical techniques to the discourses on sustainable and rights-based ways of living that speak of inclusive and democratic governance structures, enabling history to be re-read through the lens of the subaltern.

The negotiation of everyday caste-ethnic-based and sexist violence enables some to question the existing history and begin to write new accounts that contest the powerful voices that silenced them in the past. Subaltern bodies, the sites of vulnerability and marginalization, are also the sites of resistance. Their struggle to rewrite history includes their claims to participate in the political spaces. Decentralised governance is commonly defended on the grounds that it will bring the government closer to the people and create political structures that are more transparent and accountable to the poor and marginal groups in society. Reservation policy that mandates proportional representation in governance is one step toward the establishment of inclusive political spaces.

The 9th plan of the state of Kerala, India (1996-2001), conceived as a vehicle for deepening democracy, was a unique experiment introduced by the Left Democratic Front—a coalition of the Left parties led by the Communist Party of India (Marxist)—that attempted to transform decentralization from an exercise in administrative reform to the use of planning processes as instruments of political mobilization. In contrast to technocratic and neoliberal prescriptions that de-politicize poverty by characterizing it as a technically manageable problem best left to administrative experts or market mechanisms, the People's Planning Campaign (PPC), with the motto "power to people," conceptualized poverty in relation to a host of growing inequalities, such as economic dispossession and political marginalization. Kerala's participatory planning accredited ways of seeing and forms of knowing, grounded in local experiences that emerge in reflexive reasoning and dialectical engagement with citizens, instead of placing faith in either rational comprehensive decision-making or incremental institution building, championed by public administration and managerial sciences.

This book engages with the critical analysis of three important components of the PPC: Women Component Plan, Tribal Sub Plan, and Media Plan. While the first two tried to address the developmental issues of the most marginalized citizens in Kerala-- women and the Adivasi or Scheduled Tribes-- the third one attempted to understand the flow of information dissemination to multiple and heterogeneous stakeholders, deploying both vertical and horizontal communication between and among elected representatives, bureaucrats, policymakers, and citizens.

Through a detailed examination of the processes of mobilization and conscientization targeting these groups, this volume assesses the possibilities and limitations of planning processes devised to politicize and redress the grievances of the dispossessed. As my analysis of the complex effects of the PPC for women and Adivasi indicates, the depiction of PPC as a counter-hegemonic project does not tell the whole story. Although the planning process was designed to challenge the power structures in socio-economic spheres, certain aspects of the implementation process reinforced the political and social hierarchies.

Kerala's experience with the PPC demonstrates that the mobilization of civil society presupposes institutional frameworks, both formal and informal, that can be put into place through the strong agency of the state. As John Harris (2004) has argued, it is not social capital alone but the interplay of civil society, social capital, voluntary and mass organisations, and a strong state with a development agenda that sets the rules for a new vision of development. Yet, as my analysis documents, the new vision of development may replicate imperial logics that could threaten indigenous existence.

This book is a collective effort. My special mention goes to the tribals of Wayanadu and members of SHGs in Ulloor, the focus of my study in two chapters, who cooperated with me in making my study participatory. Recording their involvement was necessary to understand the process of the study itself. The elected representatives and people of the panchayats I studied in Kerala cooperated with me and supported me at every stage. I am thankful to the officials and NGOs who gave valuable information on the PPC. They helped me to understand decentralised governance deeper.

Prof. T. M. Thomas Isaac gave a clear vision of the approach of the Study. Though the findings of the study, to a great extent, exposed the fissures in the PPC, Prof. Isaac, the architect of the PPC, was articulate and honest to keep his political stance off my academic study. This book evolved from my Ph.D. thesis, which I did under the guidance of Prof. Isaac.

I am grateful to Mr. J. Rajasekharan Nair, my strength and support, for editing the text and helping to structure the book.

I don't know how to acknowledge the love my little kid Aamy has showered on me; her effervescent presence and love gave me the strength to overcome the fatigue of hard work. I have no words to describe the care and concern my husband gave me. As always, he was there for me, who picked me up when I needed it and kept my foot on the ground when I deserved it.

And my Mother, whose blessings makes the impossible possible for me.

I hope the study has done justice to the collective endeavour. Any mistake is mine.

Manjula Bharathy

Contents

Tables

Figures

Charts

Chapter 1

The Power Matters

In the beginning is the Power.

Power is the result of the convergence of forces, causing a centre-marginal relationship between those who wield power and those on whom power is exerted. If it was a social contract that created the State, it means the individuals who lived in the world of idyllic happiness had surrendered a part of their individual power to create the collective power, the State, with the specific objective to protect the society from a few recalcitrant people who were disturbing their idyllic happiness. A more logical approach would trace the genesis of the State and power to the tribal headman. As wealth became collateral to power, the headman- ship evolved into monarchy, giving rise to the Theory of Divine Origin and the unquestionable inheritance of power.

Since power converges, it obviously diverges when it cascades, creating varying shades of power until it trickles down to the outer linings of the periphery, where power is felt only as something imposed upon. The power-haves and have-nots existed even in the Grecian republics that saw the emergence and eclipse of direct democracy.

The nature of power is that it cannot but create a counter-power centre, one challenging the other. It is this nature of power that saw the emergence of the papacy to counter the power of the monarchy. While the king checkmated the Pope, elsewhere, a king had to sign the Magna Carta, and in France, the power of people guillotined the power of the king and declared liberty from power, the newly discovered power of the people, little realising that the very same guillotine, which they had used to end the tyranny of power, would create the Reign of Terror.

Representative Democracy is built on the premise of people's power. Over the period, democracy matured to include each and every individual in its power structure. But this maturing also witnessed the erosion of the essence of democracy, the power of the people. At a certain juncture in the history, democracy was appropriated by a dictator, who used the democratic tools to build a Fascist State, and for whom power meant both the means and the end. Democracy lost its shape because too many heads chose to wear it. Finally, with capitalism exploiting the fissures in democracy and redefining democracy, to suit the interests of an economically powerful minority, the supposedly government of the people, by the people, and for the people turned out to be one of a few, by a few, and for a few.

Communism emerged from the shrill voices of the exploited majority, the *de-jure* wielders of power, who were pushed to the periphery by the *de-facto* power centres. It was, therefore, natural for Communism to negate the apparatus of State power. The bloom of Communism, when the State would wither away, is the humane vision of a State without power, where a socially conscientised individual would contribute to the national pool her/his share, according to her/his ability, and draw from the pool her/his share, according to her/his need. Communism prescribed socialism and centralised planning as the ad hoc mechanism for welfare of the citizens and doctored even their thoughts to enable Communism to happen and the State to wither away. But instead of the State withering away, Communism withered away, after their leaders had metamorphosed into leviathans, leaving behind dreadful memories of the brute force of the State power. Once again, capitalism drew blood from the dead, redefined democracy as neo-liberalism in a global economy, and ensured the capitalists rule the world, wielding the absolute power in economics and politics.

Today, there is a growing consensus that the government should be decentralised with multiple layers of freedom, and this approach has learnt a lot from Gandhiji, who envisioned the Grama Swaraj. Decentralisation and participation of people in the planning process, devolution of power to the Panchayati Raj Institutions (PRIs) revitalised through the 73rd and 74th Constitutional Amendments, giving constitutional status to the local bodies, and making the elections to the PRIs mandatory are important landmarks in the socio- economic and political history of India.

People's Plan, launched by the Government of Kerala on 17th August, 1996, based on decentralisation and restructuring of local self-governments with 35- 40% of State plan fund devolved to the local bodies, was a bold political initiative towards democratic decentralisation, the first of its kind in India. It was a major departure from the earlier models of planning in its procedures, financial affairs, and institutional setup. The People's Plan aimed at bringing in structural changes in the power relations of local societies with thrust on sustainable development, local self-reliance, and political empowerment of the weaker sections.

People's Plan, with its motto, *power to people*, demanded a brief analysis of the relation co-existed between power, People's Plan, and participatory development. Power is a strong concept in the People's Plan, as it is a process of devolution of power. There are a number of positions based on a complex conceptualisation of social power, operating as invisible forms of domination. Social power identifies the determining moment of social life with economic forces and relations, and establishes a correspondence between production and power.

Most of the theoretical constructs emerge from the continuing intellectual exchange of social and political ideas located within the Marxist perspective. Any critical theory that ignores these realities runs the risk of becoming itself ideological. All theoretical analyses understand the concept of power as located not on the surface of society's structure but as deeply woven into a complex contextual social web. Theorists like Althusser, Gramsci, Foucault, Habermas, and Friere, analysed the concept of power from socio- cultural, psychological, political, and structural perspectives. Power, effected through an unconscious subjection to ideology in an Althusserain framework; power in the Gramscian hegemony that involves the colonisation of popular consciousness or common sense through the articulation of specific social practices and positions within the ideological codes or chains; Foucauldian notion of power as crucial to the construction of reality, language, meanings, and rituals of truth, and the power resulting from knowledge in an information economy, according to Habermas, all analyse the concept of power.

It was Friere who emphasized the power of participation, which promotes empowerment through the development of common knowledge and critical awareness, suppressed by the dominant knowledge system. The power that comes from true dialogue and participation in a decentralised democracy, he believes, is the real means and ends in achieving the development of humanity. Friere's entire philosophy of education and his orientation towards participation is based on the notion that the historical vocation of human beings is to be free from the shackles of material and psychological oppression, and from the patterns of life that are imposed from above, which do not provide for involvement of people in the process of change. Action and reflection are not separate activities, but an organic whole, and it is this dialogical interplay of action and reflection that contributes to the process of *conscientizacao* (conscientisation). In other words, authentic participation leads to freeing; it is an emancipatory experience, resulting in actual liberation (Friere, 1994).

Many theories and theoreticians support this new development approach that emphasises the devolution of power. White (1982) used the term power and power to people not as a revolutionary concept but as the generative power that is less threatening, more humane, and realistic in approach. People, according to her, should be allowed to explore and organise themselves to enjoy the freedom of 'dialogue' as prescribed by Bubber (Freedman, 1983) and to look for their own sources of power. This would enable them in introspecting and reflecting their own life experiences and the ways in which they engage, confront, negotiate, and succumb to them in their life world. This demands conscientisation, critical awareness, and a dialogic mode of training. It does suggest that action is more likely to be an outcome when people engage in dialogue and search together (Friere, 1983). However, the history of power is ridden with the silences and absences of the marginals in its narratives and is void of any form of authentic dialogue or participation.

Though the Kerala Model of Development could enhance the social status of the marginals, through the historical legacies of the sustained mass-based movements, their socio-economic position is still an issue of grave concern. At the PRIs, the marginals are targets of attack whenever they challenge the power structures and systems, or question the corrupt practices prevalent at the PRIs. They face miserable experiences in the public domain, especially when they start exercising their agency in the PRIs, where they are *de facto* challenging the hegemonic power centres at the local level. Most of the time, it manifests as violent backlash against Dalits, women or the tribals, especially against those who question or dare to challenge the power positions of the male–centric bureaucratic and patriarchal order.

Devolution of power is the opening-up of new channels of power through which power could penetrate deep down into the social spaces to help the people, up to the outer layers of the social fringes— who had hitherto experienced power only as something exercised on them— to reframe themselves as wielders of power to make them powerful and have the due share of the social cake; to express their opinions that evolve from their lived experiences in the language of power, and to bridge the social gulfs that had once reduced them to floating islands of social and economic spaces, using their politics of presence and power of position.

The most significant contribution of the Constitutional Amendments is that it has deepened democracy, political inclusion, and participation of the marginals in the society. The mandatory reservations for women, Scheduled

Castes and Scheduled Tribes and Other Backward Classes have brought more than a million new representatives to the democratic spaces. There is empirical evidence to suggest that the politics of presence of these marginals at the decision making spaces of local governance are changing the power definitions of the body politics substantively, and are asserting their political rights and are beginning to emerge as active citizen-subjects in the discourse of local governance and development.

It is only natural that those sections at the Centre who had been wielding power as their birthright would feel threatened of being stripped off their power bases and commands .They would then exploit the technical or legal snags to undermine the new equations of power or cling on to the infructuous structures of power to deny power to the neo-power wielders in total disregard to the macro effects the 73 and 74 amendments to the Constitution had envisaged through the newly activated micro power centers in the periphery.

So when devolution of power causes the feminsiation of power, genderisation of power, and tribilisation of power, to cite a few power centres in the periphery, resulting in a Dalit woman unfurling the national flag at the panchayat office as the president of the panchayat in one place, elsewhere the reluctant centres of power who had been using power as their birthright resorted to threatening a Dalit woman of dire consequences if she dared to unfurl the flag at the panchayat office, though she was its President, or to behead her when she dared to ignore the threat.

Any discourse positions people as social subjects. It is this discourse that constructs commonsense, attitudes, and opinions, observing what we take to be matters of commonsense as largely ideological. This 'ideological commonsense' contributes to maintaining the status quo, whereby sustaining unequal relations of power (Fairclough, 2001). It is this uneven strand of power relations that one could see operationalising at the panchayats in various forms: between bureaucrats and panchayat representatives; between panchayat representatives and people; between panchayat presidents and panchayat samiti; between technocrats and elected representatives; between panchayat samiti and planners, and so on.

The People's Plan envisaged devolution of power on one hand and enlarging and deepening the social spaces of power through democratizing the power spaces so as to access the new power spaces by those in the fringes and help them exercise these power spaces to build the power structure from the grassroots, on the other. Creating new power centres implies weakening the existing power centres and bringing down the concentration of power. While it means those who have been wielding power need to sacrifice their vistas of power and capacitate the neo-power wielders—in whose favour they had to shed their power—since the new comers are too new to understand the nuances of power and to exercise it effectively and functionally.

In a patriarchal society like India, where men, especially those at the higher rungs of social and economic ladders, man every institution and agency of power, democratization of power meant the very same men had to equip the 'usurpers of power' to sit comfortably on the pedestals they had been occupying for long . To think and act in these lines is expecting too much from them for more than one reason. If they had understood the essence of democratisation of power, they would not have occupied these power spaces as their birthright in the first place, and would have volunteered to opt out had they ever attempted to read the writings on the wall. The marginals then would not have evolved, and even if evolved, would have been assimilated into the mainstream. We would then have more women, tribals, and other weaker sections on positions of power in political parties, governments, and bureaucracy. That it never happened on its own, speaks volumes about the concentration of power in the hands of a few and the denial of power to a great majority.

Instead, it needed two Constitutional Amendments to impact upon the existing power wielders to shed a good chunk of their power—administrative and financial— to those on whom they had been exercising power as if it was the law of nature. The legally exercisable right to hold power thus had to be exercised in a legal manner. It gave legal channels to those in the margin to walk into the power zones and to exercise power. Besides, it declared any intentional block to the passage, an offence. But those who had been in power for long and who knew the snags in law, both in its interpretation and application, could pose invisible blocks, like moral gaze, and force the newcomers to freeze or return with disgrace. For instance, the recently concluded "Expert Committee on Leveraging Panchayat Raj Institutions for more Efficient Delivery of Public Goods and Services" revealed that except for the Mahatma Gandhi National Rural Employment Guarantee Act (MGNREGA) and the Backward Regions Grant Fund (BRGF), none of the over 150 centrally sponsored schemes had provided a role for the PRIs, despite the Cabinet Secretary's explicit directions through a circular dated November 8, 2004 and the guidelines of the Planning Commission. These are still managed by the line departments of respective States. In short, Panchayats are yet to evolve into full-fledged self-governing institutions of local governance, mainly because of the continued resistance from certain sections of State political leadership and bureaucracy that feel the rise of panchayats would make them redundant.

The People's Plan implanted the dual function of devolution of power and democratisation of power, and addressed the visible and invisible blocks in the meaningful implementation of the 73rd and 74th Constitutional Amendments by treating the whole issue from different political, social, and economic angles and by evolving flexible tools to dethrone the rigid caste-based, gender-based, and financial-based power equations. While some States like Kerala and West Bengal have devolved as many as 26 departments to Panchayats, several States have devolved only a few functions, even as low as 3 functions. Therefore, Article 243G of the Indian Constitution that requires the State governments to devolve distinct functional items to Panchayats, remains a constitutional promise even today. Democratisation of the local governance is essentially the empowerment of the people by giving them not only the voice but the power of choice as well, in order to shape the development they feel is appropriate to their situation. It implies maximum decentralisation of power to the elected bodies to function as autonomous units with adequate power, authority, and resources to discharge the basic responsibility of bringing economic development and social justice.

Though the People's Plan, initially made conscious and cautious efforts to smoothen the process of devolution of power and democratisation of power space, it either failed or bungled where it needed the most. Two instances—the case of women and tribals— are worth mentioning. The tribal intervention programmes of the People's Plan did not meet expectations due to many factors, including total absence of tribal-sensitive initiatives, antipathy or apathy of bureaucracy and politicians, and ignorance or misinformed nature of the tribals. The People's Plan could make no meaningful intervention to undo the hitherto practised policy or implementation strategy of tribal development that only deepened the underdevelopment in the tribal areas.

In the case of women, the People's Plan saw women occupying the legally allowed seats of power, but could make no dent in the patriarchal power fortress that halted the progress of women at the legally mandatory points by blocking their way ahead. For instance, no political party has made a decision reflecting the essence of 73rd and 74th Constitutional Amendments in their party forum, which, for all practical purpose, remain the man's forte. Even those women on the newly found seats of power were made to suffer humiliation, citing lack of sound knowledge of the language and technicalities of power. Those who sought the help of men in the office to empower themselves in the application of power were either branded as proxies or were forced to crouch back, fearing moral gaze.

The demand for historicising the structures of forgetting and exposing the hidden mysteries of hurt and humiliation animates the contemporary claim for including marginalities an important category of social life, as an intimate and embodied form of sociality. Moreover, the different positionalities among the marginals, arising out of their class, caste, religion and ethnicity, make one think about multiple hegemonies, distinguished by the customary practices of caste and religious communities. These 'differences' between and among the marginals, arising from this multiple hierarchies, place them in different positionalities which, in turn, expose them to different forms of violence- both explicit and implicit.

Moreover, the language used for discourses on the marginality is problematic. The language of the marginals' rights is deeply disturbing because it involves separating the identity of the marginals as citizen-subjects from their identities as the subject of social relations. This positioning of the social identity of the marginals in the political spectrum itself is a marker of violence. On the other hand, the powerful in the society is not burdened with this ambiguity. The marginals experience this violence not only from outside but also from within, since their agency and subjectivity itself, to a large extent, are conditioned by the hegemonic, systemic, and patriarchal interests. When one tries to understand violence towards the marginals, this inbuilt, structural violence also needs to be contextualised.

Meanings are moulded, refashioned, and regurgitated to suit the established order of things. In the process of resistance and negotiation of power, they set the limits of our thought and imagination. The 'politics of imagining the marginals' refers to non-articulation, an exclusion from the peculiar process of the creation of meanings. In art, literature, media, culture, and politics, the 'marginal' is compelled to assume the form of the 'incognito' and pose many questions into the foreground. What governs the 'exclusion? What grids of exclusion are used to define the 'marginal'? What disciplinary mechanisms work to reproduce the site of the 'marginal'? Whose politics makes it marginal? Is the distinction between the centre and marginal more amorphous than what we imagine? How does the marginal manifest itself in the everyday life and in the realm of governance and governmentality?

The histories of exclusion and relegation have kept the marginals away from the centre- stage of discourses and debates in civil society that forms a decisive power in framing the public opinion, which legitimises 'histories' as the stories of people with power. Any initiative to re-position the marginals in the phenomenology of these carved absences in all the spaces, especially in governance, needs to unravel this discourse of power which, through the hegemonised ways, made them inaudible and invisible. These silent spaces need to be deconstructed for exploring the ways in which the marginals exercise their agency to negotiate with the power structures.

Brick by Brick: Democratising Local Governance in Kerala-Insights from the People's Planning Campaign

The Left Democratic Front Government of Kerala took the major initiative—People's Plan—aiming deep and wide socio-political and economic changes to effect the revolutionary impacts of the 73rd and 74th Constitutional Amendments, brick by brick, mainly through the People's Planning Campaign built on the principle of democratising the local governance through devolution of power and equitable redistribution of the power spaces, enabling the marginals to access the power spaces and to equip them to exercise their agency in the process of governance as subject-citizens.

Chapter two tries to position the People's Planning Campaign (PPC) in the broad contexts of decentralisation and in the historicity of the local governance initiatives and interventions at the national and state levels. Viewed from a communitarian perspective, chapter three analyses People's Plan as a participatory communication process in the decentralised planning context of Kerala and delineates its communication gaps and dysfunctions, in the context of power. Changing paradigms of the theories of development, from modernisation to participation, are discussed in this chapter, focussing more on different perspectives of participation, the central focus of the People's Planning Campaign (PPC). Chapter three analyses People's Plan as a participatory communication process and explains its main components. Decentralised nature of People's Plan demands an organic model of communication to ensure participation and enhance conscientisation. Characteristics of the Organic Model of Communication, adopted in People's Plan, are discussed in the chapter three to evaluate the changes in its communication approaches. Unlike the earlier development plans, which adopted a top-bottom vertical communication, People's Plan adopted a bottom-up vertical communication to suit the process of decentralisation. Transformation of the top-bottom vertical communication, in power relations, to a two-way horizontal communication process is explained in the communication approaches adopted in the training imparted to resource persons and the representatives of the local bodies, as part of the communication process of the PPC. The multi levels of communication, operated simultaneously, in different contexts, at different levels, to suit its needs is analysed in the communication process of the PPC. The chapter argues that the PPC deconstructed the *we- know - all-* attitude of bureaucracy and facilitated resource persons and elected representatives to understand the intricacies of the system to work within the system, and enabled them to acquire the power of people under democracy to challenge the hegemony of bureaucratic power that challenges the essence of democracy. This chapter also discusses how training had created a pool of resource persons, from among the common man, who could have a dialogic communication with the top brass in the system, on equal terms, using the language of the system, and create an atmosphere of horizontal communication, which could not have been thought of earlier. Obstacles in the participative process of communication in People's Plan with respect to source and message in the communication process are also looked at.

What were the variables in the development approaches of the PPC that helped the success of the Women Component Plan (WCP)? What were the changes effected in the intervention strategy of the WCP to cater to the needs that emerged during the process of the PPC? What were the reasons for the dysfunction of the development approaches in the tribal context? Chapters four and five focus on the development strategies of the PPC in the case of two marginalised sections of the society— women and tribals— respectively, through participatory case studies.

Convergence of a few positive variables that caused the success of the development intervention of the WCP is the point of discussion in chapter four. Women in Kerala, in general, were on a fermentation process with respect to gender relations, when the PPC, through its refined gender sensitive approach, gave them visible and audible platforms to air their views and caused the shift in gender perspective to happen. One could trace the conscious application of a theoretical and ideological perspective, with respect to gender in the WCP that helped it to succeed. Interventions and modifications of the WCP, at critical junctures, enabled it to effect the shift from the Women Integrated Development (WID), which focused mainly on the practical needs of women, to the Gender And Development (GAD), which addressed the strategic needs along with the practical needs. Micro-credit and Self Help Groups enhanced the economic and social position of women and helped them to gain self-esteem and think beyond the family parameters to reach out for a national cause, as exemplified in the case of Samatha Self Help Groups of women in Ulloor Panchayat. The SHGs freed women from the clutches of moneylenders, besides enhancing their self-respect, first in front of their family members and then, before the society. Qualitative changes in the perception of the women elected representatives vis-a-vis the WCP also played a crucial role in the success of the WCP. The role of a committed and well-informed external local agent, like the Kerala Sastra Sahitya Parishad (KSSP), as an inevitable and facilitating variable in bringing about a change in gender relations, is also explained. The process, which began with feedback from the intense women training sessions, progressed through the resultant conscientisation of their gender roles, facilitated the women to break the spiral of silence and invisibility among women.

The tribals in Kerala, cut off from the mainstream, are generally living a secluded life. Any development intervention, unless specially designed, taking into consideration the ethnic identities and unique nature of different tribal communities, would not succeed. Chapter five discusses this aspect. Though the PPC effected some positive quantitative changes in the tribal hamlets, it was not successful in making any qualitative change in the living conditions of tribals. The new strategies attempted by the Tribal Sub Plan of the PPC - like convening of special grama sabha (ooru sabha), introduction of the Social Activists and changes made in the TSP- to intervene into the development problems of the tribals, and the changes it adopted during the PPC, proved to be ineffective in achieving its envisaged objectives. This is explained with the help of participatory case study done in the tribal hamlets of Panamaram Panchayat. The study reveals that the Social Activists, Tribal Extension Officer, and elected representative took cover under the oft repeated *blaming the victim theory* to save themselves from owning up responsibility for the failure of the TSP. The chapter discusses why even the Social Activists, who were educated tribals assigned to be the change agents among tribals, failed to be so, besides becoming an appendage of bureaucratic system, which the PPC wanted to revamp. The participatory strategy applied in the TSP failed to exploit the existing strong organic links among the tribal communities to disseminate the message of the PPC. Besides, it could not cash in on the communicative potential of the folk media to convey the message of the TSP.

Role of the media –print, electronic and folk— in the PPC is examined in chapter six. It looks at the role of media in an information economy, where information becomes the power, and analyses the role of media in the planning process of the IX Plan. The PPC made a strategic error vis-a-vis its media strategy. It gave too much emphasis on print media, which in general, was antagonistic, passive, or apathetic towards this development initiative that questioned the power structure in the society. This is shown through the content analysis of four newspapers. The chapter shows that media failed in its role as the fourth estate in a democratic system. Media could not cope up with what was expected of it in its approach towards the radical economic, political, and social reforms the People's Plan aimed at. Instead, the chapter discusses that media was more keen in airing its political and business vested interests, disregarding the far reaching damage such doctored, distorted, prejudiced, and concocted reports could cause in a society like Kerala, where newspapers have a tremendous impact. Media proved to be a strong ideological apparatus to manufacture the consent against the PPC, which tried to challenge the hegemonic notions of power prevalent in society. The content analysis reveals that Malayala Manorama, an anti-communist propaganda machine and the largest circulated newspaper in India, took a clear editorial policy to undermine the PPC, as it was reflected in its wide coverage of negative evaluative reports on the PPC. Mathrubhoomi, which was opposed to any radical change in the status-quo of the society, played a passive role in its attitude towards the PPC. Though Deshabhimani, the CPI (M) organ, eulogised the PPC as a new dawn, its reach was limited to the party supporters. Use of the electronic media in the PPC was minimal. Both the public broadcasting (Doordarsahn) and the private television channels (Asianet TV and Soorya TV) didn't give adequate time slots for broadcasting one of the important and innovative development projects of the State. The chapter analyses that C-DIT, the official agency entrusted to produce documentaries, did not have a well-designed media strategy to suit the requirements of the PPC. Even the training sessions did not fully utilise the screening time for the documentaries for further discussions and analysis of the issues featured in the documentaries. Communicative potential of the video was not exploited in the PPC and this had a very adverse impact on the overall information dissemination of the PPC, both among people and elected representatives. Apart from the training sessions, the use of indigenous media was limited to the initial phase of the PPC. In short, the chapter argues that media strategy vis-a-vis the PPC was faulty with respect to the print, electronic, and folk media. Further, planners of the PPC did not have a decentralised media strategy to disseminate the message of decentralisation. Thus, the chapter contends that PPC could not gauge the significance of the media in disseminating the concepts of the PPC.

The concluding chapter introduces and discusses the 'Trans power', in the moment of hegemonic crisis, which is designed by the dominant class to sabotage any subaltern movement of the war of positions. 'The crisis consists precisely in the fact that the old is dying and the new cannot be born; in this interregnum a great variety of morbid symptoms appear' (Gramsci, 1921). Trans, by being temporary, fluid, floating, and rootlessness could be easily appropriated by the vested interests of the centre and could make it appear like a permanent structure designed to better the life world of the marginals by engaging with the hegemonic apparatuses. In the case of the democratic decentralisation also, though we had departed from the normative understanding of the centralisation and its rigid technocratic and bureaucratic procedures and languages, we are yet to reach the devolution of the power phase of the decentralisation and are still groping in the trans phase, which is a fertile ground for seizures and appropriations. The conclusion also discusses the post-decentralisation phase of the PPC and the relevance and significance of the deepening of local governance process in Kerala that enabled it to arrest the COVID-19 pandemic to a large extent. However, the chapter contends that the all-pervasive market logic privileges the consumer-centric discourses above the citizen–centric and rights based discourses, where the apolitical and apathetic masses in the feudal and bourgeois public sphere (Habermas,1989) become antithetical to the process of deepening of the democratic decentralisation.

As in many cases, Kerala became a model to the world by putting into practice the theoretical concept of decentralisation and, more importantly, effecting financial devolution to the grassroots level to give expression to the essence of decentralisation, against the backdrop of the threats of globalisation. That it could not sustain the initial euphoria it had created in the socio-economic and political realms of Kerala, even as its news was spreading across the continents, is a different story. The PPC, with its objective to challenge the power structures in the socio-economic spheres was, in fact, questioning the hegemony. But the flip side of hegemony is that the PPC had to pay a price – in the form of succumbing to sectarian interests of the politically and socially powerful sections, with the sectarian interests gradually overshadowing common developmental interests. It is a logical interplay of civil society, social capital, voluntary and mass organisations with a strong State with the development agenda that would set the rules for a new vision of development (Harris J., 2001).

Chapter 2

Situating People's Plan in the Context of Decentralisation and Local Governance

Decentralisation: A Snapshot

During the preceding three decades, the idea of decentralization, like participation and civil society, has become a ubiquitous catchphrase for policy makers and scholars from a variety of perspectives, and most countries have placed it on their development schema. The changes in government, associated with decentralization, are thought to hold the potential to deepen democracy, make for more accountable and efficient institutions, increase citizen input, and foster cooperation across the public-private divide. Policymakers consider it a panacea for various ills concerning development and implemented it as a way of reducing the role of the state as the centralised state has lost a great deal of legitimacy on account of its many failures (Bardhan and Mookherjee 2002). Decentralisation can be understood as a political process whereby administrative authority, public resources, and responsibilities are transferred from central government agencies to lower-level organs of government or to non-governmental bodies, such as community-based organisations (CBOs), 'third party' non-governmental organisations (NGOs) or private sector actors (Crook and Manor, 1998; Meenakshisundaram, 1999; World Bank, 2000.) Decentralization of power aims at improved and faster communication, participation, and guarantee of the people in development, mobilisation of backing and use of resources in a grander fashion for national development, lessening of suspension in decision-making, better equity in apportionment of resources, and investments as well as reduction in indifference of administration (Rondinelli et al., 1989). Stiglitz (2008) argues decentralisation as the transfer of decision-making power from the Centre of an organization to its subunits.

The notion of decentralisation in the context of fiscal federalism is concerned with the structure of the government which would have the greatest success in resolving the problems related to the three functions of public sector—allocation, distribution, and stabilization problems. Oates (1972) puts forward a powerful argument for federalism from this perspective and reasons that decentralization, to an extent, ensures better distribution and growth.

Most rationalizations of decentralization are assembled around the postulation that greater participation in public decision-making is a positive good in itself or that it can improve efficiency, equity, development, and resource management. By bringing government decision-making closer to citizens, decentralization is generally understood to increase public–sector accountability and therefore efficacy. At its most basic, decentralization aims to realize one of the essential goals of just political governance—democratization, or the aspiration that humans should have a say in their own activities. Many analyses of decentralization consider the transfer of powers, and Manor (1999), in this context argues that to have significant promise, decentralization must entail a mixture of all three types: democratic, fiscal, and administrative.

One important component of decentralised planning has been its emphasis on the politico-administrative activities in order to facilitate local participation. Democratic decentralization at the grassroots level is envisaged as an important approach to make democracy meaningful and accomplish greater goals of a responsive, corruption free, effective, and transparent administration and delivery of services to the population (Sherwood,1969). If more equitable development is to be achieved, popular participation and the decentralisation of authority ought to be encouraged (Allen and Thomas, 1992). The alleviation of rural poverty, which has been the primary objective of most alternative development projects, is thought to have been hindered by the failure to decentralise decision-making and management structures. Moreover, increased decentralisation could promote the rise of forceful and innovative local leaders who can identify with and invest in the regions in which they live (Dubey and Gangopadhyay, 1998).

To position the varying degrees of decentralisation, one may speak of (a) deconcentration; (b) delegation; (c) devolution and (d) privatization (Feslar, 1960; Collins, 1974; Boodhoo, 1976). Deconcentration is the least extensive form of decentralisation, in which political, administrative, and fiscal responsibilities are transferred to lower units within central line ministries or agencies (Crook and Manor, 1998; Rondinelli et al, 1989; Meenakshisundaram, 1999). Delegation implies the transfer or creation of authority to plan and implement decisions concerning specific activities or a variety of activities within specific spatial boundaries, to an organization that is technically and administratively capable of carrying them out (Boodhoo, 1976). Delegation of decision-making and management authority for specific functions to organisation that are only under the indirect control of central government ministries mark the second degree of decentralisation, in which responsibilities are transferred to organisations that are outside the regular bureaucratic structure and are only indirectly controlled by the central government (Meenakshisundaram, 1999). Devolution is the extreme form of decentralisation in which sub-national units of government are either created or strengthened in terms of political, administrative, and fiscal power (Blair, 2000; Crook and Manor, 1998; Rondinelli et al., 1989). Some administrative theorists argue that devolution is a concept quite separate from decentralisation, because it denotes the divestment of functions by the central government and the creation of new units of governance outside the formal command structure of the central government (Sherwood, 1969). Devolution in this framework is an arrangement in which there is a reciprocal and mutually benefiting co-ordination of relationship between the central and state governments. It is the devolution of political, fiscal, and administrative responsibilities and powers from the central government to intermediate and local governments that is the true measure of decentralization (Shah and Thompson 2004). Privatisation is the other end, in which all responsibilities of government functions are transferred to nongovernmental organisations (NGOs) or private enterprises independent of government (Meenakshisundaram, 1999).

Decentralisation measures are often advocated to promote more appropriate forms of development and to assist the mobilisation of local human and material resources. In decentralised planning, adequate caution and importance should be given to the intra-and inter-linkages of the various existing linkages of planning.

- Physical linkages: road networks, river and water transport networks, railroad networks, ecological interdependencies.
- Production linkages: economic flows, capital flows, (backward, forward, and lateral), consumption and shopping patterns, income flows, sectoral and inter-regional commodity flows, cross-linkages.
- Population movement linkages: migration (temporary and permanent) and journeys to work.

- Technological linkages: technology interdependencies, irrigation systems, and telecommunication systems.
- Social interaction linkages: visiting patterns, kinship patterns, rites, rituals, and religious activities and social group interactions.
- Service delivery linkages: energy flows and networks, credit and financial networks, education, training and agricultural extension linkages, health-service delivery systems, professional, commercial, and technical service patterns and transport service systems.
- Political, administrative, and organisational linkages: structural relationships, government budgetary flows, organisational interdependencies, authority-approval-supervision patterns, inter-jurisdictional transaction patterns and informal political decision chains.

Another line of argument for decentralisation of planning is based on the premise that information cost is monotonically increasing functions of the distance between the action point at which the information is generated and the point at which the decision is made (Marshach and Marshaċh, 1959). If the decision-making is pushed down to the lower level, the smaller will be the units, better will be the situation, other things reaming the same (Chakravarthy, 1972; Mathur, 1973).

The above theoretical acceptance of the decentralisation at the global level enabled it to emerge as a dominant trend in world politics. In 1998, the World Bank estimated that all but 12 of the 75 developing and transitional countries with population greater than 5 million had embarked on a process of political devolution (Crook and Manor, 1998). At the heart of this transformation are a number of complex yet inter-related themes. One is an ideological shift, in which the legitimacy of central state-led development has been challenged on the grounds that it produces systems of governance that undermine national economic performance and effective public policy (Gore, 1973). The second is a political agenda, which asserts that the decentralisation of public administration and the introduction of locally elected bodies will produce systems of governance that are better able to meet the needs of poor and politically marginal groups in society. A third and related theme suggests that democratic decentralisation is a political strategy that national élites have used to maintain legitimacy and control in the face of political disintegration. Here it can be been argued that economic liberalisation, political regionalism, and the rise of powerful inter- and sub-national actors have weakened the traditional nation-state and created the conditions under which more local identities could emerge (Giddens, 1999).

Historical Review of Decentralisation in the Context of Indian Five Year Plans

In the Indian context, the often cited argument for decentralisation of planning is that, given the wide regional variation in natural endowments, levels of development and potentials, no single strategy of development for the whole country is appropriate (Gadgil, 1967; Raj, 1971; Biswas, 1973; Mathur, 1973; Aziz, 1993; Jain et al, 1985). All analysis from different theoretical perspectives postulated that standardised development schemes that are centrally drawn up cannot take into considerations the local variations in the development sectors.

In pre-British India, the Indian economic life was primarily built around land, the principal means of subsistence. Since the village community generally owned land, a communal spirit developed in all the economic activities. Such a communal social life, it is clear, originated from below. The village, therefore, came to be the very hub of this life (Majumdar, 1918). It was again in the village that local government had its birth. What, therefore, goes today under the name of decentralisation –which denotes delegation or devolution of authority or autonomy from above – had its organic growth from the traditional Indian soil.

Village has been looked upon as a unit of administration since the early Vedic period. The earliest reference to village (grama) is found in the *Rig-Veda*, claimed to be the oldest of the ancient Hindu scriptures (Altekar, 1955). Altekar, however, notes two important functions of the village headman: defence of village; and collection of government revenue. The village was governed by an assembly, which in the Rig Vedic period, was known as Sabha (Altekar, 1955). It was this assembly that managed the affairs of the village and took collective decisions. But this practice did not seem to have endured long. At a later stage, particularly during the Gupta period, the village assembly was supposed to have given place to a smaller council consisting of persons from among the village elders of the assembly. These councils were known as *Panchmandalis* in Central India. Later, these village councils developed into formal bodies regularly transacting administrative business, and came to be known as Panchayats (Bhargava, 1979). They were concerned primarily with adjudicating civil disputes of residents related to rights in land and administering criminal justice. They also performed regulatory functions related to village commons (grazing lands, woods, and water bodies). Responsibility for payment of tithes and taxes was, strictly speaking, not their concern; the revenue systems introduced since the times of Sher Shah Suri took care of these. They did, nevertheless, have some say by way of counseling the village residents on matters related to allegiance owed to different political masters like zamindars/ subedars/riyasats and so on. Village life had both caste and village panchayats, where caste panchayats were concerned with issues related to jajmani, marriage, and rituals and village panchayats comprised elders of prominent households in a village, usually from the upper caste families and feudal land lords. Village panchayats were generally casteist and sexist in nature. Participation in the affairs of panchayat was limited to the higher castes where the lowest section of the village, the Sudras, had no voice in the decisions of the council as they were not represented (Dutta, 1960).

British Rule and Indian Village

The self-sufficient character of the village system had two facets, agriculture and handicraft (Mookerji, 1958). The village systems were based on a combination of agriculture and cottage industries. Those small and extremely ancient Indian communities, some of which have continued down to this day, are based on possession in common of land, on the blending of agriculture and handicrafts (Karl Marx, cited in 1961).

The introduction of private ownership in land, combined with the breaking up of the village industries during the British rule was the main cause of the disintegration of the village communities in India (Prasad, 1971). Main functions of the village community were twofold. The village was an economic unit. As an economic unit, it used to regulate its economic affairs after paying off the royal dues through its headman. It was also a politico-judicial body in the sense that all disputes arising in the village were decided by the village panchayat itself. These were the two bases on which collective life of the village rested. But these were the very bases that were undone by the British (Mookerjee, 1958). The role of panchayats as institutions administering justice was eliminated by the British Raj. Legislation in 1860, such as the Indian Penal Code (IPC), Criminal Procedure Code (Cr.P.C.), Contract Act etc., along with Baden Powell's schema for land revenue settlements supplanted the customary/traditional law. Collectorates and courts usurped powers of caste/ village panchayats to establish the rule of law (UNDP Report, 2015).

Among many changes India witnessed with the advent of the British rule, the significant change was the virtual extinction of the old forms of self-government and the disappearance of those ancient village communities of which India was the first home among all the countries (Apte, 1960). The Royal Commission on Decentralisation was appointed in 1907-08 to go into this question of village as the base of local administration. The Commission on Decentralisation, for the first time, made comprehensive recommendations regarding the place of village in the administration of the country (Prasad, 1971). Recommendations of the Commission received no serious attention from the government for about six years. It was in 1915, the first step towards the implementation of the Royal Commission recommendations was taken. The government of Lord Harding issued a resolution on local self-government reviewing the position and largely endorsing and accepting the recommendations of the Commission (Bhatnagar, 1978).

When village panchayats were re-legislated to life in India as 'local bodies', their character had been transformed. These legislations were not prompted by any regard for customary law or traditional wisdom that might express itself as the general will of the people. They were considered necessary as agencies for development of the rational-legal institutions of representative government. Arguing for budgetary freedom for development functions to be performed by local bodies, Lord Ripon's Resolution of 1880 stressed that the educative principle of training people to participate in representative institutions of government should not be subordinated to demands for efficiency in development activities. In 1919, to ease the burden on imperial finances and bring to bear local supervision and vigilance on development activities, local bodies were re-legislated to life in other presidencies. The taluka/tehsil served as the basic unit for local boards, assigned subjects such as sanitation, education and health, with powers to levy fees and taxes. Provincial governments in 1935 wrested the power to enact legislation on local self-government. Acts were voted by provincial governments to vest powers of administration, sometimes including criminal justice, with the panchayats.

Gandhi and Villageism

The emergence of Gandhi at the head of the Indian national movement was, in fact, the unfoldment of the subdued expectations of India's village at the conscious level of political processes. The new direction in which he turned the whole current of the national movement was towards the village. Naturally, in the ultimate order of society, which he visualised, village came to be the very pivot. His concept of decentralisation was derived from his concern for the village (Pyarelal, 1958).

Gandhian concept of Sarvodaya describes a democratic socialistic pattern of economies and institutions suited to the conditions, realities, and needs of the Indian society. He stressed for village reconstruction rather than urban industrialisation. His ideology was based on the concept of villageism (Bose, 1948). In practice, this was an attempt to produce powerful village communities by initiating participatory communication, developing self-reliant village republics in the form of panchayats, enforcing reform of land ownership, and encouraging the development of rural industries. Gandhiji envisioned village as the unit of social planning (Pyarelal, 1958). His vision of villageism anticipated that the natural and necessary co-operation among villages in everyday matters of social, economic, and political life would produce popular participation.

In the Gandhian plan, development was thought of in terms of human beings with the first objective of improving the quality of life by providing the basic minimum needs. Next, the plan envisaged to record the society by structural changes like removing exploitative linkages, caste impediments and social and economic inequalities. He identified three aspects of traditional social structures as contributing elements to the problems of the society:

- First, the feudal system institutionalised social roles, in which people were linked by the exploitation of one by the other;
- Second was the rigid caste system, which institutionalised the marginalised, who were completely isolated from the economy; and
- Finally, the traditional attitude towards family and children resulted in a population that, literally, swallowed any increase in material resource (Bose, 1948).

Communication tools at that period, especially mass media channels, were insufficient to connect people to the government and to each other. Gandhi stressed the need for interpersonal channel and oral communication (Gandhi, 1937). These channels, while advising a top-down advisory role for the government, also included a bottom-up channel from people to the government and a bottom-bottom channel among people themselves. Thus, the Gandhian model advocated for a horizontal and a two- way communication in the planning processes. This notion of mass participation in development through a mass consensus carried with it a radical decentralisation of power. Gandhi envisioned a government that would build from below and govern as little as possible (Pyarelal, 1958). It would raise the consciousness of people against exploitation, injustice and poverty, encourage conscious efforts for socio-economic equality, and enable people to articulate for development. These concepts were most specifically focussed on the untouchables and suppressed classes in order to bring them to the mainstream of society.

Gandhi recommended two communication efforts for this:

- First, the government should initiate special track interpersonal communication programmes in the form of mass meetings and group persuasion programmes;

- Second, special programmes of interpersonal as well as mass communication, especially for print media, to be initiated to get the untouchables and other lower castes accepted by the social elites (Gandhi, 1937).

This clear understanding of the future plan of the village system led him to challenge the whole basis of modern technological society. His critique of the present society has therefore, two focuses: economic and political. Economic is conceived the technology– a phenomenon that leads to centralisation of power, economic as well as political (Bose, 1948). The political critique, therefore, is the direct outcome of the economic.

Concentration of economic power brings corresponding centralisation of political power in a few hands. Concentration of economic power was what he considered to be the result of the large-scale industrialism of the present age. Exploitation follows concentration and, in the longer run, will result in violence. Violence in any form was the very negation of truth. Gandhi, therefore, was opposed to such a technology, and was a strong advocate of decentralised planning in India.

Thus, Gandhi provided the Meta model of Indian development. It was never implemented as such, but its various parts were the basis of much of the subsequent development experiments in India during the initial plan period.

Three experimental participatory community projects based more or less explicitly on the Gandhian model were conducted as pilots for the future developmental efforts:

- On the eve of the attainment of independence, the former Madras state launched a new scheme of village development known as Firka development scheme. The scheme emphasised a perfect coordination of different state departments that were engaged in rural development. The scheme was evaluated in 1952 and was found that with some drawbacks it was a successful story. However, when the community development projects were started in 1952 the Firka scheme was merged in it. The experience of Firka was much useful for running the community development projects.
- Etawah project in Uttar Pradesh with three objectives– development awareness, self-development, and self-reliance through agricultural extension programme– was the forerunner to the Community Development Project (CDP) which later on started in 1952. It should also be observed that the project was supervised by experts in different walks of village life. The project personnel were expected to provide expert guidance but the people were required to make the project self-running. No financial assistance, however, was given to the people. The project belonged to them and, therefore, they had to run it.

- The Nilokheri experiment in East Punjab was started with the basic idea of self-reliant agro-industrial townships to serve as the nerve centre of rural development, providing technically trained manpower, creating a traffic of goods and ideas, and being sustained through agricultural supplies and the product of cottage industries. The Nilokheri project was launched for the settlement of refugees who migrated to Punjab during the riots which took place soon after Independence.

Though Gandhi's notion of decentralisation and Panchayati Raj was accepted in principle, it was not implemented in the subsequent five-year plans. To fulfil the desires of peasantry, as an ethical responsibility of the nationalist movement, the Indian government after the independence, initiated land reforms and institutional change to do away with despicable traditions of discrimination and domination based on religion and caste. This required the will of strong Central and State Governments to be pitted against local vested interests, whether landlords or 'superior castes'. Moreover, land revenues had to be reduced and since income levels were low and highly skewed between individuals and regions, reliance on the spread of indirect rather than the narrow incidence of direct taxes were necessary which naturally resulted in a centralised system of finance. These constraints, along with others related to the legacy of the Raj, partition of the country and the enthusiasm for a planned economy, shaped centralism (UNDP Report, 2005).

However, starting from the first plan, need for a disaggregated planning exercise was recognised, incorporating the ideas and concepts like village plan, District Development Councils, Community Development Programme, and National Extension Programme, Integrated Area Approach that resulted in some states preparing district plans, The Lead Bank scheme for preparation of district credits plans, Command Area Development, and Small Farmer Development plans. While distributing powers between the Union and the States, the Constitution of India in Article 40 (Directive Principles of State Policy) vested local bodies and Panchayati Raj as a subject with the States but did not further elaborate on the relations between the States and this third tier of Government. Meanwhile, several committees were constituted to look into the prospects and challenges of the decentralisation process in the country.

The Balwant Rai Mehta Committee in 1957 that suggested the setting up of Village Panchayats, Taluk Development Boards, and Zilla Parishads underlined the role of elected Panchayat Samitis at the community development block/ tehsil level as the basic unit of democratic decentralisation. Only an advisory role was contemplated for the Zilla Parishads, constituted of panchayat samiti heads, and chaired by the Collector. The committee pointed out that one reason for the failure of the panchayats was the absence of an organic link between different levels, and suggested restructuring the old programme as a three-tier system with a view to ensuring the people's involvement in development programmes. The Committee also argued, "So long as we do not discover or create a representative and democratic institution ...invest it with adequate power and assign it appropriate finances, we will never be able to evoke local interest and excite local initiative in the field of development" (Balwant Rai Mehta Committee Report 1957). Recognising a clear distinction between delegation of power and genuine decentralisation, it called for the establishment of panchayats at the village level and municipalities at the towns and a primary unit to undertake responsibility for development work at the local levels. This shifted the thrust from the panchayat as a development organization to the panchayat as a political institution. The government accepted these recommendations and the State governments enacted appropriate legislation to usher in a new era of Panchayati Raj Institutions (PRIs). However, the PRIs worked well only in a few States like Gujarat, Maharashtra, Karnataka, and West Bengal (Misra, 1983).

Recommendations of the Ashok Mehta Committee (1977) were: (i) The district should be the key administrative unit for planning, coordination and resource allocation, and the management of rural and urban continuum; (ii) The PRIs should be a two-tier system, with the *mandal* panchayat (block/taluka) at the base and the *zilla parishad* (district) at the top; (iii) There should be population-based representation of the Scheduled Castes (SCs) and Scheduled Tribes (STs) in the election to PRIs; (iv) There should be participation of political parties in elections, and (v) There should be financial devolution consistent with the devolution of developmental functions to the district level.

The Dantwala Committee (1978) looked into the issue of achieving full employment through block level planning. It also suggested linking planning to generation of income and employment, upliftment of the weaker sections, building up of social overheads etc. It cited the case of Command Area Programme of West Bengal as justifying the choice of block as a proper unit for planning (Bhattacharya, 1991).

The Hanumantha Rao Committee Report (1981) emphasised the need for strengthening the district level planning process. The Hanumantha Rao Committee stressed the need to involve groups of the poor at every stage of development–pre-planning, strategy setting, scheme formulation, implementation, monitoring, and review. The Working Group (1984), which surveyed the earlier ad hoc efforts at district level planning, concluded that the

States which had done this were not enthusiastic about it and also were ill-equipped to undertake the same. The G.V.K. Rao Committee recommended that the Zilla Parishads and the idea of district level planning should be strengthened and argued for an integration of block and local level planning with the lower level of PRIs.

Though Article 40 of the Constitution of India requires that "the State shall take steps to organise village panchayats and endow them with such power and authority as may be necessary to enable them to function as units of self-government", decentralisation got a constitutional status only through the 73rd and the 74th amendments.

Figure 2.1 graphically represents the changes in perspectives of planning across a span of 5 development decades (1950- 2000) in India.

Fig 2.1
Shifting Perspectives in the Indian Planning (1950- 2000)

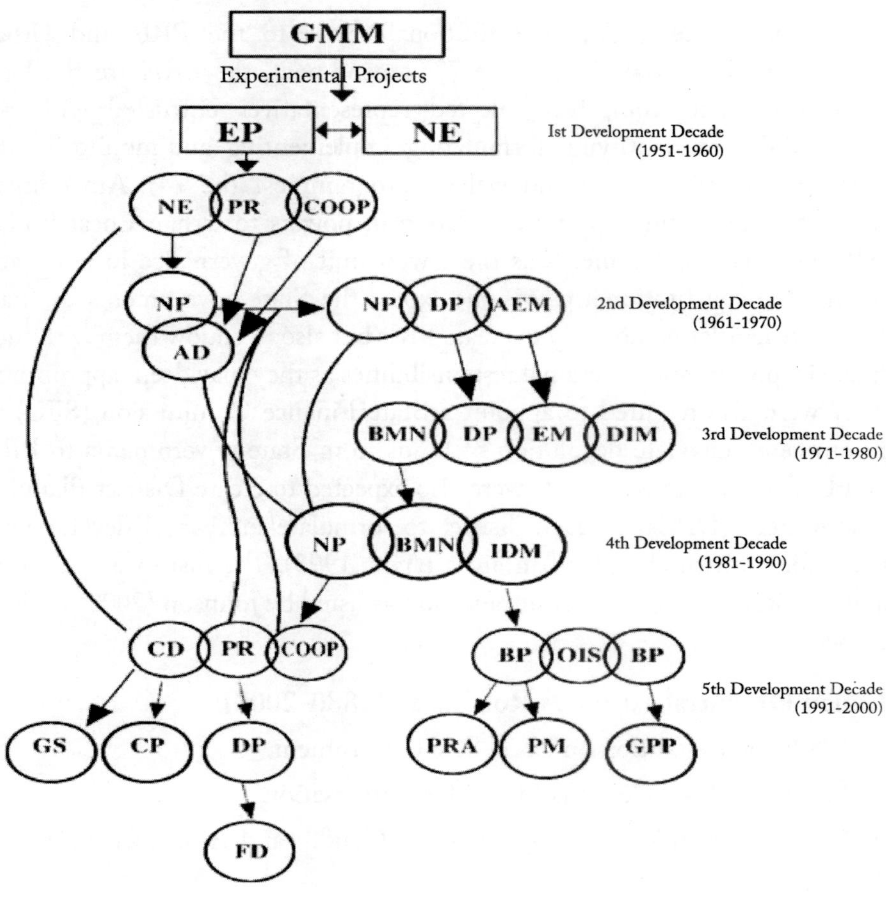

AEM- Agricultural Extension Models	GPP- Gram Panchayat Plan
AD- Administrative Decentralisation	GMM- Gandhian Meta Model
EM- Extension Model	NP- Nilokheri Project
DIM- Diffusion of Innovations Model	CD- Community Development
IDM- Integrated Development Model	DoP- Dominant Paradigm
OIS- Operational Integrated Strategy	GS- Gram Sabha
PRA- Participatory Rural Approach	PR- Panchayati Raj
MAL- Multi- Disciplinary Approach at Local Level	COOP- Co-operatives
CP- Community Plan	BP- Block Plan
DP- Decentralised Planning	PM- Participatory Model
FD- Financial Devolution	DP- District Plan
GPP- Gram Panchayat Plan	

The amendments gave constitutional status to the PRIs and Urban Local Bodies (ULBs). As per the 73rd amendment, the PRIs are the local level institutions comprising elected representatives entrusted with the responsibility of identifying, formulating, implementing, and monitoring the local level developmental and welfare programmes. The 74th Amendment mandated the setting up and devolution of powers to Urban Local Bodies (ULBs) or city governments as the lowest unit of governance in cities and towns. The constitutional provisions expect the State governments to enact necessary legislation not only to create PRIs but also to endow them with such financial powers and functional responsibilities as they may deem appropriate. They were also required to appoint a State Finance Commission (SFC) to recommend adequate devolution of funds from State governments to PRIs and ULBs. State governments were also expected to create District Planning Committees (DPCs) in each district to formulate local level development plans for both rural and urban areas (Aziz, 1993). The historical trajectory and milestones of Indian decentralisation as listed by Johnson (2003) is given below.

Indian Decentralisation: A Road Map (1880-2000)

1882: The Resolution on Local Self-Government.

1907: The Royal Commission on Decentralisation.

1948: Constitutional debates between Gandhi and Ambedkar on Gram Swaraj, 'self-rule'.

1957: Balwantrai Mehta Committee – an early attempt to implement the Panchayat structure at district and block (Samithi) levels.

1963: K. Santhanam Committee – recommended limited revenue raising powers for Panchayats and the establishment of State Panchayati Raj Finance Corporations.

1978: Asoka Mehta Committee – appointed to address the weaknesses of PRIs, concluded that a resistant bureaucracy, lack of political will, ambiguity about the role of PRIs, and élite capture had undermined previous attempts at decentralisation, and recommended that the District serve as the administrative unit in the PRI structure. Based on these recommendations, Karnataka, Andhra Pradesh, and West Bengal passed new legislation to strengthen PRIs.

1985: G.V.K. Rao Committee – appointed to address weaknesses of PRIs, recommended that the block development office (BDO) should assume broad powers for planning, implementing, and monitoring rural development programmes.

1986: L.M. Singhvi Committee – recommended that local self-government should be constitutionally enshrined, and that the Gram Sabha (the village assembly) should be the base of decentralised democracy in India.

1993: The 73rd Amendment to the Indian Constitution – PRIs at district, block and village levels are granted Constitutional status. The Gram Sabha is recognised as a formal democratic body at the village level. The 74th Amendment, granting Constitutional status to municipal bodies, was passed soon after.

1996: The Panchayati Raj Extension to Scheduled Areas (PESA) Act – Powers of self-government are extended to tribal communities living in 'Fifth Schedule' areas.

Decentralisation and Local Governance in Kerala: Historical Overview

Under the British rule, Kerala was divided into three areas; Travancore and Cochin were princely states, while Malabar was part of the Madras Presidency. The local self-governments in Madras Presidency were urban in origin. The recommendations of the Royal Army Sanitary Commission regarding the urgent need to redress the filthy urban conditions and the financial constraints of the provincial governments to meet these civic requirements were important factors that contributed to the Madras Towns Improvement Act of 1865 (Santha, 1993). The Town Improvement Act of 1871 was the reason for elections of the councilors by the tax payers and for an elected vice-president. The Madras Municipal Act of 1884, introduced the three- tier structure and enabled to enhance the number of elected councilors to three fourth of the total membership. Amendments of the Act in 1920 and 1930 enhanced the scope and functions of the democratic process of the municipalities. In 1930, the Malabar District Board became an elected body with its first elected president as a local landlord. Madras Village Panchayat Act of 1950, after the independence, substantially increased the powers of the local bodies, which provided direct election for the office of the president (Menon, A, 1978). Under this Act, panchayats had certain limited judicial powers and the main sources of revenue were taxes on buildings, vehicles, and entertainment. The 1954, elections gave a sweeping majority to the Leftists and signaled a dynamic period for the local bodies in Malabar.

In Travancore, the Town Improvement and Conservancy Regulation of 1894 enabled the formation of Trivandrum, Nagercoil, Alleppey, and Kottayam Town Improvement Committees. The Municipal Act of 1920 enlarged the scope of the urban local bodies beyond the focus of sanitary arrangements to education and health sectors. In 1941, Trivandrum was made into a corporation with an elected Mayor. Meanwhile, the rural local governments were active only from 1930s and the Travancore Village Panchayat Act of 1935 entrusted the local governments to declare any revenue village/s to be a panchayat with an elected or nominated committee to perform a variety of civic duties.

The urban local bodies were also evolved in the state of Cochin to mainly monitor the sanitation work, and in 1910, Municipal and Sanitary Improvement Regulations were passed, providing the scope of Town Councils with elected members. One of the important achievements was that women could vote and get elected to these local bodies (Menon, A. 1978). The Cochin Village Panchayat Regulation Act of 1914 was one of the earliest legislations, and in 1922, election was introduced for the rural local bodies.

During the integration time of Travancore and Cochin in 1949, there were 197 village unions in Travancore and 100 panchayats in Cochin. The Travancore Cochin Panchayat Act was legislated in 1950 and the elections were held in 1953. When the Kerala State was formed in 1956, there were 495 reconstituted panchayats in Travancore-Cochin area and 399 panchayats in the Malabar area. Despite the integration, the two-tier system in Malabar and single-tier system in Travancore-Cochin continued to be the administrative structure of the local bodies for a longer period of time.

In 1957, Kerala became the first democratic space in the world where the Communists came to power through the ballot box. The first democratically elected communist government in the state strongly believed that democratic decentralization is the best possible alternative to de-bureaucratize governance and to ensure people's participation, and initiated a number of political interventions to augment the decentralisation process in Kerala. One such significant intervention was the appointment of the first Administrative Reforms Committee (ARC) in the state, formed in 1957 under the chairmanship of E.M.S. Namboodiripad, the then Chief Minister of Kerala. E.M.S.Namboodipad, a leading Left political ideologue, who strongly believed in democratic decentralization as it facilitates the protection of interests of the working class and other common people. His scholarly engagements and writings on decentralization were strong imperatives towards conceptualising and implementing the legislative and policy framework, systems and procedures of decentralization in Kerala for more than four decades after the formation of the state. The ARC recommended a two-tier Panchayati Raj system, both directly elected, with village panchayats and district councils at the bottom and district level, respectively. The report envisaged the local bodies in the realm of self-governing units, much beyond the scope of development agents. Prominence was given to the assimilation of revenue and development functions, where village panchayats would be empowered to collect land revenue to be remitted to the government.

Recommendations of the ARC laid the foundations of the Kerala Panchayat Bill and Kerala District Council Bill of 1958. However, the dismissal of the Communist government stalled the enactment of the bills, which had an adverse impact on the course of development of the local governments in Kerala. During 1960-1961, when Shri. Pattom A. Thanu Pillai was the Chief Minister, the Kerala Panchayat Act, 1960, the Kerala Municipalities Act, 1961, and the Kerala Municipal Corporation Act, 1961 were enacted, unifying the existing laws in the Malabar and Travancore –Cochin regions of the state and enlarging the functions and financial resources of local bodies (Ramachandran, 1994). Village Panchayats everywhere were found discharging a wide variety of functions which had, however, been broadly divided into two categories – obligatory and discretionary—as was seen in the concerned laws of the different states (Santhanam Committee Report, 1963). Another noteworthy feature of the Kerala Panchayat Act 1960 was the provision of reservation of seats for Scheduled Castes, Scheduled Tribes, and women. Section 7 of the Kerala Panchayat Act 1960 stipulates "where the number of electors belonging to Scheduled Castes and Scheduled Tribes in a Panchayat area is not less than five percent of the total number of electors in that Panchayat area, one seat shall be reserved in the Panchayat for Scheduled Castes and Scheduled Tribes." It was also provided in the Act that one woman member could be co-opted by the Panchayat, in case no woman was elected to the Panchayat

(Kerala Panchayat Act, 1960).The first round of elections to 922 panchayats in Kerala took place in 1963.

However, it is important to record that Kerala Panchayat Act of 1960 and Municipal Corporation Act of 1961 majorly ignored the recommendations of the ARC and substantially diluted the spirit of the decentralisation envisioned in the ARC. For instance, the powers vested in the Panchayats were not commensurate with the duties and responsibilities assigned to them and as a result of this, many of the proposals even on trivial matters, had to be sent to higher authorities for their approval (Visalakshi, 1967).

Despite the Act being impressive in exhaustively listing out the duties and functions of the local bodies, the actual experiences were different where they could only exercise on the traditional civic functions. Besides, the absence of an intermediary tier at the district or block level adversely impacted on the functioning of the local bodies, as there were abysses in the convergence of political leadership between the state and the local bodies. Though in 1964, the then Congress government tried to enact the Panchayat Union Council with an intermediary zilla parishad in tune with the Balwantrai Mehta Committee, the ministry lost the power before the Act could be enacted.

In 1967, the Left government introduced the Kerala Panchayati Raj Bill with a two tier system, which envisioned panchayat as the basic unit and zilla parishad at the district level, but could not enact the Bill due to the fall of the ministry. In the amendment of the Kerala Panchayat Act 1967, provision has been made for the direct election of women for each Panchayat by reserving one seat for women (Visalakshi, 1967).

When C. Achutha Menon became the Chief Minister in 1970, efforts were again made to create Zilla Parishads at the district level. In 1971 the Kerala District Administration Bill was introduced in the Legislative Assembly. However, due to a variety of reasons it was left to the next government under A.K. Antony to enact a slightly modified legislation called Kerala District Administration Act, 1979 (Oommen, 2009). When it received the assent of the President on May 18, 1980 a new government under the Chief Ministership of E.K.Nayanar had come to power (Ramachandran,1994).

There was a long interval before the second round of elections to panchayats took place in 1979 and then the third in 1988. Following the general elections in March 1987, a new Government again headed by E.K.Nayanar came to power in Kerala and efforts were made to implement the District Administration Act, as clearly mentioned in the election manifesto of the Left Democratic Front (LDF) government. The LDF government made sincere efforts to establish a democratically elected and responsible government at the district level. Though the successive governments in the state introduced several bills for empowering LSGs in Kerala, all the initiatives failed to meet the desired results, as they were poorly executed. The political differences over the powers to be enjoyed by LSGs further slowed down the process of decentralisation in Kerala.

The major breakthrough in this direction came in 1991-92 experiment with the District Council under the Left government. The LDF government took serious steps towards setting up district councils in the state and overhauling the local self-government system (Isaac and Franke, 2000). The LDF government also took the initiative for formulation of the Eighth Five Year Plan of the state with a clear vision on decentralization, and the District Development Councils (DDC) and the Block Planning Committees (BPC) were assigned some responsibilities to submit their proposals. Unfortunately, the district level authorities including the district level officials did not have the capacity to formulate sound and viable proposals to be included in the state plan based on the specific development needs of the district. Only a few districts carried out the planning in the manner visualized in the State Planning Board guidelines (Isaac and Franke, 2000). The UDF Government that came to power in May 1991 in the state wanted to reverse the decentralization initiatives taken (Oommen, 2008), and the short-lived district councils were dissolved. Thus, the first experiment of democratic district administration came to an end as a result of the hostile attitude of the UDF government towards decentralization.

People's Plan in the Context of Participative Democracy

The 73rd and 74th Constitutional Amendments made the Panchayati Raj and the Municipal Institutions as intrinsic structures in the political framework of India and opened up a new phase in the history of decentralization and local government system in Kerala, as in the case of other states in India. Conducted from 1996 through 2001, the IX Plan of Kerala— the People's Plan for Decentralized Planning— envisioned to promote participatory democracy by establishing structures and processes to maximize direct involvement of citizens in planning and budgeting. Linking planning and budgeting to the efforts to eradicate poverty, mitigate inequalities, and empower historically disadvantaged citizens, the PPC sought to capitalize on local knowledge, while also using participatory decision-making as a means to change attitudes and behaviors associated with sexist, class-based, and anti-caste prejudices that impede the egalitarian civic culture.

For more than a century, development has been claimed as the means to reduce poverty through modernization and economic expansion. Yet across the global South, poor growth performance, falling levels of agricultural productivity, environmental damage, structural decay in the industrial sector, and deterioration of services in the crucial sectors such as education, public health, and transportation have raised key questions about the adequacy of hegemonic approaches to development. Within governments, international institutions, and academic communities, proponents of change have debated the comparative merits of technocratic interventions, neoliberal market mechanisms, and participatory deliberative decision-making as remedies to persisting underdevelopment and mal-development. These debates reflect the fundamental differences about whose knowledge (experts v. local people) and which processes (rational administrative v. market v. mass participatory) will be most effective in remedying the serious environmental, agricultural, social, and political issues that confront the world in the twenty-first century.

The People's Planning Campaign (PPC) offers helpful insights into multiple dimensions of these debates and was an innovative response to the dire economic and political challenges confronting Kerala. In contrast to technocratic and neoliberal prescriptions, which de-politicize poverty by characterizing it as a technically manageable problem best left to administrative experts or market mechanisms, the PPC conceptualized poverty in relation to a host of growing inequalities such as economic dispossession and political marginalization.[1] Rather than placing faith in either rational comprehensive decision-making or incremental institution building championed by public administration and managerial sciences, Kerala's participatory planning accredited ways of seeing and forms of knowing grounded in local experience that emerge in 'reflexive reasoning and dialectical engagement with citizens' (Heron and Reason, 1997).

Conceived as a vehicle for deepening democracy, the 9th plan of the state of Kerala was a unique experiment that attempted to transform decentralization from an exercise in administrative reform to the use of planning processes as instruments of political mobilization. In keeping with the motto, "*power to people*," the People's Planning Campaign sought to promote participatory democracy by establishing structures and processes to maximize direct involvement of citizens in planning and budgeting. In stark contrast to the decentralization models espoused by the multilateral development agencies like the World Bank, the Kerala State Planning Board (KSPB) delegated new decision-making power to the local panchayats governing municipalities and

1 For critiques of the technocratic vision, see Harriss (2001) and Heller (2001); and for critiques of neoliberal prescriptions, see Escobar (1995), Ferguson (1994), and Harris (2004).

rural districts, blocks, and villages. These local state government institutions (LSGI) were given discretionary authority over 35-40% of the state's annual development budget and charged to create and implement development plans through a series of nested participatory exercises in which citizens shaped (rather than choosing among) policies and projects.[2]

Informed by the belief that the people know best what is good for them, the People's Planning Campaign sought to achieve a sustainable model of development, local empowerment, and environmental protection through people's participation in the planning and implementation processes. From the outset, clear tensions existed between respect for local knowledge and efforts to transform beliefs that sustain gender, class, and caste hierarchies. These tensions played out in the campaigns that were designed to encourage mass participation in local assemblies convened at rural village and municipal ward levels to identify pressing needs and priorities for development; training seminars for participants; development seminars where members of the local panchayats attempted to draft development proposals from the diverse views aired in constituent assemblies; task forces chosen to prepare annual development plans, and in District Planning Committees where statutory bodies were responsible for approving final plans. Tensions also arose during implementation pertaining to criteria for selection of beneficiaries, formation of beneficiary committees to distribute funds, and in monitoring committees whose task was to ensure maximal participation and transparency without compromising the technical requirements of planning.

As the "most ambitious and concerted state-led effort to build local institutions of participatory democratic governance ever undertaken in the subcontinent" (Heller, Harilal and Chaudhuri 2007), the PPC was envisioned as far more than a means to devolve power to the local level as mandated by the 73rd and 74th Amendments to India's Constitution. It sought to build the capacities of citizens, improve the quality of local decision-making by creating government responsiveness and accountability, and reducing power imbalances and corruption, especially in the life world of the people living in the marginals.

The politics of/by marginals should be understood through the realisation of the fact that the politics from centre to the grassroots operate in a social reality that is hierarchical and complex, in which caste, religion, gender, and

2 Prior to 1996-97, LSGIs received approximately Rs. 20 crores in discretionary funds. By 1997-98, discretionary funds increased to Rs. 749 crores, growing to Rs. 950 crores in 1998-99, Rs. 1020 crores in 1999-2000, and Rs. 1045 crores in 2000-01.

community differences etc., are intensely engraved in everyday socio-political relations, and its influence in the political rostrum gets manifested in all layers of political processes. Hence the apprehension shared by Dr. B. R. Ambedkar (1952) towards the PRIs when he commented that "what is the village, but a sink localism, a den of ignorance, a narrow mindedness and communalism". The political processes through different ways at different points in time define and redefine the state's margins and centre. The abstract nature and character of the state authorizes it to delineate and maintain the category of marginals through the tactics and apparatus of administration. However, the ideas of equality, representation, and participation that require imaging of marginals in a manner that suits the principle and ethics of democratic politics and participative democracy as an engagement with the marginals, become significant in this context. People's Planning Campaign with its motto, 'Power to the People', was trying to make ruptures in the hegemonic power structures and the normative value frameworks in both formal and informal structures that make discriminations, exploitations, humiliations, and social injustice stemming from the structural inequalities and inequities as commonsensical and normal.

Chapter 3

People's Plan: Combining Theory and Practice of the Participatory Communication

Creativity, communication, and community are the three major factors that connect human beings, and the organic link thus produced positions them in their habitats which are rooted in political, socio-economic and cultural frameworks. One of the crises of the postmodern context is the breakdown of the organic links between creativity, communication, and communities. When the tools of communication determine the content of the message, communication gets increasingly alienated from real communities. This often gives rise to hypothetical communities, which are mechanically connected but organically alienated from each other. When communication ceases to have organic links with communities, it becomes dehumanised dissemination of information. Communication, as dialogue and debate, occurs spontaneously at any time of social change. But, it is the participatory communication, like in the PPC, a deliberate intervention to effect social and economic change that holds the most interesting possibilities.

Participation, by putting emphasis on the needs and the viewpoints of individuals and groups, is recognised today as an integral part in deepening the discourse of the people-centred development. Participatory communication is understood as communities and individuals engaging in meaning making, which is a horizontal and deinstitutionalized multiple processes, in which all the stakeholders have definite and interchangeable roles, and are concerned with transforming social conditions. Participatory planning, therefore, is making people aware of the various facets of the real development problems in their region; organising to react collectively and effectively to these problems;

bringing to light the conflicts that divide the various interest groups; becoming politicised and learning to provide alternatives to problem situations and finding solutions to various problems, and becoming technicised, obtaining the necessary tools to put to concrete use the solutions provided by the community. It has allowed people to be subjects of their own development and not simply objects of technology or processes.

People's Plan, viewed from a participatory perspective, had three processes. First, the IX Plan of Kerala, popularly known as the People's Plan, based on the premise of decentralized planning, demanded, mainly, a bottom-up communication process. Second, the People's Planning Campaign (PPC), the communication strategy evolved to disseminate the message of the People's Plan, adopted a two-way vertical and a two-way horizontal communication at the intermediary phase. Third, training imparted to the resource persons and the elected representatives of the local bodies, as part of the communication process of the PPC, transformed the top-bottom vertical communication to a horizontal communication process.

Connecting People's Plan and its Phases to the People

Realising the necessity of decentralised planning as a structural pre-requisite for empowering people through their participation and mobilisation of resources, the Kerala Government resolved to allocate 35-40% of the State plan fund for schemes and programmes to be formulated and implemented by the elected local bodies. A non-partisan campaign of people- the People's Plan Campaign (PPC) - was envisaged to successfully complete the task of plan formulation and execution within the stipulated time frame of the IX five year plan. The ninth plan of Kerala- the People's Plan- started on 17 August 1996.

The PPC was organised in a phased manner with well-defined objectives for each phase. Each of the six phases had a nodal event, and involved a separate round of training at the state, district and local levels. Figure (3.1) gives a graphical representation of the organisational structure of the People's Plan.

A High Level Guidance Council was formed comprising eminent personalities in the State. Apart from representatives of all political parties and major mass organisations, the Council included the vice-chancellors of universities, heads of centres of excellence and cultural leaders.

Figure 3.1
Organisational structure of the PPC

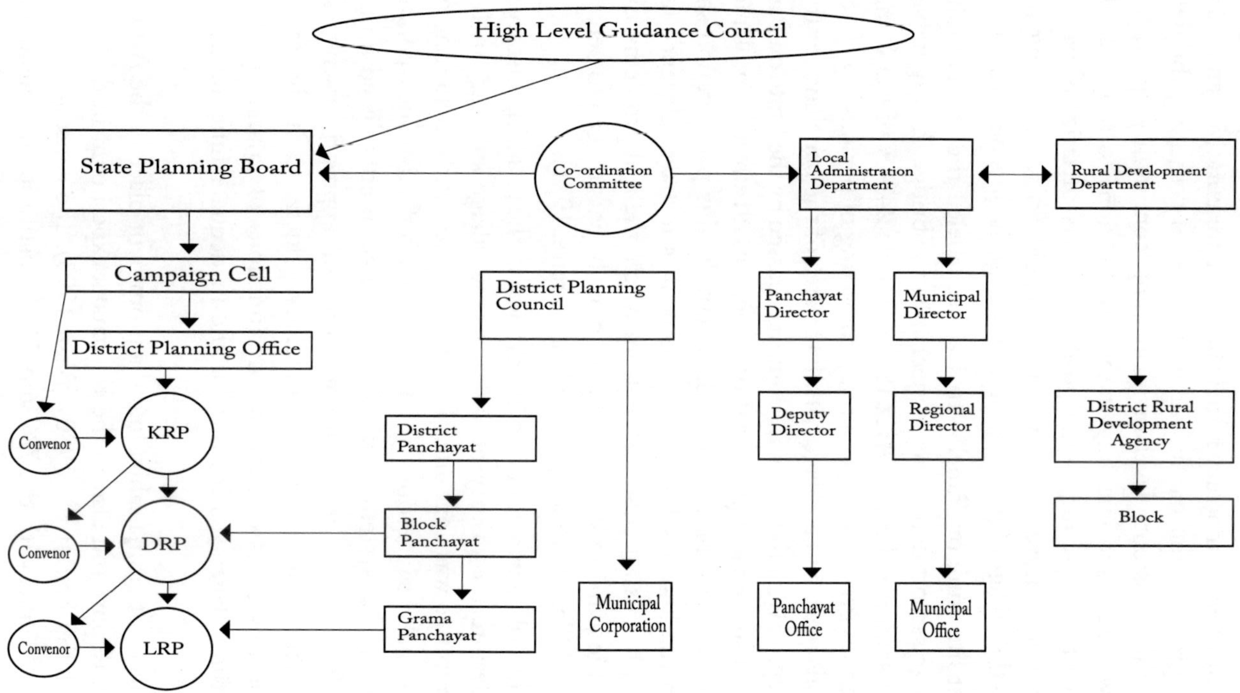

HLCC - High Level Guidance Council, SPB - State Planing Board, SC - Special Cell, DPO - District Planning Officer, KRP - Key Resource Person, DRP - District Resource Person, LRP - Local Resource Person, C - Convenor, CC - Coordination Committee, DPC - District Planning Committee, JP - Jilla Panchayat, BP - Block Panchayat, GP - Grama Panchayat, M/C - Municipality / Corporation, LA - Local Administration Department, PD - Panchayat Directorate, DDP - District Director of Panchayat, PO - Panchayat Office, MD - Municipal Directorate, RD - Rural Development Department, DRDA - District Rural Development Agency, B - Block

The Six Phases of the PPC

The grama sabha— the assembly of citizens in every village to discuss and decide the local issues—has always been an integral part of the concept of a village government or grama panchayat. Decisions of the grama panchayat were valid only if the grama sabha endorsed it. Therefore, the grama sabha was an institution of direct democracy rather than of representative democracy (Aziz, 1996). The grama sabha has an important role in activating the democratic process at the grassroots level in inculcating community spirit, increasing political awareness and enabling the weaker sections to progressively assert their point of view. It highlights positive aspects of citizens' participation, calling for more innovative efforts and strategies in reconnecting the sabha (people) to the villages (grama) to strengthen grassroots democracy.

The vast literature on Panchayati Raj has labeled the grama sabha as the gateway to grassroots democracy, a mechanism to bridge the gap between civil society and state panchayats (Aziz,1996). Article 243-A of the Constitution of India defines grama sabha as a body consisting of persons registered in the electoral rolls related to a village within the area of the panchayat at the village level. In keeping with the Constitution, Acts passed by the State on Panchayati Raj tried to ensure greater participation of people and effective implementation of rural development programmes. Deductively, this participation should be reflected in the grama sabha. If development is to have relevance to people who needed it most, it should start from where the real problems and needs existed. People living in such peripheries must be encouraged to perceive their felt needs and identify their real problems (Freire, 1971).

The grama sabha was not given importance in the planning history of India. This was despite the history of a very strong village structure in India. An official committee was appointed in 1962 to review the functioning of grama sabhas and make suggestions for their formal effective incorporation into the Panchayati Raj system (Isaac, 2001). The committee listed a number of procedural factors, like the absence of a common/appropriate venue, selection of inconvenient time, inadequate publicity, reluctance of the members to convene meetings, unawareness of the functions of grama sabha, and the apathy of the villagers, as reasons for the inadequate functioning of grama sabha.

The concept of grama sabha found a prominent place in the Ashok Mehta Committee Report and also in the Karnataka experiment in decentralisation during the latter half of the 1980s (Aziz, 1993). The concept received a new constitutional status with the 73rd and 74th Constitutional Amendments. The grama sabha was reconstituted as the base of the three-tiers Panchayati Raj

Institutions (PRIs). In Kerala, the Panchayati Raj Act of 1994 endowed the grama sabha with substantial powers and functions. They have to be convened at least twice a year.

Grama sabha symbolised and manifested the very objective for which the PPC was evolved— participation of people at the grassroots level. A typical grama panchayat has 10 to 12 wards. Thus, on average, even when the grama sabha is defined as the assembly of voters in a ward, there would still be 1,500 to 2,000 members. Such a large membership made even these assemblies unwieldy.

One of the first achievements of the PPC was to find a practical solution to this problem. Instead of grama sabha meeting as a general body of several hundred people, it was decided that after a brief common gathering, the participants would divide into small groups, each group dealing with a particular development sector and discuss, in depth, the problems of that sector. Twelve groups were proposed: Agriculture and Irrigation, Animal Husbandry and Fishing, Education, Drinking Water, Sanitation and Health, Industry, Transport and Energy, Housing and Welfare, Culture, Women's Development, SC/ST Welfare, Co-operatives and Resource Mobilization.

Identification of the felt needs of people was the first step in the decentralized planning. The grama sabha provided an ideal forum for people in every locality to meet and discuss their local development problems, cause of the problems and possible solutions. In order to ensure maximum participation, the grama sabha was convened only on holidays. Squads of volunteers visited the households and conscientised the people about the programme. A vigorous publicity campaign, using all possible media, was resorted to disseminate the information on the PPC.

Aims of the group discussions were mainly three-fold: to elicit both qualitative and quantitative information on the development sector of that ward; to list the development problems and to prioritize the needs of the ward with reference to the sector, and to select representatives from each groups for deliberating on each sector at the development seminar. A semi-structured questionnaire was distributed in grama sabha to smoothen the flow of discussions. Resource persons were mobilised and were given training to act as facilitators in the discussion groups. A three-tier training programme was drawn up— the state level training for Key Resource Persons (KRP), district level training for District Resource Persons (DRP) and panchayat/municipal training for Local Resource Persons (LRP). It was made mandatory that all district and block panchayat members participate in the district level training and that other elected representatives participate at least in the local level training.

A special campaign cell was set up at the Kerala State Planning Board headquarters. It was estimated that more than two million people participated in the grama sabha and the urban ward assemblies.

After the identification of the felt needs in the grama sabha, the next step in the planning process was to make an objective assessment of the natural and human resources of the locality. The planning perspective had to be a judicious blend of the local needs with local resource availability. A series of participatory studies were undertaken in every grama panchayat/ municipality and their outcome resulted in a Development Report of 75-100 pages. The reports had a uniform structure with chapters covering a review of administrative and local history of panchayats and analysis of natural and human resources of the locality. Besides, the report had twelve chapters covering the various development sectors of the particular panchayat.

Development Seminars were organised in each Panchayat/municipality to discuss the Development Reports. Main objectives of the second phase included: generation of an extensive local database; a comprehensive survey of all development sectors for all panchayats and municipalities; list of plausible solutions to the development problems, and formation of a task force to prepare development projects for each development sector. Discussions at the development seminar were held in small subject-wise groups.

The task force, the third phase was elected by the group to prepare the project. It was formed at the development seminars to projectise the recommendations and suggestions that emerged from the development seminars. Twelve task forces were constituted in each local body to cover the development sectors. The projects in different development sectors were broadly classified into three: projects in material production sectors; in infrastructural sectors, and in service and welfare sectors. To ensure uniformity, every project proposal was envisaged to have eight parts. A hand book on project preparation covering explanation of project proposal formats, methods of financial analysis, brief overview of the development perspectives for each sector, and selected model projects for various sectors were printed and published to facilitate the process of project preparation. Separate set of guidelines for the preparation of Special Component Plan (SCP), Tribal Sub Plan (TSP), and Women Component Plan (WCP) were also given. The task force prepared around one lakh projects for consideration of the panchayats (Isaac, 2000).

Elected representatives of the grama panchayat samitis and municipal councils had the right to select the projects and programmes to be included in the annual plan. For the local bodies, the total general sector allocation was made between grama panchayats, block panchayats, and district panchayats in the ratio 70 : 15 : 15. Within each tier, the allotment was made solely on the basis of the population of each local body.

Table 3.1

Guidelines on Sectoral Allocation to the Local Bodies

Development Sector	Rural Local Bodies (%)	Urban Local Bodies (%)
Productive	40-50	20-30
Service	30-40	40-30
Infrastructure	10-30	10-35

Source: KSPB Hand Book

Plan allocation for each local body was separately indicated in the State budget, with broad guidelines regarding sectoral allocation to be made by each local body. While 40-50% of the plan allocation was to be invested in the productive sector and 30-40% in the social sectors, 10-30% of the plan allocation was given to the infrastructure sector, as shown in table (3.1). The plan document had eight chapters which included the development strategy, the pattern of finance, projects by sector, integrated programmes, and programmes for women, SC, ST, and monitoring system (Isaac, 2000).

In the PPC, the basic unit of planning was village and municipality. Block panchayats were to be built up primarily by integrating the plans of grama panchayats. Every block panchayat was to prepare a Development Report, in printed form, in which the problems identified in the grama panchayats in the block area and the type of projects included in their plan for each sector were integrated.

In each sector, all major development problems identified were listed in rows. In each column, under the relevant grama panchayat, the rank order of the problems was marked according to their relative gravity. Thus, a matrix of relative importance of different types of projects for each grama panchayat was prepared. These matrices gave, at one glance, the problems and solutions identified by the grama panchayats.

Project integration of the campaign encompassed three major dimensions: the integration of projects across sectors; the integration of projects across local bodies or tiers, and the integration of the schemes of the central and

State Governments implemented through the local bodies in the local plan (Isaac, 2001).

Thus, all development activities at every level should be integrated with the local plans. The block plan document, a combination of the development reports and the plan documents from the grama panchayats, had four sections: first section covered the history, natural and human resources, and review of the ongoing plans; second section covered the development sectors; third section was on the development strategy for the block, pattern of finance, TSP, SCP and WCP, and the fourth section had annexures with selected documents, statistical statements, texts of the projects, and recommendations to the district panchayats.

Each district at the district panchayat level prepared its Developments Report integrating the analysis and programmes of the lower tiers. Block panchayats and district panchayats also organised seminars to discuss their plan documents.

A pilot review of the projects prepared by the local bodies revealed that a significant portion of them had to be modified to ensure their technical soundness and viability before they were approved for implementation. Hence, a new phase- the sixth phase- was added for the technical and financial appraisal of the projects and plans. More than one lakh projects had to be evaluated to rectify the technical and financial weaknesses of the project proposals. Further, the official machinery was not able to complete the task of evaluation within a span of three to four months (Isaac, 2000).

Consequently, the concept of Voluntary Technical Corps (VTC) was evolved. Retired technical experts and professionals were encouraged to enroll themselves as volunteers to appraise the projects and plans. The experts were required to spend at least a day a week to give technical assistance to the panchayats. Expert Committees were formed at the block (BLEC), municipal (MLEC) and corporation (CLEC) levels. The expert committees had no roles to change the priorities set by the local bodies. Their task was limited to the technical and financial appraisal of the projects and providing suggestions for modification. Objectives of different phases and sequences of various events of the People's Plan are graphically represented in the figure (3.2).

Figure 3.2

Objectives of the Phases and Sequences of Various Events of the PPC

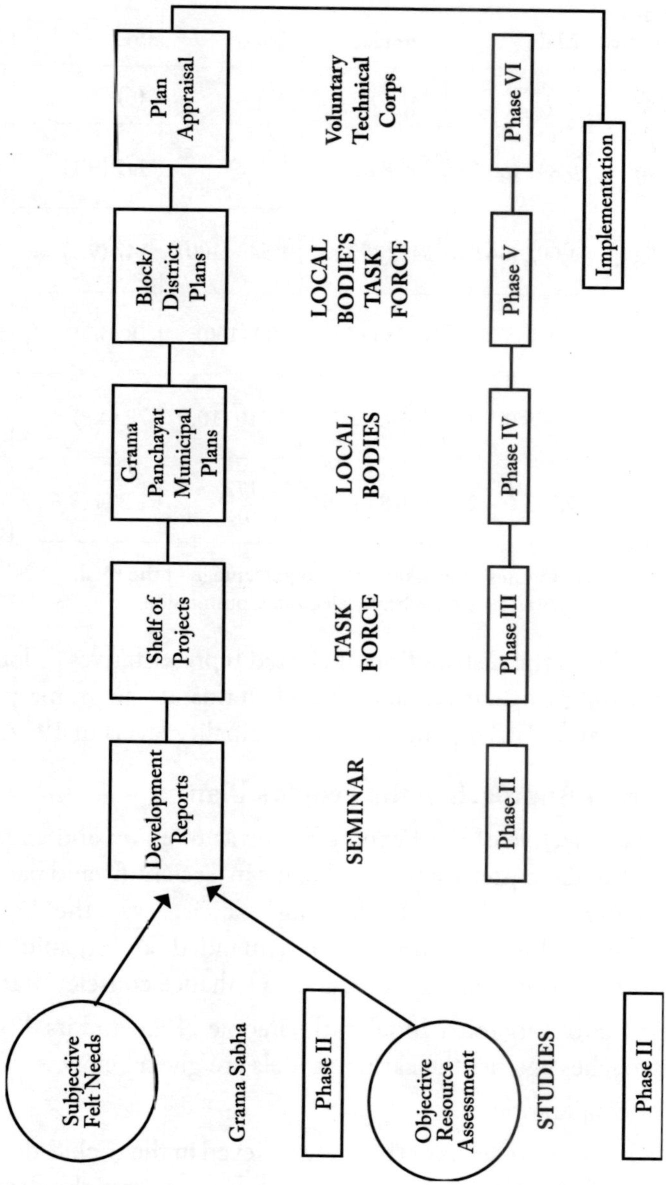

Table 3.2

Distribution of the Elected Representatives of Local Bodies in Kerala, 1997

Type of Local Bodies	**No. of Local Bodies**	**Number of Representatives**				
		Male	**Female**	**Total**	**SC**	**ST**
(1)	(2)	(3)	(4)	(5)	(6)	(7)
Grama Panchayat	990	6,842 (63.8)	3,878 (36.2)	10,720 (100)	981 (9.1)	96 (0.9)
Block Panchayat	152	1,002 (64.9)	541 (35.1)	1,543 (100)	147 (9.5)	11 (0.7)
District Panchayat	14	196 (65.3)	104 (34.7)	300 (100)	18 (6.0)	3 (0.1)
Munici-palities	58	1,055 (65.3)	555 (34.7)	1,610 (100)	78 (4.8)	3 (0.0)
Total	1,214	9,095 (64.2)	5,078 (35.8)	14,173 (100)	1,224 (8.6)	113 (0.08

Note: Figures in brackets refer to percentage of the total.
Source: Kerala State Election Commission

Table (3.2) shows the distribution of elected representatives of local bodies in Kerala, according to their sex and SC/ST status at the grama panchayat, block panchayat, and district panchayat/ municipality levels in 1997.

Communication Approach in the People's Plan

The primary objective of the People's Plan was to equip and empower the local bodies in Kerala to prepare the local plans in a scientific and participatory manner. Decentralised nature of planning exercise was the hallmark of the People's Plan. This decentralisation demanded an organic model of communication to ensure participation and to enhance conscientisation.

Characteristics of Organic Model in the People's Plan and its difference in planning approaches against the earlier models are given below.

- Motive for cooperation

Earlier planning approaches of the State believed in the trickle-down theory and followed a diffusion of innovation approach to address the development problems of the region. Hence, the motive for co-operation in the earlier plans was that people *need to be helped*. Organic nature of the People's Plan was built on the understanding that *people can help themselves*.

- Assumption about the user groups

Former plans believed that *people lacked abilities and resources to develop themselves*. The plans considered masses as passive and helpless, and thought to deliver development projects to help people. The participatory approach of the PPC took the notion that people have the *ability to develop themselves.* Devolution of 35- 40% of the State plan fund to the elected representatives of local tiers testified this belief of the PPC.

- Attitude towards problems

Planners of the previous plans delineated the problems of people and considered themselves on a *problem solving* chair. But the strategy adopted in the grama sabha of the People's Plan was not even to pose the developmental questions before people, but to ask them to *identify and prioritise the development problems* of their locality.

- Attitude towards participation

Previous plan models considered participation only as a tool for the effective delivery of programmes. The People's Plan, on the other hand, did not consider participation as a *means to achieve the end.* The campaign itself was participatory and hence, a *never ending* process.

- Learning relationships and valuation of knowledge

The People's Plan challenged the earlier notion that the *planners know all and people know nothing*. The very concept that people had to prepare their own local plans confirmed the participatory idea that *everyone has something of interest to share*, for the People's Plan considered that the experiential knowledge was equally relevant for development. The concept of taking *western knowledge* as superior to the *traditional and indigenous knowledge* was given a back seat in the Peoples Plan. The People's Plan recognised the significance of the practical wisdom, which people had gained through their daily life experiences.

- People were seen as subjects

The very term target group, in the earlier planning process, identified people as *targets and objects.* The People's Plan made a shift in the thinking process where people were seen as *subjects and actors.*

- Media used

Earlier plans relied mostly on the *mass media* for information dissemination of the messages of the plan. Though, not very effective, the People's Plan attempted to *integrate the media,* including the folk media, for conscientisation.

- Communication process and organisational structure

Earlier planning models relied mostly on the vertical, *top- down and one-way* form of linear communication. The People's Plan adopted a *bottom-up, two- way communication* with a strong feedback mechanism operating in the planning system. An attempt was also made to replace the *hierarchical vertical* form of organisational structure with *horizontal* structure in the People's Plan.

- Mode of communication and the time perspective

Monologue and consultation were the modes in the earlier plan models whereas, the People's Plan was based on the *dialogic mode* of communication. The project/ programme format of the earlier plans worked on a *short-term,* time specific format. The People's Plan had a long-term perspective, for its objectives were to challenge the power structures inherent in the socio-economic and political system of the society.

Figure 3.3
Differences in Communication Approaches between Earlier Plans and the PPC

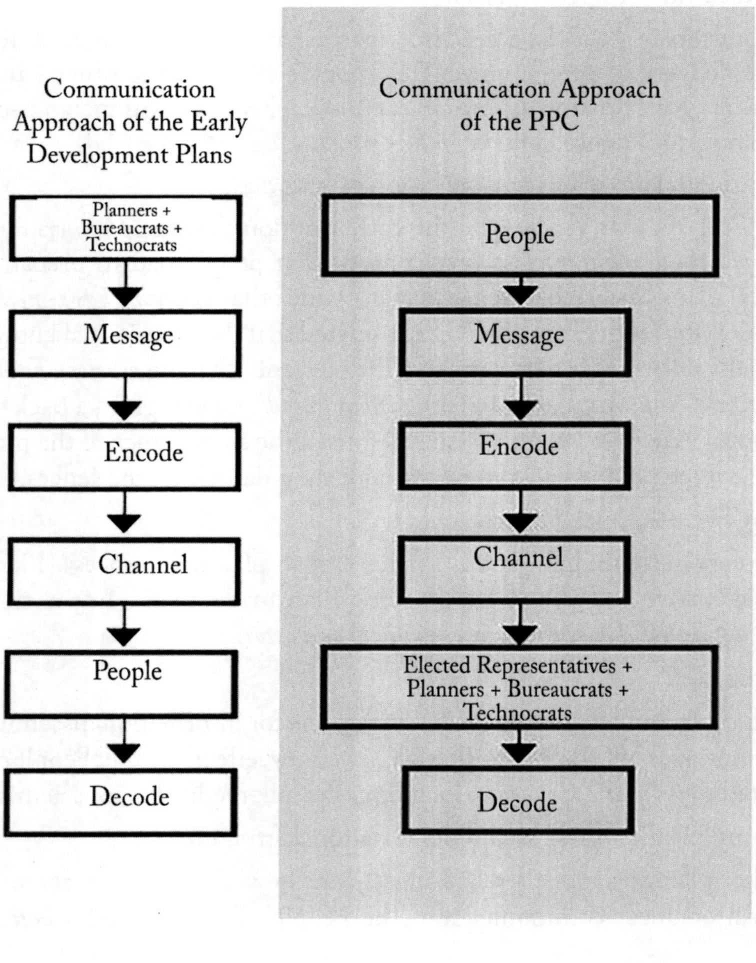

Figure 3.3 shows the difference in the communication approaches between the early development plans and the People's Plan. While the earlier plans adopted a top-down communication approach (from planners + bureaucrats +technocrats to people) towards planning, the PPC chose a bottom-up communication process (from people to planners + bureaucrats +technocrats+ elected representatives).

Communication Approaches in the Training Process of the PPC

The People's Planning Campaign was the communication strategy adopted by the Kerala State Planning Board (KSPB) to disseminate the message of the People's Plan. The communication approaches in the PPC had two stages.

Stage 1: Top-down Communication Process in the Training Modules

Training was an important component in the People's Planning Campaign. Much confusion was developed around the norms and rules of the People's Plan, the new financial procedures, the role of the bureaucrats, panchayat members etc. This demanded extensive and intensive training programme modules to be conducted at various levels—panchayat, district and state—depending on the context and need of the problems and requirements. The KSPB constituted a pool of resource persons, Key Resource Persons (KRP) at the state level), District Resource Persons (DRP) at the district level) and Local Resource Persons (LRP) at the panchayat level). Training preceded each phase of the campaign, and orientation workshops were organised at various levels. The State level orientation was of five to seven days duration, and was attended by 400-600 KRPs. The KRPs helped the DRPs to organise the district training programme on an average duration of three days and imparted training to around 12-15,000 DRPs. The DRPs, in turn, helped to organise one- day workshops at municipal/panchayat level and gave training to around 1,00,000 LRPs.

Training in the first phase focused on the organisational tasks involved in the convening of grama sabha. The resource persons were also introduced to the philosophy, approach, and broad phases of the campaign. In the second round, the focus shifted to Development Seminar and preparation of Development Report. Certain model integrated sectoral programmes that could be implemented at the panchayat level were also introduced. The third round dealt with the evaluation of the ongoing programmes, preparation of new schemes and elements of cost- benefit analysis. The final round focused on various guidelines to be adhered to while prioritising the schemes and drawing up the draft plan. Thus, each round of training was expected to concentrate upon the immediate task in the phase of activity that was to begin.

As this planning exercise from below itself was a novel and complete deviation from the past, local bodies lacked the needed expertise, experience and information base to prepare the local plans. This demanded intense conscientisation and communication among people about the objectives and characteristics of this new development culture.

Communication process in the first stage of the PPC followed a vertical and top-down (from the planners + bureaucrats+ KRPs+ technocrats to the elected representatives +people) training method as in the earlier development plans. This was because:

- The People's Plan involved devolution of 35-40% of the State plan fund to the Panchayati Raj Institutions (PRIs) to carry out the development objectives in a given period;
- The mammoth nature and massive scale of activities of decentralised planning demanded a cascading form of training modules;
- Training in the form of top-down had to be given to organise and mobilise the planning activities at different stages of the PPC;
- Preparation of the local level plan involved a lot of technical details; and
- More than 75% of the elected representatives at the local tiers were holding office for the first time.

Inexperience of the representatives, coupled with the technical nature of planning, demanded a top-down communication. The training had to synchronise with the different phases of the People's Plan making the top-down communication imperative for the PPC. This first stage, with this vertical one-way communication in the training modules, lasted only for a short period. Once the elected representatives, who received the training to implement the activities of the planning process, confronted with ground realities, they gave their feedback, thereby initiating a bottom- up communication process (from elected representatives + people to the planners + bureaucrats + KRPs+ technocrats), which is reversal of the first stage that functioned along with the existing top-down communication process. This initiated the second stage of the PPC.

Stage 2: Two-way Vertical and Two-way Horizontal Communication

Besides the two modes of vertical communication, the second stage also saw the emergence of horizontal communication. Horizontal communication began from the grassroots when representatives of the panchayats discussed among them the practical problems they faced at the implementation stage. This created a vibrant communication culture at the grassroots level. What had churned out from this vibrancy was fed back to the planners at the next training session in a direct communication context. This triggered layers of horizontal communication, this time among the planners and the bureaucrats. Result of these layers of horizontal communication took the form of vertical communication when they were disseminated to the elected representatives and resource persons, activating a series of horizontal communication among them, causing yet another stream of bottom- up vertical communication and the subsequent two- way horizontal and vertical communication interplay, making the whole communication context vibrant and dynamic at the panchayat, district, and State levels. This created a homophilic communication interaction on a new development culture, which was framed into a participative frame of reference.

Communication in the training modules of the PPC was top-down, dialogic, and interactive to sensitise the elected representatives at the local bodies, and to conscientise them of their basic rights of participation and power in a democracy to plan, design, and decide their future. Training, per se, demands a top-down communication process. In the case of the training modules of the PPC, this top-down communication process had a specific objective other than the overt dissemination of the messages of the PPC. Its primary and fundamental objective was to capacitate the trainees to evolve a bottom-up and participative communication, the very essence of the PPC. Thus, the top-down communication process of the training modules of the PPC was aimed to deconstruct the prevalent power structure between the trainers and the trainees.

Distinct from the earlier plan experiences of top-down approach, this Plan had adopted a participative approach to implement the development projects. Any development programme that regards people as mere recipients, rather than as its actual participants, usually fails. Meaningful discussions generated by people can help the community to identify its true problems and priorities and locate where its capabilities and needs lie. This self-analysis helps a community to generate realistic proposals for new development initiatives and stimulates tremendous interest to see these initiatives succeed. The spirit of the PPC ensured the communication potential in the participative planning process.

Communication Approaches in the PPC

PPC is the communication strategy of the People's Plan to connect with the people and to enhance the organic links between the planners, bureaucrats, elected representatives,and the people. Source, message, channel, receiver, feedback, and noise are the general elements of communication process.

Source

The original source, the Government of Kerala, delegated its power to disseminate information regarding the People's Plan to the Kerala State Planning Board (KSPB), which, in turn, became the source of the PPC.

In the initial phases of the PPC, ministers, leaders of the ruling alliance, pro-left NGOs like Kerala Sastra Sahitya Parishad, members of KSPB, all were its spokespersons. This was understandable as the Left Democratic Front (LDF) government initiated the PPC. Being a new process, and that too a participatory one, the message had to be disseminated to people to ensure their participation in planning.

The PPC was presented as an alternative development initiative to tide over the crises of the Kerala Model of Development. Though a general cynical attitude, the hallmark of Kerala society, was evident towards the PPC, the initial credibility of the source was high.

At the same time, there were certain inherent variables which affected the credibility of the source right from the beginning .The LDF was led by the Communist Party of India (Marxist), a cadre party with centralized and hierarchical organisational structure. Since the concept of the People's Plan, which aimed decentralisation and devolution of power to the grassroots was mooted by the CPI (M), conflict between the concepts of decentralisation the CPI (M) was advocating and the centralised nature of the party itself affected the credibility of the source. The bureaucrats, who were following the hierarchical pattern of functioning, too did not enjoy the much-needed credibility to air the message of decentralisation. However, these unavoidable negative elements were countered effectively, to an extent, by a pool of resource persons, who, though belonged either to the CPI (M) or to the bureaucracy, could overcome these inherent limitations with their non-partisan attitudes and past experiences in the development activities, like the Total Literacy Campaign.

Media covered the news of the PPC in a very positive framing along with the networking of activities designed by the Planning Board for its information dissemination. But after the initial high pitch, the mammoth nature of the PPC, coupled with its teething problems (inexperience of elected representatives of the local bodies, reluctance of bureaucracy and legislators to devolve power to the panchayat bodies, inadequacy of resource persons, and problems with expenditure of the fund allocation) and inappropriate handling of issues by the ruling coalition, tarnished the image of the PPC in the minds of people. The derived credibility of the KSPB, hence, was lower than its initial credibility.

In the next stage, political problems within the LDF snowballed. One of the major constituents of the LDF - the CPI- started criticising the PPC. This, along with the evaluatory mode of the reporting *(agenda setting nature of media and its role are detailed in chapter 6 on media)* and the politically motivated negative campaign of the opposition parties, gave a thoroughly distorted image about the credibility of the source. The government failed to counter criticisms aired by political parties and the media.

Lack of proper leadership in the LDF to effectively counter these criticisms accentuated with the demise of E.M.S., the legendary figure in Kerala politics, who had been writing articles airing the thought of decentralised planning, since 1956. Thus, the terminal credibility of the source was lesser than the derived credibility. These factors took the wind out of the sail of the PPC, which started as a development initiative. Still, the KSPB continued to be the most important and reliable source of information of the PPC.

At the same time, it is worth mentioning that the credibility of the KSPB remained high among the panchayats, which were the actual implementing bodies of the People's Plan.

The source, in a participative process, has to continuously modify its messages, respond to interaction with receivers focusing on their needs, share knowledge and integrate indigenous knowledge. This shifting of role to cater to the changing contextual needs was not effective in the PPC.

Channel

As this planning process was a total deviation from the past system of planning procedures, the KSPB deployed various communication modes like interpersonal, group, and mass communication to conscientise people, elected representatives, bureaucrats, and resource persons.

Figure (3.4) shows the flow chart of the different channels of communication used in the PPC. It details the interpersonal, group and mass communication used in the PPC.

Figure 3.4
Channels of Communication in the PPC

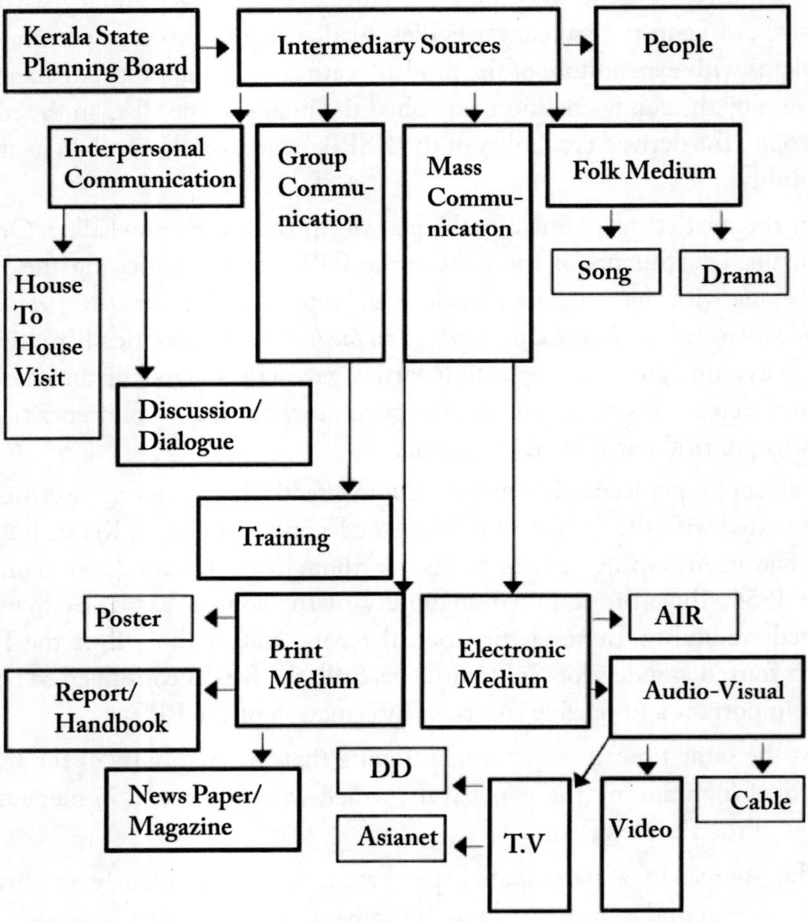

Message

Considering the shift towards decentralisation in the planning process, understanding the concept of people's participation, realising that all individuals have the capacity for reflection and conceptualisation for taking decisions and choosing alternatives and planning social changes for development, the message designed for the PPC was very much participatory.

In the PPC, the planners adopted a combination of constructionist and dialogical model for encoding the message of the IX Plan as against the usual transmissive mode (messages transmitted from the sender to the passive receiver) approaches of the earlier plans. Message was designed in a dialogical process through continuous interaction with people. Transaction between source and receiver reflected the felt needs of the receiver. Message was shaped using the appropriate technical and scientific input from the source, and was interfaced with the indigenous knowledge of the people.

Though a participatory process was adopted for designing the text of the training materials, studies conducted by the KSPB revealed that even the elected representatives or the resource persons were not quite clear about the concepts of decentralised planning. Even those women, who were active participants of the PPC, were unaware of the concepts, like, five year plan, participative planning and the unique nature of the PPC, as shown in table (3.3) taken from a survey of women elected representatives conducted by the KSPB in 1998.

Table 3.3
Clarity of Women Elected Representatives Regarding the Activities in Different Phases of the PPC

Document	Grama Sabha	Dev. Seminar	Task Force	Plan
1. No response	258 (20.3)	509 (40.0)	649 (50.9)	692 (54.3)
2. No clarity	110 (8.6)	58 (4.6)	65 (5.1)	56 (4.4)
3. Average Clarity	692 (54.3)	513 (40.3)	398 (31.2)	367 (28.8)
4. Good Clarity	203 (15.9)	187 (14.7)	157 (12.2)	155 (12.2)
Total	1274 (100	1274 (100)	1274 (100)	1274 (100)

Source: Survey of Women Elected Representatives, KSPB, 1998.

Most women and tribals considered grama sabha as a forum for grievance redressal, and not as the one for which it was envisaged. They saw the PPC as the means to get benefits from the government, which really defeated the very purpose of the PPC. Inadequate or lack of user specific approach in the message design, to some extent, accounted for the non-sustainability of the PPC.

Figure 3.5
Development of the Messages in the PPC

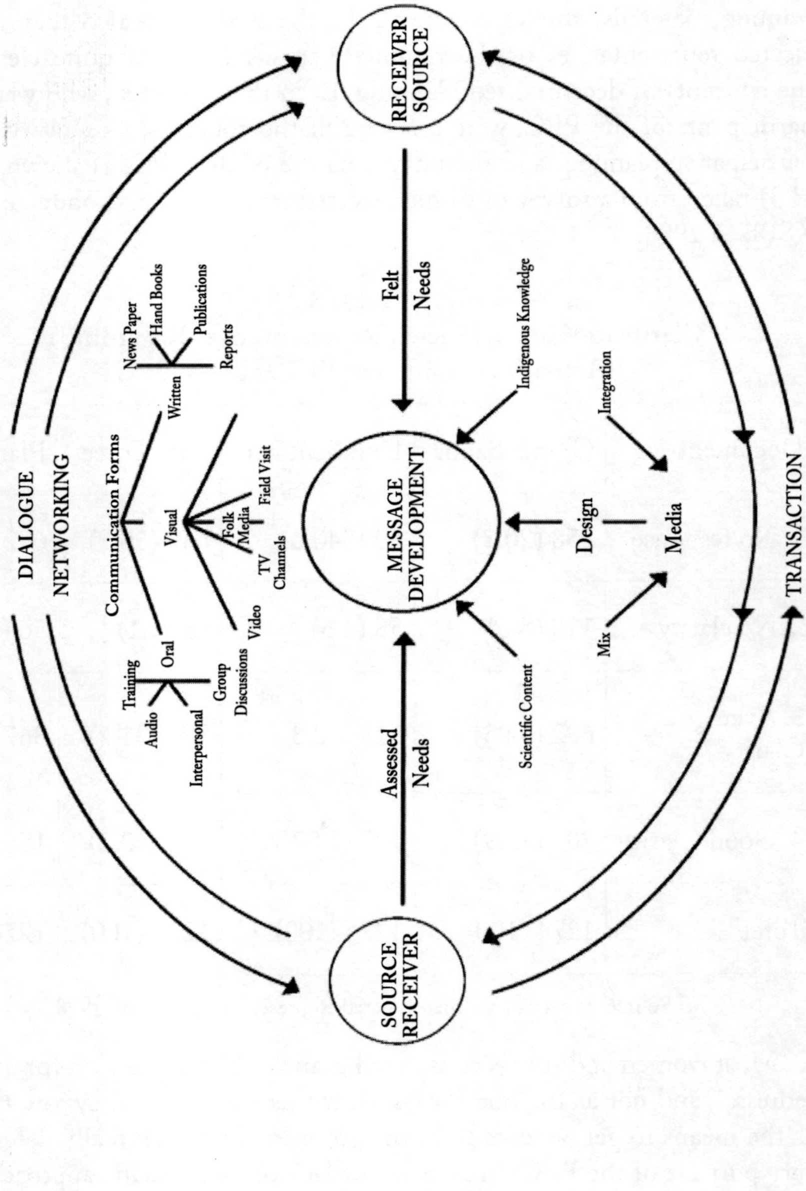

Receiver

In a participatory process, like the PPC, roles of the source and receiver were continuously shifting, i.e., source became a receiver and the receiver became a source as the participative planning process gained momentum. They ceased to be the source and the receiver and functioned as participants, though the receiver was considered as the dominant party. Participants grew and changed, each influenced by the interpretations of the other's message, changing feelings and beliefs, as the dialogue progressed. Informed decision-making utilised the indigenous knowledge and was based on access of information necessary to make those decisions. The receiver was in a position to make a strong statement as to what was perceived as right.

In the PPC, grama sabha gave this platform for people to be heard and to express their development needs and problems. But beyond this, neither the KSPB nor the people were successful in extending this participation to own up the PPC as a development initiative. Studies conducted by the KSPB revealed that participants who attended the grama sabha belonged mostly to the lower income groups. They expected economic benefits from the PPC and viewed it as a forum to avail the welfare packages. Hence, the main objective of the PPC—to make people the real participants of the planning process and to empower them to decide on their future— was not achieved.

Noise

In the PPC, the semantic noise—noise due to the complexity of the message— was high, due to its innovative and novel content. The six-phased campaign process with various rules, procedures, and jargons made it difficult for the common man, especially those who wanted to join the PPC at a later stage, to comprehend it.

The Kerala polity, in general, was unaware of the development spirit of the PPC. This had an adverse impact on participation, which was the fundamental requisite for the effective communication of the PPC. The source was unsuccessful in reducing the semantic noise, either by redundancy or by simplifying the messages, so that the general public could comprehend it. Even the women and tribal elected representatives found the handbooks and training materials too technical. Though the PPC tried to demystify the technical nature of the planning process by teaching people to write development projects and reports, the source was unable to completely break or deconstruct the technical jargons of the planning process.

Feedback was a continuous process and its potential was exploited at all phases of the planning process.

Figure 3. 6
PPC as a Dialogic Communication process

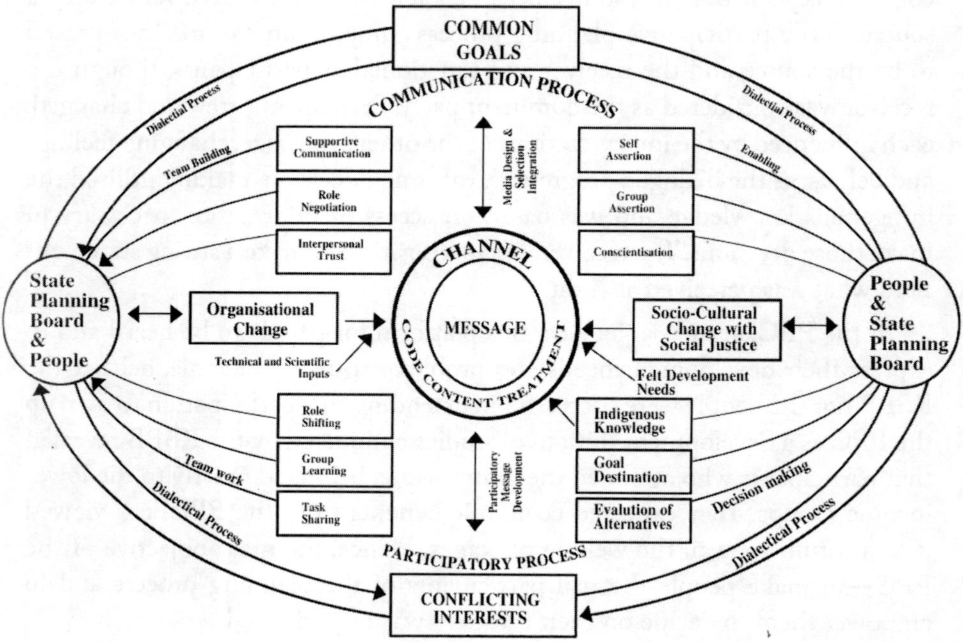

Figure (3. 6) *[an adaptation of the transactional model of communication: Shirley A. White]* illustrates the participatory nature of communication in the context of the PPC. Dialectic processes between the common goals and the conflicting interests in development are shown in the figure. The interchanging roles of the KSPB and people as source and receiver, participatory development of messages, selection and integration in the media design, and organisational changes to effect the PPC are shown in the figure. The conflict and common goals in the process of development and the dialogical participative approach adopted in the planning process to address the divergent interests of the locality are detailed in the figure.

The Participatory Communication Approach of the PPC

The essence of what makes a communication process participatory was evident in the communication strategies adopted in the PPC of the People's Plan.

Training modules, environment creation, and review mechanism were the three main components of the PPC.

Training modules enabled the transformation of vertical communication to horizontal and the horizontal one to vertical, both simultaneous and creating positive impact.

Environment creation aimed to set the stage for the mammoth decentralised planning activities at various levels–State, District, Block and Panchayat/ Municipal—involved the application of various communication strategies that made the process of communication operate at various directions, simultaneously.

Review mechanism, another cardinal component applied on all activities of the PPC at all phases, too created multi-dimensional communication processes, enabling the PPC to churn out a new communication context and development culture hitherto unknown in the process of planning. This change in the communication approach is detailed in chart (5.1).

Chart 3.1
Changes in the Intervention Approaches of the PPC

	Intervention approaches in the early Five year Plans	**Intervention approaches in the PPC**
Societal source	Ruling class or dominant Elite	Competing political, socio-cultural interest groups
Structure	Hierarchical, bureaucratic	Horizontal, egalitarian
Production	Standardized, controlled, synchronic	Creative, free, original, diachronic
Content and ideology	Selective and coherent, decided from 'above'	Diverse and competing views, decided from below
Audience	Dependent, passive, organized on large scale	Fragmented, selective, reactive and active
Effects	Strong, rigid and confirmative of established social order	Multiple and flexible

The multi-faceted and multi-directional process of participative interventions were evident at every phase of the PPC in different communication contexts. Three specific contexts— participative communication in the grama sabha, participative modification of Government Order in the PPC, and the District Plan—exemplifying the decentralised and participative nature of communication in the PPC are detailed below.

Participative Communication in the Grama Sabha

Participation of people in the grama sabha determined, to a great extent, the success of the PPC, since the plan was based on the discussions and the subsequent decisions emerged in the grama sabha. Effective functioning of the grama sabha was vital for ensuring transparency in the preparation and implementation of the plans. Transparency was a major check against corruption and misuse of public funds.

As mentioned earlier, one of the first achievements of the PPC was in making discussions in the grama sabha in small groups. These small groups allowed very strong horizontal interaction among the group members, where people participated actively. This was more visible in the case of discussion among women group members, where they came up openly with problems that affected them from their experiential understanding. These small group discussions facilitated more focused discussions, pertaining to the subjects chosen in the group. Horizontal processes of communication within the groups really helped the subject experts, bureaucrats, and political leaders to have a unique and different understanding of the process of planning. This planning process, through the grama sabha discussions, showed drastic changes in the communication approaches.

In the grama sabha, communication process was vertical, circular, and horizontal in nature, since there were inter and group communication between and among the local participants. There were multiple modes of communication processes—two-way vertical, two-way horizontal and circular—in the grama sabha between and among its participants. Grama sabha witnessed serious and intense arguments, discussions and even confrontations on the immediate local development problems to be addressed in the PPC. A basic factor in participation was self-expression, and true participation arises from dialogues and discussions through interpersonal and group communication.

Grama sabha as the first phase of the PPC, was successful in attaining the participation of the above- mentioned nature. Nearly two million people participated in grama sabha, all over Kerala (Sep-Oct, 1996) as shown in table (3.4).

Table 3.4
Attendance Patterns at the First Grama Sabha of the PPC, Sep-Oct, 1 996

District	Average atten-dance by pancha-yat	Average atten-dance by ward	Average as % of voters	Female as % of attendees	SC/ST as % of attendees	SC/ST popula-tion in pancha-yat
(1)	(2)	(3)	(4)	(5)	(6)	(7)
	N=979	N=979	N=979	N=932	N=967	N=566
Trivandrum	1928	171	11.25	35.01	17.61	13.43
Kollam	1810	150	9.37	28.11	13.13	9.45
Pathana-mthitta	1562	162	12.43	28.9	15.36	14.26
Alappuzha	2140	203	14.12	31.49	4.12	6.76
Kottayam	1519	143	9.89	26.89	12.38	15.97
Idukki	1507	153	12.51	22.45	16.87	12.38
Ernakulam	1280	122	8.38	20.26	14.58	12.32
Thrissur	1560	142	9.43	27.54	1.48	1.02
Palakkad	1477	140	10.44	22.29	4.58	2.82
Malappu-ram	1973	167	12.661	27.43	11.48	16.81
Kozhikode	2440	219	15.32	26.76	n.a.	n.a.
Wayanadu	2081	185	13.98	22.39	16.15	10.64
Kannur	1563	147	11.20	21.94	5.57	16.58
Kasaragod	1635	150	11.81	20.80	13.11	16.73
All Kerala	1737	159	38	26.22	8.94	9.99

Note: n.a., no data reported.
Source: Tabulated from Statistical Returns of First Grama Sabha, 1996-97.

Table (3.4) presents the average participation levels for grama sabhas by district. In 979 panchayats, 1737 persons attended. This represents 11.38% of the voting age population of the panchayats. For the 932 panchayat's male/ female break- down, the female participation rate was 26.22%. Among the 567 panchayats submitting the SC/St data, average attendance was 8.94%, a figure similar to the all Kerala population average of SC/ST. The 11.38% of voting age persons attending the grama sabha probably represents about 20- 30 % of all grama panchayat households, assuming that on an average one person per household attended. Suggestions and ideas from women and SC/ST were given special significance at the discussions.

Communication activities in the grama sabha helped people, even those from different social groups within a community, to share information and exchange ideas in a positive and productive manner. Understanding how development issues affected them, discovering what others think in other communities, and seeing what other communities had achieved, enriched this dialogue. These were the effective methods that helped the people in grama sabha to reach a consensus and find common grounds for action, based on their own needs and capabilities.

Dialogues in grama sabha were initiated and guided by resource persons, who were trained at various levels, to facilitate discussions of the localities. Discussion tools, such as flip charts, posters, slides, and video, were used to help people visualise and reflect their own reality. These activities led to a serious diagnosis of problems and a search for solutions in the grama sabha.

Participative Modification of Government Order in the PPC

Government orders are normally perceived as rigid and top-down communication. For the first time in India, the PPC proved how a Government order could be modified, even seven times, to incorporate and reflect the needs and demands of people, expressed through the elected representatives and resource persons. A classic example of the bottom-up communication that helped the top-down communication to re-work its strategy for the benefit of the common man in a democratic system is given below.

The guidelines on various aspects of the procedure for the selection of beneficiaries, like determination of criteria, publicity, application form, verification, grama sabha, selection of beneficiaries, and transparency were issued by the Local Administration Department vide G.O. (P) No. 220/97/LAD dated 2ndOctober, 1997. One or more changes were made in each or all aspects. For instance, in the *determination of the criteria*, eligibility alone was prescribed in the original order. It was modified to incorporate "prioritisation" also in the second order dated 2nd September 1998, exactly one year after the original order.

Similarly, in *publicity*, it was stated in the second order that "model application form would be published in newspapers."This was not there in the original order.

In *Grama Sabha,* the modification that the "list finalised in the grama sabha cannot be changed under any circumstances" was made in the second order.

In *selection of beneficiaries*, a new clause that reads, "thereafter the final list shall be printed and published in the grama panchayat office, ward notice boards, libraries, markets, government offices and schools," was incorporated in the second order to give maximum publicity and transparency to the beneficiary selection process.

Vide Circular No: 46996/P3/98/LAD dated 6th November, 1998, changes were made in the procedures to be followed when income was a criterion for the selection of beneficiaries. When it was found that it would be difficult to determine small differences in income, if it is taken as a criterion, the circular advised "to avoid income as a criterion and instead" depend on "other indicators reflecting income like type of house, land owned, and assets owned etc."

Circular No: 46997/P3/98/LAD dated 6th November, 1998 *(the same day on which the previous circular was issued)* made it clear that "any applicant would be free to submit his application form in the prescribed Performa in manuscript or in photo copied form."

It was also made compulsory that acknowledgement slip "indicating the application number, name of applicant, scheme number and date of receipt" should be given by the local body.

Circular No: 2801/P3/99/LAD dated 24th January, 1999, regarding the selection of beneficiaries through the grama sabha by grama panchayats for schemes being implemented by the block and district panchayats, made it clear that if the list of selected beneficiaries did not reach the block panchayats and district panchayats on or before 31 January "they may select the beneficiaries omitting the grama panchayats which have not furnished the list."

G.O. (P) No: 138/99/LAD dated 9th July, 1999, has made the following among other modifications to ensure objectivity and transparency in the selection of beneficiaries: "each local body may fix its own last date for receiving application; photocopies, handwritten or typed application in the prescribed performa should be accepted; and eligibility criteria and prioritisation criteria should be published in the application form itself showing the marks to be awarded to each criterion."

Circular No: 25421/ D.P.1/2001/LAD dated 30th July, 2001, made the modification that "not more than one member from a family should be selected as beneficiary for the same purpose."

All these modifications to the original government order dated 2nd October, 1997, through government orders or government circulars, were incorporated after giving proper attention by the government to the feedback from the elected representatives and resource persons, so as to make the guidelines for procedure for the selection of beneficiaries transparent and meaningful, reflecting the true nature of the decentralised planning process.

District Plan

The decentralisation planning process of the People's Plan, through its different phases, aimed to equip people to prepare their local development plans based on the participatory studies conducted on the available local, natural, and human resources.

Grama sabha discussed and prioritised the local problems and issues based on the needs and demands of the local people. These were reduced to printed development reports at the Development Seminar. Task force prepared the projects based on the needs and demands emerged from the local levels. Finally, there was convergence and integration of the panchayat plans at the block level and then, at the district level, to formulae the grassroots-level plans.

The block panchayat plans were to be formulated primarily by integrating the plans of the grama panchayats. Based on the Development Report, the problems identified by the grama panchayats in the block area and the type of projects included in their plan for each sector were integrated.

Integration of plans at the higher level was confronted with many technical and practical problems:

- All local plans at the panchayat level were independent;
- There were disparities and contradictions between the panchayat plans; and
- There were gaps in the panchayat plans.

All these plans at the district level were routed back to the respective block and panchayat levels for dissemination among people and to get their feedback. This review mechanism, applied at all stages of the PPC, formed a crucial component that gave the PPC it's participative and decentralised nature.

District plan under the People's Plan was a total reversal, in a very positive sense, from the earlier plans. It brought in, for the first time, the integration and convergence of bottom-up planning, which reflected the needs and aspirations of people at local level, and applied participative communication and a strong review mechanism to incorporate the feedback for formulating the district plan.

PPC and Power

The idea and practice of empowered participatory democracy, as opposed to the liberal constitutional understanding of democracy, is now part of an emerging global discourse. It is increasingly capturing the imagination of a rapidly globalising technocratic world, marked by citizen- apathy. The impact of globalisation has been multi-faceted. While globalisation has created new forms of interdependence across and within nations, the asymmetrical nature of these patterns of interdependence has resulted in certain sections of people and communities feeling marginalised and without voice. It has also brought about a technocratic revolution, where law making and public policy have acquired an 'exclusive' tag, and are seen as the prerogative of a few chosen specialists, well beyond the scope of understanding of ordinary citizens. Increasingly, even the systems acclaimed for their democratic nature are excluding the voice of the common, and make the agenda and policy making a forte of the specialists. This is tellingly described today as the 'green room effect' (Kent Jones, 2009), where the acting or the performing are confined to the 'specialists' or 'experts', making the common occupy the position of spectators in the periphery with minimal role to play in the activities of governance. This has resulted in a majority of the population being sidelined which, in the course of time, makes them apathetic towards the process of governance.

Power of the knowledge society is derived not simply from technological advances, but also from the growth of new elites who embody and institutionalise them (Stuart Hall, 1989). The truth-claim and the procedures for gaining access to that truth have historically privileged the pronouncements of trained experts over the discourses of ordinary people (Foucault, 1980). Today, this ideology manifests itself in the deference of people to the expert, and ultimately the subordination of their own experiences and personal meanings to expertise. As a result, decisions affecting ordinary people are shown to be based on expert knowledge, denying the rationality of individual citizens and their life experiences. Understanding human nature and the problems of living have become the purview of scientists, rendering people dependent on experts to explain and oversee their life experiences. Hence, the specialists dominate any debate concerning issues of public interest because ordinary people are unable to enter the scientised debate, as they lack the technical terminology and specialised language of argumentation. Unequal relations of knowledge are, therefore, a critical factor that perpetuates class or elite domination in the modern information society (Stuart Hall, 2001). Inequalities exist in access to information, production and definition of legitimate knowledge and in the domination of expertise over common knowledge in decision making. Underlying all these elements of the power of expertise is the expert's lack of any accountability to the ordinary people affected by his or her knowledge. A knowledge system that subordinates knowledge of ordinary people also subordinates common people.

The normal bureaucratic practice of keeping people at a lower level, with respect to the working of the system, was achieved mainly through the complexity of the bureaucratic process and its language. The imposed ignorance of people about the working of the system gave space to the common man to have only vertical communication with the system, which always occupied the pedestal of the omnipotent and omniscient source.

The training programmes of the PPC showed an explicit shift from the positivist- instrumentalist approach of the modernisation programme towards a model which was manifested in the training at different stages of the planning that was more qualitative and normative. In this training programme, the priorities were more contextualised catering to the needs and problems of the individual panchayats than the universal applicability of the earlier plan models. Also, this started an intense process in which the exogenous and endogenous reasons for the development problems of the panchayat were analysed and prioritized, based on the development experiences of the representatives from the local tiers of administration.

Through the training, the PPC, equipped ordinary people to speak to technocrats/bureaucrats / experts in their language, challenging the power of the technocrats/bureaucrats / experts they had enjoyed due to their command over scientific information and language about the administrative system, and thus helped ordinary people break the authority of power dynamics in the administrative system. Series of training programmes on the nuances of planning, technicalities of project preparation, complexities in the procedures, bureaucratic bottlenecks and impediments at the implementation stage gave the ordinary people an understanding of the functioning of the administrative system that was expected to deliver the new concept of decentralised planning. This capacitated a strong pool of elected representatives and resource persons who got well versed in the functioning of the system, and who could question the fissures in the hierarchical system, challenge its centralised nature, and see through the system to cross over the hurdles. Besides, training equipped them to comprehend the crux of the system, bypassing the administrative jargons and the labyrinthine process, which quite often, posed real hurdles for the common man to understand the system that had been designed to serve him.

Training programme, in a sense, reversed the communication process from horizontal to vertical too, but in a very positive way. Some of the grama panchayats like Kanjikuzhy *(People's vegetable cultivation programme)*, Kunnothuparambhu *(water conservation programme)*, Thaanalur *(health programme),* Olavanna *(drinking water programme),* Thrikunnapuzha *(sanitation programme),* Ulloor *(Self-Help Groups programme),* to cite a few, gained expertise in the above mentioned programmes. Training sessions that aimed to help them correlate their needs with the locally available natural and human resources were successful in some panchayats. This expertise in the plan process and effective implementation of the projects with people's participation made these panchayats stand above other panchayats. This newly gained status, thanks to the effective utilization of the potential of training, placed these panchayats on a pedestal from where they were giving lessons, based on their experiential knowledge and technical know-how, to other interested panchayats and bureaucrats. Though vertical and top- down in nature, this communication process proved to be a landmark in the whole process of the PPC, the very aim of which was to empower people.

Unlike the familiar classroom training, which seldom contemplates the practicality of the lessons, the training modules of the PPC were so designed that they preceded the actual infield experience of the different phases of the PPC. The trainees, enriched by theoretical knowledge and practical experiences, confronted the trainers at the next session with newly gained awareness, and gave effective feedback, which helped the planners to remould the Campaign process. Thus, the multi-faceted interplay of different contexts of two-way vertical and horizontal communication in the different phases of the training helped to concretise the objectives of the People's Plan.

The training programmes in the PPC deconstructed the *we- know - all-* nature of bureaucracy and technocrats and facilitated resource persons and elected representatives at LSGIs to understand the intricacies of the system to work within the system. This knowledge empowered them to have a face to face communication with the top brass in the system, communicating with them using the language of the system, creating an atmosphere of horizontal communication, which could not have been thought of earlier. This pool of over 50,000 persons in the length and breadth of Kerala from among the common man, who could communicate with the higher ups in the bureaucracy on equal terms - the very essence of democracy- perhaps, is the long lasting positive result of the PPC. This capacitated pool of resource persons in all panchayats today work as the Forward and Backward Level Information Ambassadors and as interlocutors between the community and the LSGIs, and collectively, form the central radar to capture details of the innovative programmes developed by the panchayats/ municipalities/corporations.

Communication Gap in the People's Plan

Though the right to communicate is widely shared theoretically, it is difficult to practice it. As most scholars admit, genuine participatory communication in the Freirean (1983, 1994) sense hardly exists, except, in a very limited way, in a number of small localised experiments (Berrigan, 1977, 1979; Lewis, 1993; Louw, 1993). While translating broad policies to specific practices, obstacles arise. The PPC, being a participative planning process at the State level, was massive in nature and hence, confronted with many obstacles.

The inherency of conflict and the propensity to avoid it is one of the barriers to participation. Besides, the participative endeavours are not in the interest of those seeking high visibility. When participatory efforts were implemented in the PPC, real world realities and sharp political conflicts complicated them. This conflict of decentralisation at one level and centralisation at other level was very much evident in the PPC, and that retarded the process of participation.

Authentic participation addresses power and its distribution in society, directly. It touches the very core of power relationships. While the multiplicity paradigm argues for structural change, it also asserts that the route to individual and social development is precisely the route to increased participation. Development and participation are inextricably linked. Participation involves equitable sharing of both political and economic power, which often affects the privileges of certain groups. Therefore, Bordenave (1994) observed that the major resistance to participation was most often not such overt, cataclysmic actions. Rather, the main obstacle was the much less visible, yet insidious and continuous reluctance to organisational change. Bureaucrats and members of the Legislative Assembly, in general, adopted apathetic or negative attitudes towards the PPC, since the PPC took away much of their powers.

Criticism of People's traditionalism, under-education, and recalcitrance nature are often cited as major obstacles to change. However, far less attention was given to other aspects like institutional or bureaucratic intransigence. Structural change alone would accomplish little. Participation is necessary but not sufficient for this to happen. The chicken and egg paradox is that, while the existing structures were a substantial impediment to participatory processes, valid and applicable restructuring could occur only through some degree of authentic participation. Therefore, unless policy making and the social process are themselves participatory, it is unlikely that the result will be a democratic pattern of communication.

There is no magic formula for injecting participation into projects or communities. It must come from within. Further, barriers to participation are most certainly not limited to government-populace or powerful-powerless relationships. Communities are seldom-unified groups of people having the romantic image of one big family. Each of the sub-communities or factions has its own self-interest to protect and endeavour which may or may not serve the needs of the community at large (Kennedy, 1984).

Figure 3. 7
Communication Gaps in the PPC

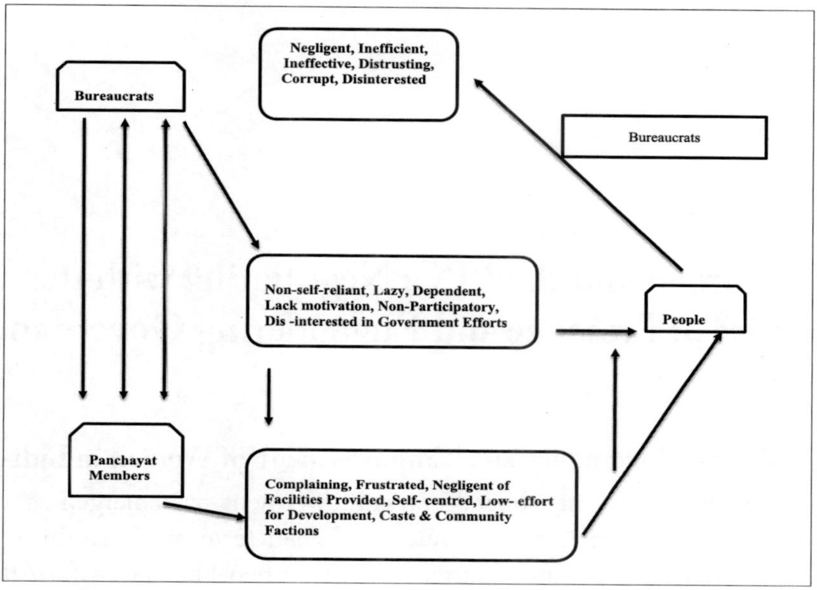

All these revealed a clear communication gap in the PPC. Both bureaucrats and panchayat members perceived People's participation in different ways. Bureaucrats took people as passive and politicians saw people as a never satisfied lot; demanding more and more development activities. It was observed that people's enthusiasm waned when their solutions and suggestions were not taken care of immediately, when their demands raised in the grama sabha were not met, and when their problems were not redressed. Same attitude was very much visible among the tribal communities. They perceived panchayat members as corrupt, and bureaucrats as indifferent. Hence, in most cases, people adopted development projects that were in their immediate self-interest.

The People's Planning Campaign, through its concept of devolution of power, was challenging the hegemonic notions of power that were present in the socio-cultural and political life of Kerala. But this demanded not only sensitization from the part of the planners, but co-operation from elites who held power and conscientization among people to hold power. This triangular function had to work in harmony for the effective implementation of the PPC. This demanded a well-planned communication strategy to counter the hegemony of power equations. That, to an extent, was missing in the People's Planning Campaign.

Chapter 4

Women and the PPC: Negotiating with the Politics of Presence and Engendering Governance

Engendering Governance and 'Empowerment' of Women in India

In the contemporary neo-liberal era, empowerment has emerged as a key word, effectively replacing the much maligned term, welfare. The recent focus on empowerment is an important part of the neo-liberal transformations taking place around the world, as the states attempt to downsize their welfare interventions and reinvent themselves. Empowerment has now been recognised, worldwide, as a development concept: UN Millennium Development Goals coming with Gender Equality and Empowering Women; World Bank's new 'human' face with Poverty Alleviation and Empowerment (Khan, 2000); US Agency for International Development introducing Empowerment Programme; and Government of India declaring 2001 as the Women Empowerment Year (Menon, Sen, 2001). The skeptical developmental inquiry of the term 'empowerment' and the anxiety posed by Harriss is relevant and evident when he asks the question, "is empowerment yet another engagement in the armory of the anti-politics machine that is constituted by the practices of international development"? (Harriss, 2002).

It is in this premise of complex and engaging debates that one has to deal with the empowerment concept, as it is a risky and a political act. It is better to describe it as "a power relationship, which deserves careful scrutiny" (Cruikshank, 1999). When one tries to understand an intervention that engages with local governance in India and women empowerment, the interplay between de-politicisation and re-politicisation, surveillance and subversion, and regulation and unruliness comes to the foreground. Modern governmental systems are altering the relationships between those who govern and those who are governed; this relation, in turn, is defining political society's struggles in India today (Chatterjee, 2004). The ways in which the state associates itself with or against the question of women empowerment and engendering governance in the public spheres becomes critical here. In this context, both counter-hegemonic and hegemonic usages of the empowerment are following Foucault's (1991) governmentality in that they aim to produce aware and active subject- citizens who participate in the project of governance and mould their behavior towards certain ends; they all, therefore, involve both subjectification and subjection (Crusikshank, 1999).

Empowerment, writes Jo Rowlands (1998), is nothing if it is not about power and, therefore, it is a fiercely political issue. How did gender questions advocate conceptualised power, disempowerment and empowerment? Kabeer (2001) differentiates between the powerful and the empowered, arguing that those who exercise a great deal of choice in their lives may be very powerful, but they are not empowered… because they were not disempowered in the first place. Like the one made by Frank (1969), who distinguished between un-development and under-development, Kabeer views disempowerment not as an original lack, but as the outcome of oppressive forces. Empowerment, thus, is concerned with overcoming disempowerment and the related inability to make strategic life choices, and challenging unequal power relations.

What constitutes women's strategic life choices and interest around which they are supposed to mobilise? Here, Maxine Molyneux's (1985) work on practical and strategic gender needs proves to be influential. Using her analysis, feminists argue that empowerment approaches need to specially (although not solely) address women's strategic gender needs and strategic gender interests. This implies challenging women's subordination through gender and other systems of domination that would lead to emancipatory outcomes. It is recognised widely that the phenomenology of absences woven around the life world of women made her invisible and inconspicuous in the public sphere and in the decision-making bodies. This being one of the reasons for their disempowerment and could possibly be countered by the gendered citizenship through the politics of presence of women in the public sphere as a form of resistance. Affirmative policies and subsequent representation of women in the decision-making bodies and the theoretical arguments around this representation, and the ways in which they alter the discourses around the gender questions therefore assume significance in the context of engendering governance.

It is often argued that with substantive/ numerical representation, i.e., increased presence of women in public life, women's interest will be better represented (Mohanty, 2008). Substantive representation stresses and gives importance to what an elected individual thinks and does, rather than emphasising who the person is. It requires deliberate actions. One of the most influential works and complex interpretations on the concept of political representation was done by Hanna Pitkin (1967) that goes beyond the two dimensional aspects of descriptive or substantive representation. She states that 'representing means acting in the interests of the represented, in a manner responsive to them'. She states that the shift from direct to representative democracy has shifted the emphasis from the politicians to what (policies, preferences, and ideas) they represent and, in doing so, has made accountability to the electorate the pre-eminent concern. Representation is seen as an important concept in a democratic context. As Niranjana Seemanthini (2003) argues, 'similarly working within the larger framework of representative democracy, this axis of representation – especially the relation that is posited between the political representative and the represented – needs to be understood more deeply than it has been till now'.

Going one step further, an argument is made in terms of 'critical mass' by Drude Dahlerup (1988) for substantive changes in political decision-making process and outcomes. There are many studies that have shown that there must be at least 30 percent reservation for women, a critical mass, to make a difference in politics (Dahlerup, 1988, 2005, 2006; Grey, 2006). It states that an increase in the number of women in any decision-making body is based on both arguments of justice and participation.

However, even in this context, representation has been critically analysed. While feminist scholars make a linear connection between the representation and participation, the presumption is that the first is necessary if not a sufficient condition for the second (Mohanty, 2008). Jayal in this context (2009) reasons that women's representation and women's effective participation, though related, are distinct issues, and that representation does not necessarily translate into participation; and the relationship between representation and participation is both complex and contingent. These engaging and conflicting discourses on representation and participation at various levels are useful while analysing the ways in which women's issues are approached in the Indian development plans and subsequent changes in their perspectives. The involvement of the state and the women's movement are important while contexualising gender discourses in India, which are briefly mentioned below.

In the development trajectory of India, growth with stability, in the 60s was changed to growth with social justice, thereby showing concern and care towards the marginalised. Women, despite half the population, in general, are considered marginalised in society, irrespective of their class, caste or race. The situation of women as producers in their own right, present or potential, and not merely in their role as child bearers was not recognised in the erstwhile plan documents. Gradually, issues related to women's work and employment, women's role and social change, education of women and children, health of women and children, and violence against women gained increasing centrality. Kabeer (1994) brings out this shift in the development perspectives when she argues that 'reversed' development must begin from the perspective of the most marginalised and places human life and enhancement of human well-being and creativity at the forefront. According to her, production needs to be organised around human needs rather than around market mechanisms, because the market is not the most efficient allocator of resources. The state, she thus avers, has a key role to play in the areas of poverty alleviation and development (Kabeer, 1994).

The involvement of the state as a key player in the process of engendering governance in India dates back to 1984 when the government of Rajasthan implemented the Women Development Programme (WDP), which was structured as a tripartite partnership between government, NGOs, and academic institutions. Beginning with the launch of the WDP in Rajasthan in 1984, a shift in attention from 'delivery mechanisms'—that so far had looked at women as objects of compassion and welfare— to subjects in the development process was made. The Indian states turn towards women empowerment as a desired development strategy and its goal is the cumulative result of multiple and intersecting local, national, and transnational processes. These include: rise of peasant, dalit, leftist, and women's movements around the issues of equal rights, citizenship, land distribution, and political participation in the post-colonial India; failure of state-initiated modernisation strategy to alleviate poverty and address growing inequalities; increase in the number of NGOs during the late 1970s; personal initiatives of powerful individuals within the government for a different kind of development trial; the relative success of non-formal education and adult literacy campaign in mobilising women to lead struggles such as anti-liquor movement; and national-level feminist interactions with state agencies resulting in the passage of the 73rdand 74thconstitutional amendments reserving one-third of seats for women in the local level legislative bodies.

The panchayat legislation enacted, in the wake of the 73rd amendment, facilitated a new presence of women in the institutions of rural local governance, and it was heralded as a silent revolution. The increasing number of women in public spheres has demonstrated that reservation challenges the societal image of women's roles. It has also given recognition to the need to increase women's spaces and support structures to enable their effective political participation. Even though India's perspective on gender development has been articulated in the Constitution and the relevant strategies were envisioned, there exists a definite gap between ideas, institutions and practice, if one follows the postulates of Amartya Sen (2000). There is a gap between the idea (participative democracy) and its institution (PRIs), and their manifested practices in the local governing institutions. It is very difficult to estimate the gap using conventional indicators as it tends to expand and collapse at various contexts, based on the lens with which you are looking at the gap. Even with the critical readings that recognizes the inadequacies of the affirmative policies in the local governance, the mere presence of the elected representatives at the three tiers of local governance from the marginals comprising women/SC/ST made a marked shift in the hegemonic nature of the erstwhile classist, sexist and casteist structure of the local governance.

As discussed before, besides the state, women's movement and collective mobilization of the women at multi levels which questioned the gender dimensions of the oppressions and hegemonic status quo of the male-centric patriarchal system of government and governance were successful in bringing the question of power to the centre-stage of development discourses. The terrain of Indian women's movement is one of contestations and negotiations. The term Indian here entails a connotation of political and cultural singularity that obfuscates the variances, differences and pluralities in women's movement. Nussbaum (2003) argues that both feminist theory and feminist practice are highly plural, and it would be deeply mistaken, in any writings on gender and decentralization, to impose from the top-down normative understandings of development that rejects or marginalizes many of the understandings women actually hold. Placing the argument of Katzenstein regarding movements (Katzenstein,1987) in the context of women's movement, one could argue that even the so-called 'unsuccessful women's movements' also influenced discourses in ways that profoundly impacted civil society and perhaps the state. Whatever the particular effects of movement on institutional participation, engendering governance is a product of the conjoined and interacting influences of the pluralistic and diverse women's movements and struggles.

In deepening and widening the democratic decentralisation, women's movements played a great role in persuading and even to an extent compelling the State to devolve power to the fringes. Over the last two decades, ranging from State and National Policies for Women to various policy and legal initiatives focused around gender, women's movements played a key role in formulating and implementing these policies. In 1974 the Indian government published a report, Towards Equality, that put the status of women forcefully on the national agenda by arguing that the position of Indian women had declined, not improved, since 1911 (Committee on the Status of Women 1974). The National Policy for the Empowerment of Women (2001) reinforced that despite the plethora of policies and other initiatives in the area of women's empowerment "there still exists a wide gap between the goals enunciated in the Constitution, legislation, policies, plans, programmes, and related mechanisms on the one hand and the situational reality of the status of women in India on the other." Owing to the untiring efforts of the women's movement, the country amended and enacted various women-related legislations. The Married Women's Property Act (1874) and the Hindu Succession Act (1956) were amended and the Parliament passed the Protection of Women from Domestic Violence Act (PWDVA), 2005 to provide immediate support to women victims of domestic violence. The Sexual Harassment of Women at Workplace Act which came into force on 9thDecember, 2013 provide a safe and secure environment to women at the workplace. All these have been the result of a number of local, national and international developments/initiatives, many of them emerging from a growing movement for women's human rights and gender equity and equality. Feminist readings of the women's movement in India are very critical of the patriarchal power in governance systems and institutions and they were successful in placing these asymmetric modes of power in the public sphere. Engendering governance discourses need to address these hegemonic and patriarchal webs of power relations in institutions and structure of local governance.

Governance is presumed to be gender neutral. But, in fact, the discourses, procedures, structures and functions of governance remain heavily skewed in favour of men, in general. This unequal sharing of power leads to an unequal sharing of resources – time, income and property- between men and women. In India where the structural inequalities like class, caste and gender-based discriminations, continue to exclude the majority of people from the process of governance, gendering becomes one of the critical and structural pre-requisites for the democratization of governance. Democratic decentralisation becomes even more critical for women because of the proximity and relevance of the local governments to their lives.

Gendered governance and gendered citizenship assume significance in the light of three arguments: first, on the ground of justice, as women constitute 50 percent of the population; second, since women's experiences are different from those of men, they need to be separately articulated; and third, since women's and men's interests are different and often in conflict, they should both be represented in the decision making bodies (Mohanty.B, 1999). The importance of defining governance in broader and more far-reaching ways than it has traditionally been understood emerges from the myriad forms that women's political participation assumes at the local level — both private and public, economic, social and political.

Using the Gramscian theoretical approach, the dominant group (*read as men*) is able to maintain its status quo and hegemony as it is aware of its own strength and weakness and also the strength and weakness of its opponents, while the subalterns *(read as women*), who are aware of their own strength and weakness and also the strength of the dominant class, are ignorant of the weakness of the dominant. This inadequacy places them in a vulnerable position, which makes it difficult to appropriate the vested interests of the dominant group. It is also important to mention the applicability of the corporate consciousness (slight change in the power relations of the dominant group without altering the core area of its vested interests) in practice, which gives a tokenism of benevolence to the subaltern *(read as women*), and then celebrates it as an achievement of democracy. One has to be cautious and careful about the ways in which the corporate consciousness of the dominant class *(read as men)* appropriates democracy and its meaning. These appropriations are very much visible in the engendering practices at local governance.

Gendering of local self-governance institutions underwent serious debates in this decade. The decision of reserving 50 percent seats for women in PRIs impacted the body politic, substantively. The survey (2008) on Elected Women Representatives (EWRs) in India, carried out by the Ministry of Panchayati Raj reveals that women have expanded their representation to unreserved seats. It is indeed unique in the world that more than a million women are steering the ship of local governance, either as members or as chairpersons.

Any study to understand women's positionality needs to reconnect the empirical data with their socio-cultural history to de-articulate the prevalent notions of 'ineffective presence' of women in local governance. This rewriting of history is, therefore, relevant and significant in the context of the emerging politics of development that needs to be evaluated from the perspectives of the hitherto marginalised and the excluded. Myths were created about women's disinterest and passivity in politics, and about how female relatives of influential politicians from the well-off sections merely occupy these seats for name's sake, allowing men to carry out the real tasks. However, research data disprove these myths. Documentation of the work of young and first time women entrants from economically weaker sections indicates a high level of participation and performance. What one sees in these local bodies, today, is public patriarchy, where women are included but not allowed to participate, and where their work is consistently undervalued.

While there is evidence of new energies, women's role in the panchayat continues to be fiercely debated. The importance of women's political participation is, therefore, to be understood in the context of their socio-cultural subordination. It can, however, be argued while it is true that traditional, social, and political structures continue to subordinate women even after they are elected to the positions, the opportunity to participate in the public arenas through the affirmation policy itself is a great leap forward for women.

A survey of Women Elected Representatives (WERs) conducted in 1998 by the Kerala State Planning Board identified problems with gender trainings, particularly with respect to the flow of information, as the major contributor to the unsatisfactory performance of the WCP.

4.2 Shift in the Women Development Approaches

Seven decades of developmental plans, initiatives and programmes have not produced any significant impact on the gender empowerment of women in India. Women, who comprise half the population, in general, still remain marginalised and invisible in the socio-political and economic spheres of life. The trajectory of planning in women development reflected the paradigmatic shift in the focus of developmental demands and needs of women on the basis of their existential links with the society in which they live (Cooper, 1995).

In the fifties and sixties, the welfarist approaches in the plans viewed women as non-productive dependents, and were concerned only with family welfare. If at all women were considered in development programmes, it was, at best, as adjuncts to their husbands, or as daughters or mothers. It was assumed that women's position would improve, as did the economic prosperity of their husbands. (Cubit, 1998). Furthermore, it took for granted the notions of male-breadwinner and female housewife. Development programmes, addressed to male households, failed to recognise the work done by women.

The next shift emphasised on efficiency. The earlier attempt to equip women to be part of development process was reversed, for development without the recognition of women's productive role and without addressing gender differences would be counterproductive (Cooper, 1995). But when planners recognised the contribution and participation of women in development programmes for a permanent effect, they also realised the difficulty to design projects to incorporate women, for they effectively knew nothing about what women did. The task the planners faced was twofold: first, to uncover the range of work women did in a qualitative sense; and second, to find a way in which this work could be operationalised so that women's contribution could be quantified. These new perception of women's role in development brought in a series of studies on the historical reasons for the marginalisation of women, transition from sex to gender, their work participation in the household, women's role in the economy at the micro and macro levels and so on (Garnsey, 1981).

In the 70s, policy approaches aiming to incorporate women into development activities began on the basis of experiences, reviews and reformulations of strategies and objectives through several stages from the welfare-oriented, equity, antipoverty and mainstreaming approaches. In the 80s, the WID was accepted and adopted as a strategic emphasis aiming to achieve women's integration in all aspects of the development process (Garnsey, 1981).

The acceptance of the need to overtly place women on the development agenda was accompanied by the formulation of WID policies and the institutionalisation of various mechanisms among both development agencies and recipients of international development assistance to address the concerns, needs and contributions of women. This led to a plethora of WID programmes and projects aimed to improve the condition of women and to deliver development (Jahan, 1995).

However, targeted and segregated women-only projects helped only to marginalise women further and isolate them from the mainstream of development (Ruehl, 1983). Relegating the responsibility for improving the status of women to one department, rather than to all sectoral ministries simply ghettoized women. Treating women as a unified and special category divorced from other social relations, including economic and social processes, did not accommodate or accurately reflect the various groups of women or the different voices of women. Women-only projects were often poorly conceived and funded and, sometimes, added to women's already heavy workloads with few compensatory benefits (Ruehl, 1983).

These reviews, analyses and conclusions led to significant rethinking of the WID approach. It became evident that projects focusing exclusively on women implied that the problem, and hence the solution, could be confined to women. For example, population programmes that exclusively targeted women were often unsuccessful, since their male partners, whose consent was integral to the project success, were not targeted. Such approaches failed to recognise the critical role of men in decisions regarding women's lives (Seidman, 1994).

Relying on women as the analytical category for addressing gender inequalities meant a focus on women in isolation from the rest of their lives and from the relations through which such inequalities were perpetuated and reproduced (Seidman, 1994). This led to the major shift from women as the key focus of analysis to a focus on gender relations, i.e., the social relations between men and women that generate and perpetuate gender inequalities.

Rethinking in the WID approach also led to a move away from assessing the adverse impact of development on women to examine the adverse impact of women's exclusion from development. 'Women need development' was replaced by 'development needs women' (Moser, 1993). Social justice and equity arguments were complemented with arguments of economic efficiency. The marginalisation and isolation of women from the mainstream of the development process came to be seen as economically inefficient and hampering economic growth (Jahan, 1995). Hence, welfare-oriented and equity approaches were increasingly replaced and complemented with mainstreaming and efficiency approaches.

Attempts to redress gender inequalities by treating women in isolation left untouched the complex gender relations through which inequalities were reproduced and perpetuated (Seidman, 1994). The shift to "Gender And Development" (GAD) sought to investigate unequal relations between men and women and their naturalization as a problem in and for development. Treating unequal power as a key obstacle to women's participation in development, GAD identified empowerment of disadvantaged men and women as integral to development. Equitable development required formerly excluded groups to participate in decision making.

These shifts towards the development policies of women were reflected at its micro-level in Kerala also. The PPC's outreach to women, scheduled castes and scheduled tribes echoed GAD's prescriptions for development success. But Kerala, with its socio-development indicators, especially with regard to women, typifies the marginalisation of women through a different framework.

4.3 Marginalisation of Kerala Women in the 90s

It was the commendable progress made in the conventional gender development indicators—especially in education and health of women—that put Kerala on the pedestal of the much acclaimed Kerala Model of Development. However, Kerala could not strike a direct correlation with its improvements in gender development indicators to the corresponding changes in the status of women. Patriarchal hegemonic power structures interwoven into the everyday lives of women, and that too in all the spaces, made women internalise their subordinate position as normative and normal. The cocoon of invisibility that speaks about the phenomenology of absences spun around them is a complex process, and cannot be dismantled easily.

So women exist as non-entities, both at home and outside of the home — their presence at the power structures is obliterated by the Leviathans who are hell-bent not to give them the visibility they have the right to; their hushed up voice that speaks of the new horizons of gender equality in matters of governance is drowned in the orchestrated cacophony and clamorous voice of men; their novel initiatives are nipped in the bud, terming them as dysfunctional dreams of novices; their little failures are magnified as dangerous viruses that could stagnate the system; their silence to learn from the mistakes is dubbed as inability to speak out; and their earnest efforts to learn the nuances of the system are made to end up caught in the complex cobweb of bureaucratic jargons and technicalities; forcing the new agents of the much-needed change succumb to the multi-pronged diffusing tactics of the powers that be, and making the valuable contributions of women unrecorded, unrecognised, and unpaid; their presence made invisible, and their voice inaudible.

A brief analysis is attempted to show the stark difference in gender development indicators at the state and national levels, where Kerala stands at an advantageous position in some, but having dismissive statistics in other key indicators.

The socio-economic condition of women in Kerala is in an advantageous position compared to the rest of the country. All available data testify this. As per the National Sample Survey, illiteracy rate among Kerala rural women is 15 percent as against the national average of 47 percent. In the urban areas the corresponding figures are 13 and 26 percent. While 54 out of 100 students in Kerala are women, it is 40 for India. The figure is 69 and 44, respectively, for the post graduates. Sex ratio of the state has been consistently favourable to women and it is the only state in India where women outnumber men. The longevity of women in Kerala is high, 77, compared to the national average of 67. Infant mortality rate, maternal mortality rate and average number of children in family too are the lowest in Kerala.

Figure 4.1
Sex Ratio-India & Kerala

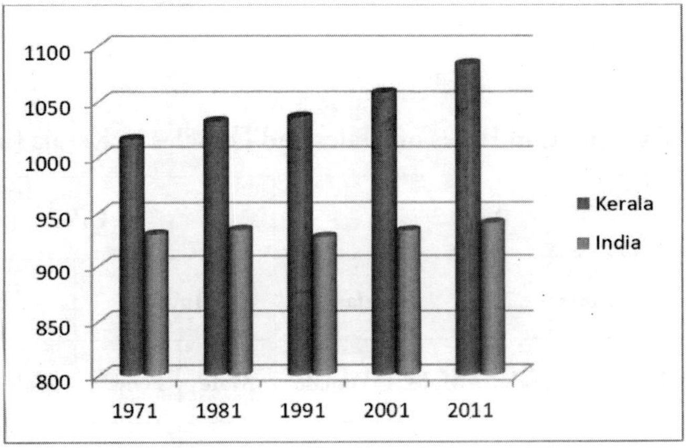

Source: Census Report of India 2011

A comparative analysis of the sex ratio (number of females per 1000 males) in India and Kerala over five decades (1971-2011) indicates the magnitude of that difference. Although national data continue to document what Amartya Sen (1990) called "millions of missing women" as a result of anti-female bias in distribution of food and health care, in Kerala women outnumber and outlive their male counterparts. The gender gap in literacy rates is four times greater at the national level (16.3) than in Kerala (4), where women have made gains in both rural and urban areas.

Table 4.1
Literacy Rate in 2011 – Kerala & India

	Liter-acy Rate	Male Literacy	Female Liter-acy	Gender disparity	Urban Male Literacy	Urban female literacy	Rural Male Literacy	Rural Female literacy
Kerala	94	96.1	92.1	4.0	95.4	90.8	97.8	93.4
India	73	80.9	64.6	16.3	77.2	57.9	88.8	79.1

Source: Census Reports of India

However, the same Kerala that ranks first among the Indian states in terms of Human Development Index (HDI) and Gender Development Index (GDI) presents a weak picture with regard to female work participation, which is contrary to the general notion that with decrease in number of children and increase in literacy rate among women, work participation of women will increase. Though work participation of women is lower compared to men, all over India, it is very much explicit in Kerala. It is the same even among the educated.

Table 4.2
Work Participation Rates of Males and Females in Kerala (in %)

Year	Rural				Urban			
	India		Kerala		India		Kerala	
	Male	Female	Male	Female	Male	Female	Male	Female
1987-88	53.9	32.3	56.7	31.6	50.6	15.2	59.2	21.8
1993-94	55.3	32.8	53.7	23.8	52	15.4	56	20.3
1999-2000	53.1	29.9	55.3	23.8	51.8	13.9	55.8	20.3
2004-05	54.6	32.7	55.9	25.6	54.9	16.6	54.7	20
2009-10	54.7	26.1	56.4	21.8	54.3	13.8	54.7	19.4
2011-12	54.3	24.8	56.5	22.1	54.6	14.7	55.2	19.1

Source: Various Reports of NSSO

The low participation rate was also partly caused by changes in the structure of employment. The sexual division of labour had resulted in the concentration of women in low paying unorganised sectors, such as agricultural labour, cottage and traditional industries and selected service sectors. The shift in cropping pattern from female labour intensive paddy cultivation to commercial crops had resulted in decline in the share of women agricultural workers from 43.6% in 1981 to 36.1% in 1991 (Isaac, 2001).

Table 4.3
Nature of the Work of Women in Kerala

Type of work	% of women in the work	The work place	The visibility of work
Salary jobs	14%	Factory/Office	Visible
Daily labour	41%	Other's backyard/ Factories	Visible
Self-employment	21%	Own backyard/ Small scale industry	Half visible
Agricultural work for self-consumption	50%	Own backyard	Half visible
House work	98%	House	Invisible

Source: Women Empowerment, Training Book, Kerala State Planning Board.

Marginalisation of women in the economic process and their subsequent invisibility in the respective work spheres is explained in table (4.3). The market centric neo-liberal policies of globalization that cater to the vested interests of the corporate and the patriarchy coupled with the hegemony of capital in the socio-political spaces (Neeraja Jayal, 2008; Melissa Butcher, 2003; Sherin M. Rai, 2003) further deteriorated the status of women in Kerala. The lack of control of women over resources has been cited as another reason towards the weakening of social status among women. Despite the general progressive political environment in the State and active involvement of women at the grassroots level political processes, they are virtually absent at the leadership level. The percentage of women representation in the Kerala State Legislative Assembly from the time of its inception is very much marginal. Figure (4.2) shows the representation of women in the State Legislative Assembly. Except in 1996, it never reached the two digit number.

Women in positions of power are invisible. Other than sharing of power at the local self-government levels—thanks to the reservation policy—women are almost invisible in the cultural, political, social and economic sectors, and are yet to hold key positions of power. The majority-minority communalizations that are gaining strength are anti-women in nature. The oppression and exploitation they face are quite different from what women, elsewhere in India, face.

Figure 4.2
Representation of Women in the Kerala Legislative Assembly (1957-2016)

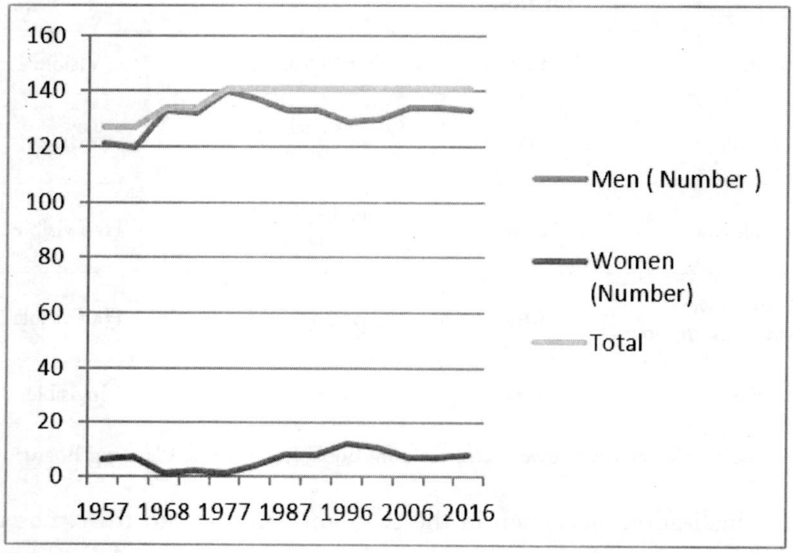

Source: Various Issues of Economic Review, Kerala

Table 4.4
Crimes against Women in Kerala (2007-2013)

Year	Rape	Molestation	Kidnapping	Eve teasing	Dowry deaths	Cruelty by husbands and relatives	Other offences	Total
2007	500	2604	166	262	22	3976	1851	9381
2008	548	2756	167	255	25	4135	1820	9706
2009	554	2539	171	394	21	3976	1699	9354
2010	617	2939	175	539	21	4788	1702	10781
2011	1132	3756	221	573	15	5377	2205	13279
2012	1019	3735	214	498	32	5216	2288	13002

Source: Crime Bureau Records

Women are subjected to multiple forms of violence right from cradle to grave. The highly gendered nationalistic discourses and social order that privilege men to wield power and exercise it, position women in a secondary status and are subjected to the panoptic and moralistic gazes. Femininity and body of women have become symbolic markings of the honour of family, society, and nation. It is in this context of unbalanced and asymmetrical gender power equations prevailing in Kerala that a gender aware and gender sensitive decentralised planning, i.e., People's Plan, assumes significance for research on gender.

4.4 Intervention of the PPC in Women Development

Reservation for women in the local bodies of Kerala was introduced in 1991 with the formulation of district councils. But this lasted only for a very brief period to make any significant impact on the status of women in Kerala. However, the entry of 34% women as councillors in the district leadership effected the first major breakthrough in the long tradition of invisibility of women in government leadership. The 73rd and 74th Constitutional Amendments made one-third reservation for women at all levels of local bodies mandatory, and significantly, made the office bearer-ship also mandatory. In 1996, Kerala had 4153 grama panchayat members, 595 block panchayat members and 116 district panchayat members from among women. As mentioned earlier, one of the objectives of the PPC was to infuse gender sensitiveness in the process. This growth process was envisaged to result in an increase in the work participation of women and to undermine the traditional sexual division of labour.

The PPC tried to intervene and then, to deconstruct the prevalent notions and realities existed in the women's programmes in the planning process, which are listed in the chart (4.1).

All the data in the subsequent sessions are limited to the time period of 90s to analyse the inferences in the context of the PPC.

Chart 4.1
Beliefs and Realities about Women's Programme in the Planning

Common belief	Reality	Possible interventions
Governance processes are gender-neutral	Structures and processes of governance consider men as the real political actors.	Disaggregate data on membership in all institutions.

Common belief	Reality	Possible interventions
Decentralisation of government functions to the local level increases grassroots participation equally for community women and men.	Women are marginalised in the process of governance within local institutions.	Support greater representation for women in local governance institutions and community organisations.
Households are homogenous units.	Inequalities within families translate into inequalities in the public sphere. Women and men have different demands for community resource allocations.	Recognition of households as space for power relations in project planning.

The following gender sensitive communication measures were initiated as part of the PPC.

- Guidelines were issued to encourage participation of women in every stage of the planning process.
- Local bodies were given instructions to elect 1/3 of the resource person for the PPC from among the women activists.
- A separate subject group on women welfare was made mandatory. A structured questionnaire on gender problems was provided to facilitate the discussions at grama sabhas.
- In the Development Report, guidelines were given to have a separate chapter on women and development, which should include a historical review of the status of women and their problems, both economic and social.
- A separate task force was constituted to prepare projects for women-development based on the recommendations of the Development Report.
- The Women Component Plan (WCP), first time in the planning history of India, was introduced.

All these indicated that there was a conscious development intervention from the very start of the PPC to make the planning process gender sensitive, incorporating the gender concerns. The major activities of the WCP in different phases of the PPC are shown in chart (4.2).

Chart 4.2
Activities of the WCP in Different Phases of the PPC

Phase	Objective	Activity	Gender Component
I (Grama Sabha)	Identify the felt needs of people.	Grama sabhas in rural areas and ward conventions in urban areas.	Special subject group in the grama sabhas to discuss gender problems.
II (Development Seminar)	Objective assessment of the resources, problems and formulation of local development perspective.	Participatory studies: preparation of development reports, organisation of development seminars.	Special chapter in development report on gender issues. Special subject group for discussing gender issues in the development seminar.
III (Task Force)	Preparation of projects.	Meetings of task force.	A special task force for women development projects. Gender impact statement of projects.
IV (Elected Body)	Formulation of plan of grass-root tiers.	Plan formulation meetings of elected representatives.	A separate chapter on women development projects. Ten per cent to be set apart for WCP.
V (Elected Body)	Formulation of plan of higher tiers.	Plan formulation meetings of elected representatives.	A separate chapter on women development projects. Ten per cent to be set apart for WCP.
VI (Volunteer Technical Corp)	Appraisal and approval of plans.	Meetings of expert Committees.	

In each of the six phases of the PPC, separate guidelines were woven into the planning process, consciously, to make the plan gender sensitive.

4.5 Critical Interim Evaluation of the WCP

An interim evaluation of the WCP was made at the end of the first year of the PPC. Certain crucial weaknesses, which hindered the actual genderisation in the planning process, were delineated.

The weakness in the first year's annual plan of the PPC was two-fold. First, the Campaign failed to ensure sufficient participation of women in the planning process. Second, the participant women were not fully empowered to effectively intervene in the process from a gender perspective.

A survey Conducted by the Kerala State Planning Board in 1998 among the women elected representatives exploring the reasons for low participation in the grama sabha in the first year of the PPC gave interesting findings as shown in table (4.5). Author, being a Key Resource Person (KRP) at the State level, was very much involved in the formulation and evaluation of questionnaires of the study among the elected women representatives.

Table 4.5
Reasons for Low Participation in First Plan Grama Sabha: Opinion of the Women Elected Representatives

Reasons	Most Important Reason	Second Most Important Reason
(i) Inadequate awareness	715 (50.9	250 (25.2)
(ii) Aversion to public activities	333 (23.7)	214 (21.5)
(iii) Burden of household duties	245 (18.40)	266 (26.8)
(iv) Discouragement from men	34 (92.4)	124 (12.5)
(v) Lack of adequate preparation	53 (3.7)	99 (10.0)
(vi) Absence of special consideration in grama sabha	18 (1.3)	37 (3.7)
(vii) Others	7 (0.4)	2 (0.3)
Total	1405 (100)	992 (100)

Source: Survey of Women Elected Representatives, Kerala State Planning Board, 1998.

Training programme was expected to mould the character and nature of the WCP. But the interim evaluation found that the training modules were very general in nature, without going beyond the basic explanations on the project preparations. Concrete details, such as how to prepare women specific projects and how to incorporate the gender component, were not worked out properly. This weakness of the training programmes contributed to many drawbacks of the WCP.

The same survey revealed that poor performance of the WCP was due to the lack of active and qualitative involvement of the women elected representatives in the Campaign. This is shown in table (4.6). The percentage of people who participated in different phases of People's Planning Campaign for namesake increased from 0.8 in grama sabha to 11.6 in the formulation of the plan document as shown in table (4.6). Even a significant percentage of the women elected representatives (17.03%) did not answer to the question of their role in the formulation of the plan document.

Table 4.6
Level of Understanding of the Elected Representatives

Document	Grama Sabha	Dev. Seminar	Task Force	Plan
1. Non-response	258 (21.2)	509 (40.0)	649 (50.9)	692 (54.3)
2. No Clarity	110 (8.6)	58 (4.6)	65 (5.1)	56 (4.4)
3. Average Clarity	692 (54.3)	513 (40.7)	398 (31.2)	367 (28.8)
4. Good Clarity	203 (15.9)	187 (14.7)	157 (12.8)	155 (12.5)
Total	1274 (100)	1274 (100)	1274 (100)	1274 (100)

Source: Survey of Women Elected Representatives, Kerala State Planning Board, 1998

The survey indicated that the women elected representatives did not have proper clarity regarding the activities of the different phases of the PPC. Table (4.6) quantifies this lack of clarity among the women elected representatives

Women elected representatives opined various reasons for the low quality of women development projects: Lack of clarity regarding the WCP; dormancy of Women Development Task Force; non-participation of the women in project preparation; and lack of interest in elected council. (Isaac, 1998).

4.6 Redefining Development Interventions in the WCP

Feedback from the women elected representatives with respect to the WCP, which was a bottom-up communication, and the horizontal communication among the planning top brass, after receiving the feedback, gave serious thinking about redefining the development interventions in WCP.

Accordingly, the following changes were made:

- Ten percent of the plan fund for the WCP was made mandatory because panchayats were not complying with the original suggestion to set apart ten percent of the plan fund for WCP;

- A member of Woman and Development Task Force was included as ex-officio member in each of the other sectoral task forces, in order to ensure that gender concerns were incorporated into the general projects;
- A new subject committee on women and development was constituted at all levels in order to appraise whether the women projects satisfied the criteria laid down for them;
- A special gender training programme, addressing women activists, was implemented; and
- Training programmes, focusing on women elected representatives, were held with the objective of developing some of them into a team of key resource persons and organisers.

Even these conscious and explicit changes could not bring about the desired gender sensitivity in the PPC. Evaluation of the projects earmarked for women revealed that though the mandatory provisions were complied with, the qualitative changes envisaged through the WCP didn't materialise because the purpose for which the changes were made were not breathed into the projects. Projects in large numbers were found to be prefixed with 'women' to make them appear as women projects. (Women latrine, women stable, women drinking water etc.)

The evaluation proved to be an eye opener to the planning authorities that even while attempting qualitative shift in the WCP, they too were trekking the same path of the WID approach, which they wanted to replace. Evaluation of previous failures of the WCP led to the realisation that the development process itself needed engendering. Hence, there was a need to refocus the strategic emphasis from a narrow WID approach to a more dynamic Gender And Development (GAD) approach. Planners, during the initial phase of the PPC, addressed the practical needs of women to tackle the problem of economic dependency. Later, the planners, through the feedback from the elected women representatives, realised that gender sensitivity could be interwoven into the social fabric only by addressing the structural realities of gender in the socio-economic linkages. Thus, KSPB, towards the latter phase of the PPC, brought in the Gender and Development perspective (GAD) into the WCP.

In the GAD approach, the strategic emphasis is widened to include women's rights, women's role as active participants and agents in development, and their role as actors with a specific agenda for development. The GAD approach recognizes that improvements in women's status require analysis of the relations between men and women, as well as the concurrence and cooperation of men (Moser, 1993). Emphasis is placed on the need to understand the ways in which unequal relations between women and men may contribute to the extent and forms of exclusion that women face in the development process. There is also an overt recognition that the participation and commitment of men are required to fundamentally alter the social and economic position of women. The GAD approach sees gender as a cross-cutting issue with relevance for and influencing all economic, social and political processes, and seeks to redress gender inequity through facilitating strategic, broad-based and multi-faceted solutions (Routledge and Flemmen, 1991).

Inherent in the GAD approach is gender mainstreaming, which is addressing women's concerns more holistically and effectively. The GAD approach, however, does not mean that stand-alone women's projects or projects with special components targeting women are to be abandoned altogether. Until there are no structural constraints and barriers restricting women's participation, projects directed exclusively at women or projects with special components addressed to women are still required, especially in circumstances wherein cultural dictates necessitate segregation of the sexes, or in situations where women require special assistance to enable their full participation in mainstream projects (Brydon and Chand, 1989).

Although the WCP was intended to shift Kerala toward a Gender and Development approach, initial evaluations suggested that the process suffered from the limitations of WID. GAD's emphasis on women's rights, women's roles as active agents and participants in development, and their unique role to redress gendered power imbalances were noticeably absent (Moser, 1993). These findings were particularly disheartening because the WCP was intended to promote conscientisation among the most disadvantaged local women.

The qualitative change in the perceptions of the women elected representatives viz.- a- viz. the WCP materialised through a long process. It began with the feedback from the intense women training sessions, progressed through the resultant conscientisation of their gender role and culminated in their self-actualisation and empowerment, so as to achieve the envisaged objective of the People's Planning Campaign - to break the spiral of silence and invisibility among women.

Developed over three intensive days at state-level workshops in which 311 women participated, the training program was fine-tuned through deliberations of 55 women faculty members, who produced the handbook "Women's Empowerment and People's Planning." In keeping with the focus on the most disadvantaged citizens, the conscientisation process included the innovative use of street theatre. Local women watched a performance of a skit, "Subhadra Madhavan and Panchayati Raj," which depicted the trajectory of one woman elected to serve in the panchayat, who braved multiple social challenges in order to fulfill her governance role. Participants were invited to analyse the plot critically and to consider how Subhadra might be empowered to work in partnership with others including men to perform her duties more successfully. Indeed, participants were encouraged to alter the plot to dramatize collaborative decision making that could produce policy benefits for women. Rather than imagining the elective office as a lonely role and onerous burden which individuals engage in isolation, local governance is envisioned as a collective process that enables social transformation in the society, and not as a lonely struggle, and they changed the skit, accordingly (Isaac, 2000).

At the district level, the handbook was distributed in conjunction with conscientization workshops at one-day conventions that were attended by 3,114 women. The conventions opened with a performance of the reworked skit "Subhadra Madhavan and Panchayati Raj." Selected participants shared testimonials about their experiences in collective decision-making in the context of the PPC and the challenges involved. All convention participants completed a self-evaluation form designed to assess diverse individuals' experiences with the WCP. Prior to completion of the questionnaire, a facilitator reviewed the questions and responded to requests for clarification. The results of this survey were used to modify the WCP in subsequent years of the campaign.

Following the conventions, project clinics were convened at the block level to review and assess WCP proposals, which led to modifications to the approved projects. The most important outcome of these clinics, however, was increased awareness of the inadequacy of the women component planning process. Despite good intentions, local level capacity-building had been totally inadequate to sustain implementation of the WCP on a massive scale. To remedy these deficits, an additional state-wide training programme was developed for women task force members. Selected members of task forces from all local governments participated in three-day workshops designed to heighten deliberation about the outcomes of the block-level workshops. These training sessions continued over two months to enable all women task force delegates to participate. This advanced training improved the quality of deliberations and substantive WCP projects in 1999-2000, resulting in two major developments: the emergence of women's collectives in the form of Self-Help Groups (SHGs). These groups played important roles in crafting Women Status Reports (Isaac, 2000).

A case study of Samatha Self-Help Groups (SHGs) at the Ulloor Panchayat in Trivandrum district illuminates complexities and paradoxes of women's empowerment through the PPC. The Samatha SHGs focused on microfinance, decentralised planning, and grassroots participation in local planning. Although the female literacy rate in the Ulloor panchayat was 83%, only 15% of the women worked in the formal sector. Close to 40% of the population lived below the poverty line and were in debt to moneylenders and traders (Manjula, B. 2002). Women worked primarily as vegetable vendors, daily labourers, domestic helpers, or as fisherwomen. In addition to social and economic problems, these women shouldered major familial responsibilities. Several women's organisations worked in these areas, but they had been unsuccessful in addressing the economic needs or the social problems women confronted. Consequently, these organisations were unpopular, especially among women from the lower socioeconomic groups. The Samatha self-help groups emerged in this context. In 1997–1998, the Ulloor panchayat prepared the Samatha SHGs project as part of the mandatory WCP. Members of the SHG were drawn from poor and lower-middle class families. Informed by the notion that poor women's problems cannot be tackled individually, requiring collective intervention instead, the groups were organised in SHGs and each was independently registered under the Charitable Societies Act. The Ulloor model accorded maximum autonomy and flexibility to each of these groups. The bylaws governing operating procedures were crafted through discussions and deliberations at the panchayat level. SHGs also had access to loans at a nominal interest rate that was much lower than that of the private money-lenders. This feature made SHGs popular among women.

The Idavacodu unit was the first SHG of the Ulloor Panchayat with 20 members, including six fisherwomen, four vegetable vendors, four domestic helpers, and four daily wage labourers. All members were from the poorest households and were indebted to moneylenders and traders. Education sessions introduced members to the objectives of SHGs, the procedures to follow in collective decision-making, and the norms and rules regarding credit. Bank officials, representatives from the National Bank for Agriculture and Rural Development (NABARD), Kerala Sastra Sahitya Parishad (KSSP) members and panchayat members took an active part in this conscientisation process.

After three months, members could apply for a personal loan by submitting a request to the group. The members decided which loans to grant, initially opting for the principle of first-come, first served. The interest rate was nominally 2%, although there was flexibility for those in dire need. Loans were made to individual women without requiring her husband, father, or son to co-sign. Loans were guaranteed by other women in the SHGs, who trusted the woman's ability to earn and repay the debt. Each SHG was locally based and comprised 15–25 members who met weekly in the homes of group members' houses. Groups operated on the principles of mutual trust, cooperation, accountability and transparency. At each meeting, the group would break for tea, and all members were expected to socialize together. Two or three members were expelled from the SHGs because of their reluctance to have tea in the home of a low caste member. Group members reported that this practice had considerable impact in addressing the caste issue, which was initially very strong in the neighborhood. After tea, members discussed the pros and cons of their microenterprises, as well as family issues and financial problems.

Within one year after the formation of the first SHG unit in Ulloor, 110 groups, each comprising 20–25 members, were registered, representing nearly half the families of Ulloor panchayat. The phenomenal growth and popularity of SHGs among women was not due to dissemination of information through the media, but rather through the word of mouth. Women who were benefiting from the SHGs passed on details about the possibilities of these local collectives to other women. This horizontal interpersonal networking and communication made the SHGs a dynamic and vibrant phenomenon at the grassroots level. Table 4 provides the details of the SHGs in Ulloor panchayat.

Table 4.7
Performance of SHGs in Ulloor Panchayat

Number of wards	15
Number of SHGs formed	100
Number of women enrolled	2,200
Asset of SHGs (savings +bank loan)	10 million
Groups assisted with bank loans	85

Source: Manjula Bharathy (2004)

Making women more visible in the public domain was the most significant achievement of the Ulloor SHGs. Participation in the SHGs generated women's increased attendance in grama sabhas, development seminars, and public functions organised by the Panchayats. Women's participation in grama sabhas rose from 26 percent in the initial stage to 60 percent in subsequent years (Manjula, B, 2010). The women's Sunday meetings attracted public attention and public acceptance.

The Ulloor experiment was significant in one additional respect. Ulloor assigned the women's SHGs a specific role in beneficiary selection at the grama sabha. PPC guidelines required that selection of projects for funding to be based on objective criteria. Yet, given the huge numbers of people participating in grama sabhas, it was difficult to assess the projects presented. In Ulloor, the women SHGs prepared project lists that clearly indicated the objective criteria used to establish priorities for funding and presented this information in the grama sabha. Given this critical role, women developed great enthusiasm for attending the grama sabha where final decisions about funding allocations were made. On many occasions when they believed that selection of particular beneficiaries deviated from objective criteria, they registered their protest. Their dissents were given due respect and corresponding alterations were made in the list (Manjula. B, 2010). The feeling of being heard and recognised boosted their confidence tremendously.

The power experienced within Samatha self-help groups was altogether new to women, who had been treated as "the second sex" (Beauvoir, 1949) both at home and in the society. Weekly meetings, discussions, attendance in the grama sabhas and training sessions enhanced their level of understanding of various issues, and their ability to articulate gender inequities. Although economic benefit first attracted women to SHGs, they gradually expanded their discussions to address problems of their neighborhoods. Economically-stressed women, who often found it difficult to make ends meet, mobilized collectively to share Rs. 5000 from their pooled savings to help women in other parts of Samatha who were suffering from flood damage. Participation in SHG deliberations expanded women's perceptions to engage the world beyond their homes. Samatha SHGs also solved many familial problems of members, such as wife-bashing and exorbitant dowry demands. They filed written complaints against suspects in dowry deaths. The training and weekly meetings instilled new confidence which, in turn, enhanced their efficiencies and abilities. They started chairing sessions attended by panchayat presidents, collectors, and other dignitaries; indeed, some became panchayat presidents. In one survey, 83% of the women reported that experience in SHGs opened a new world to them (Manjula. B, 2001). Two quotations indicate the sense of empowerment experienced by SHG participants.

I am 68. I started a family life at 18. For five decades, my family was my world. Confined within the four walls of my home, I never knew the world outside. But the gram sabha opened up my world. Today, I know there is a society outside of my family. In the gram sabha, I heard myself and through many voices similar to mine realized, for the first time, that voices like mine are important for society too, a fact which I was unaware of. This changed my world completely. (Chellama, a grassroots worker)

I have three kids. My husband and my children have different demands and needs. I manage to meet their needs without much complaint within my limited resources. Society too, I know, is not much different. I think, I can manage that too. (Jameela, 45, Chirayan Keezhu Panchayat President)

Figure 4.3

Reasons for the Successes of the Ulloor SHGs

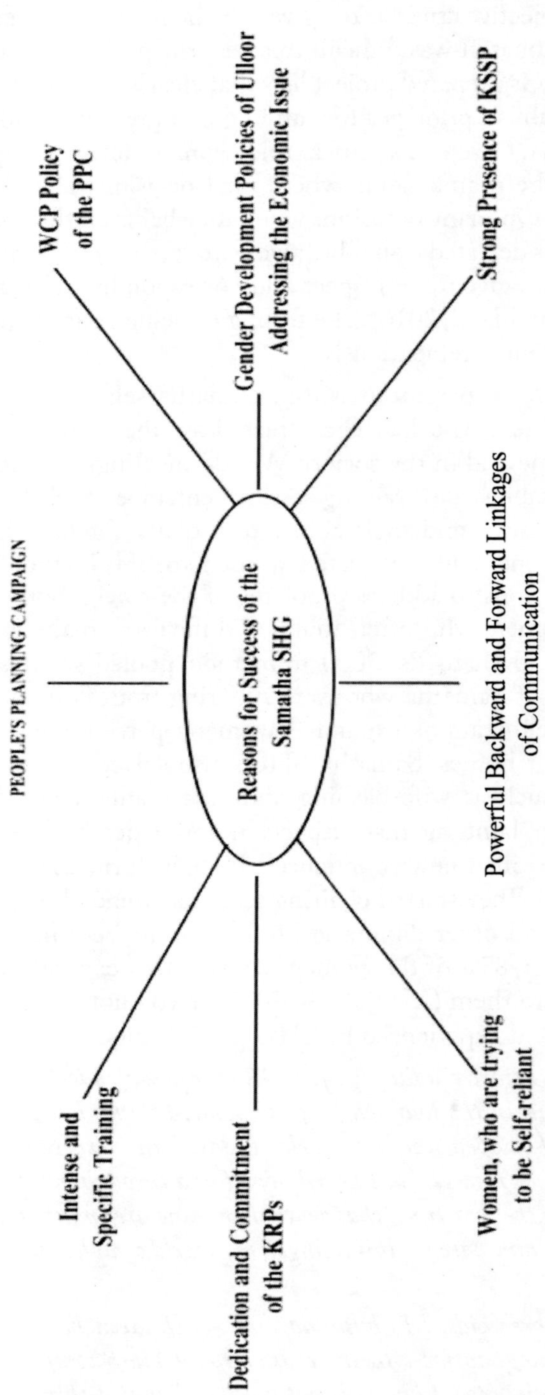

Participation in SHGs countered traditional socialization that deprived individual women of power and mobility, while also affirming women's collective right to take charge of their gendered identity. Rather than consigning themselves to inequality, SHG participants took on responsibility to redress gender-based injustices, thereby redefining the meaning of being women. In Kerala, where strong patriarchal norms prevail, women had been taught to view themselves as mirrors that reflect the figure of men at twice their natural size (Woolf 1929). When internalized by women, these sexist notions reinforce the status quo that provide visible roles to men and invisible roles to women in social, political and economic spheres. The PPC with its WCP tried to overturn women's habitual invisibility through conscious intervention. By linking women's SHGs to distributive decisions in grama sabhas, Ulloor found a potent mechanism to accomplish these transformative objectives. These interventions accounted for an increasing presence of women in the development projects of the PPC, and their increased attendance in grama sabhas and development seminars, thereby facilitating women's entry into political and economic spheres of life.

The SHGs are not a panacea, however. Much of the loan money was spent on personal loans to members, rather than on sustainable income-generating economic projects. The micro-enterprises funded, despite the enormous labor that women devoted to them, showed minimal profit margins. Soap making, for instance, involved the intensive labor of seven women over two days. With an investment of Rs. 500, the profit after covering the costs of raw materials was only Rs. 32 (Manjula. B, 2010). When divided among seven members, this yield was far from satisfactory for a long-range enterprise.

Beyond economic matters, the relationship between women's formal representation in politics, their substantive representation, and their empowerment remains unclear. Most PPC gender interventions were unsuccessful in transcending the domain of practical gender needs to focus on strategic gender interests. In Kerala, women's presence in planning and budgeting processes did not translate into the ability to use voice to politicize issues of concern to women, to use electoral leverage to press demands on decision-makers, to trigger better responsiveness from the public sector to their needs, or to enforce constitutional commitments to women's equal rights.

Although women's understanding of various issues improved, the concept of a five-year plan, or a long-term campaign remained elusive. Decision-making within SHGs generated high levels of understanding of the immediate context of their deliberations, yet they were far less clear about the wider framework of the PPC or the WCP. Although their grasp of the complex planning process was not negative, nearly 79% of the women participants reported a need for additional training to acquire more information about the PPC. Thus, the PPC has, to an extent, succeeded in disrupting long-standing patterns of women's silencing and invisibility, but their visibility is still not sharp enough and their voices often remain so feeble that one cannot hear them. Decentralization will achieve its empowerment objectives only when women's presence is felt and their voices are heard distinctly and clearly.

A participatory grassroots experiment such as the Ulloor Samatha SHGs initiative reveals that poor women — while achieving their limited task — can acquire awareness about their conditions, and the ability to use and build on their own knowledge to develop critical awareness about their economic, political and physical environments. At the same time, working collectively to improve their resource position heightened participants' confidence, brought women out of isolation, and reinforced their community consciousness. When initiatives such as Samatha are linked to participatory planning processes, they can contribute to decentralization of power and women's participation in social and economic decision-making. Recognizing these sizable challenges, in no way undermines the significance of the emergence of women SHGs. These experiments, which were almost entirely the result of local initiatives, contributed significantly to the subsequent design of Kudumbashree neighborhood networks in Kerala, which are widely acclaimed nationally and internationally as innovative interventions in engendering governance. The gender sensitive approach of the PPC, refined on the basis of lessons learned, was a crucial first step to give women voice and visibility.

Post-PPC

Politics of presence of women (Phillips, 1995) in the public sphere of Kerala and the formation of Kudumbashree Mission are the two significant contributions of the engendering phase of the People's Planning Campaign in Kerala. The mandatory nature of the WCP in the PPC had expanded the scope of spaces where women could engage with issues beyond their family in a more normative manner. The Kudumbashree Mission differs from the conventional programmes since it perceives poverty as the deprivation of basic human rights and denial of spaces to exercise one's agency and subjectivity. Kudumbashree locates collectivisation of voices as the means to enable women who are in the periphery to claim their rightful spaces in the process of governance. More importantly, as a state initiative programme, Kudumbashree brings in the unique positionality of the state in the welfare discourse and the relevance of the local self-government institutions in providing organisational support and coordination to such initiations towards poverty alleviation, democratic decentralisation and deepening of democracy. Kudumbashree, which was launched in 1998 as a community network of women, today is one of the largest community based women organizations in the world. It has 4.5 million women members who cover more than 50 percent of the households in the state. These women are federated into 2,50,000 Neighbourhood Groups (NHGs), 19,876 Area Development Societies (ADSs), and 1,072 Community Development Societies (CDSs). Formation and spread of Kudumbashree even in the nook and corner of Kerala is a manifestation of the people-centric development interventions. The SHGs of the WCP in the PPC are modified into a more holistic NHG network in the Kudumbashree, where primacy is also given to the Gender Self Learning Programmes (GSLP) and other social development interventions. The synergic interface with local governance, connects Kudumbashree with a variety of initiatives—social infrastructure, right-based interventions, employment generation, food security, health insurance, housing, enterprise development, and wage employment programmes. Conducive environment enabled by the PPC, social capital, experiences shared by the model panchayats, efficient functioning of the Kudumbashree members all have made Kudumbashree very popular in Kerala. It was this spreading of women groups almost uniformly in all wards and panchayats of Kerala, making their presence visible and active, and made the politics of presence of women through Kudumbashree significant in critical phases of COVID-19 interventions.

The participation of women in the NREGA is much higher in Kerala compared to other states. The women labour days in NREGA at the national level is only 52 percent, while it is 93.4 percent in Kerala. It is paradoxical that women prefer to participate in MGNREGS despite very low LFPR in Kerala. Moreover, studies conducted by Aruana Roy and others have shown that corruption is least reported in Kerala in the case or MNREGA. Main reason for this is that the planning and implementation of MGNREGS was initially entrusted with Kudumbashree Mission. Kudumbashree, with its vast network of women NHGs in rural Kerala, was able to rope in women in large numbers to the programme. Though Kudumbashree was relieved of this pivotal position in MGNREGS, the local women leadership of Kudumbashree continues to be a driving force-often as supervisors and mates in the MGNREGS.

Regardless of the recognition and acceptance at national and international levels, on a closer scrutiny and analysis one could discern the fissures and ruptures in the democratic values and philosophical underpinnings within the Kudumbashree network for which it was institutionalized (Manjula B, 2016). It is important for the policy makers and practitioners to discern the caveats in it and to engage Kudumbashree networks to move towards a transformative gender politics.

However, even with its conscious gender interventions, PPC did not make a drastic and remarkable improvement in the status of women in Kerala as envisaged in the People's Plan. Even the interventions to bring out Women's Status Study Reports at the panchayat that critically engaged the local issues with gender perspective to deconstruct the myth of gender equity and freedom in governance was not that fruitful. Women's increasing entry into the governance process at the local level has not been accompanied by a corresponding change in the gender division of unpaid labor in the domestic chores. As a result, working women tend to work for longer hours than working men, giving rise to the phenomenon of 'time poverty', which, to a large extent, denies them the chances of active engagement in the PRI related activities, and even socialization in the public sphere of Kerala. This multiple burdening of women adversely affects their quality of intervention in the governance process and it needs to be socially and economically understood and systematically analysed. The standalone power and representation in local bodies without commensurate power within family and in their respective political parties, often work out to the disadvantage of the women in exercising power (the women have to grapple the double subordination ordained by the gender hierarchy as well as the hierarchy within the respective political party).

Patriarchal gender ideology is deeply entrenched in the mindsets of the players in the governance system and gets manifested: for example in deprioritizing women's projects, designing women's projects to be subsequently used as general projects (a community centre to be subsequently utilised for general use), being gender insensitive (to locate yoga centre in a remote place which is inaccessible to women unless through own conveyance), to be gender blind (to allocate one room in the local body shopping complex for women and feeling complacent in doing justice to women and being blind to the myriad problems faced by women such as lack of resources for earnest money deposit, permission required from male members, social issues of operating a shop in a masculinized local market environment), giving scant regard for the privacy needs of women (such as privacy in Jagratha Samithis, PHCs etc).

The success of Kerala was realized through a holistic development approach and political will of the Left, emphasizing structural changes such as land reforms, public provisions of health, education, and other social infrastructure, a universal public distribution system, and community participation through decentralized planning. However, the same political will was not visible enough in changing the representation of women in either political parties or in the legislative assembly. Engendering the legislative bodies and political parties are important requisites towards the process of engendering governance.

Unfortunately, both these spaces are scarcely represented by women. The percentage of female Members in the Legislative Assembly (MLAs) in Kerala fell from 10.23% in 1996 to 6.06% in 2016, even as the number of women candidates contested for the elections during this period that witnessed five elections, doubled. Similar skewed presence of women is also evident at the top rungs of the organizational structures of all the political parties at the national and state levels. It creates a situation where power at the grassroots levels is divided between men and women with men still manning the power at higher rungs. In both the elected forums of governance and the party forums where major discussions aimed to alter the form and essence of the country and the political parties are deliberated, decided, and designed, the presence of women is marginal.

It is a matter of serious concern that the despotism of politics, majoritarian communalism and religious fundamentalism all has undermined the process of secularization Kerala had achieved through its social reform movements. The minoritarian caste politics echoes a significant ideological shift from the caste politics that characterized Kerala's project of modernity during the renaissance period in the beginning of the 20th century. The main feature of communalization of politics in Kerala today is the masculinization of the public spheres. Women's bodies, which were co-opted by the different movements and agendas in the history of Kerala, including conjugal, caste and agrarian reforms are now co-opted by counter-democratic forces in order to forge an ideological unity amongst them. Ethno-caste political identities are seen to establish their link with the body politic through the act of surveillance and policing of women's bodies (Meena Pillai, 2015). It is an issue of severe anxiety that a new women identity that complements this pseudo-nationalistic order is being manufactured in Kerala.

In today's gendered socio-political scapes in Kerala, the presence of an actual male gaze is no longer necessary because its possibility is constant. Society does not need to create laws for subjugation because the male gaze has already separated, isolated, and objectified each individual woman. It is quite common that women who are active in the public domain, especially in the PRIs in Kerala, are subjected to moralistic gazes and immoral framings. It is the constancy of these panoptic and moralistic gazes and their inescapable and all pervasive nature that forced many Kerala women, who were active in the local governance, to withdraw and retreat completely from the public spaces. When women challenge the structure and transcend the boundaries imposed on them that confine their locations to home and hearth, they are labeled immoral; when women succumb to the patriarchal norms and accept their subordinate position and act accordingly, they are branded proxies. Women actively involved in the process of governance, especially EWRs, and members of Kudumbashree have to carefully tread through these often collapsing and often diverging categories of 'immoral' and 'proxy'. These implicit, strategic forms of systemic GBV entwined with conditioned power encapsulate women pushed them back again to the very same spaces of invisibility and inaudibility sans subjectivity and agency.

In the economic spaces, increasing uncertainties in the organized and unorganized sectors, denial of job opportunities, wage stagnations, contract conditions and restrictions for union activities, singularly and collectively, accentuate the labour issues of women. The complexities involved in the functioning of the grievance redressal mechanisms, media trail and the resultant social ostracisation have singularly and collectively affected the working conditions of women, thereby decreasing the FWPR, substantively.

To conclude, the PPC and the post PPC phase did bring a change in the 'politics of presence' of women in the PRIs and in the public sphere. One can in no way argue that the PPC drastically changed the internalized structures of patriarchal subjugation and invisibility of women in Kerala. Patriarchy is not overturned, or even significantly eroded, overnight. But the entry of women in the public spaces via grassroots institutions leaving the private and circumscribed spaces of the home, to an extent neglecting the question of 'who will make chapatis' (Datta, 1998) is an important indicator of change. Many of the women elected representatives shared the enhanced sense of social and personal status within and outside the family. Men willingly sharing the household responsibilities and invitations to weddings of higher class families that can be treated as trivial at macro analysis becomes quite significant gains at the micro level (Manjula. B, 2008). Challenges and problems highlighted by various studies of the PPC (Chatukulam and John, 2000; Vijayan and Sandhya, 2004; Radha and Roy Chowdhary, 2002) need to be read along with the success scored by at least some elected women representatives in Kerala, both as participants in local governance and as representatives articulating the interests of the women. A dialectic view of truth must include the notion that there are always emerging possibilities, which are not yet visible.

Chapter 5

Tribals and the PPC: Participatory Processes and the Paradoxical Practices

We did not go up the stage
That was made in our name
Nor were we invited on to it
We were shown
Our place
With pointed finger
And we sat there (obediently)
We were highly appreciated
And 'they', standing on the stage
Kept telling us of our own misery
'But our misery remained ours alone
It was never theirs'
We mumbled – uttered our doubts
'They' listened intently
And roared….
Pulling us by the ear admonished us
"Say sorry….otherwise….

Vahru Sonvane : *The Stage*

Excerpts from the Tribal writing, *The Stage,* brings forth the issue of appropriation of tribal life and their ways of seeing by the dominant groups. Just 84 words! It was more than enough for a tribal poet to explain in-depth the decay from within of the experiments, paradigms, theories, discourses, redesigning and restructuring of multi-pronged, integrated, comprehensive, and organic tribal development programmes and the failure of such top-down programmes of the State for more than 70 years. Still, we toy with our failed models with the conviction that they need to be pulled out from the narrow forest tracks they use to trek—and they have been using these tracks with creepers and climbers on the sides, for hundreds of years—into the multi-tracked, highways of our corporatised development models that change every time, a new advertisement strikes the front page of newspapers or capture the prime time slots in television. What if we apply the rate of crime— rape, murder, domestic violence, and the like— or siphoning of public money as signs of underdevelopment and compare the status of our mega society with that of the tribal culture? Yet we--the smart-phone or I-phone wielders who speed up our rockets to find new space for living on the Moon or the Mars, after taking our lives on earth to the threshold of near extinction--are hell-bent to catapult the tribal people to the orbit of our perceived notions of development, oblivious of the fact that the very same tribal people have a lot to tell us for their and our own benefit if we are ready to listen to them. Yes, just listen to them.

Ramachandra Guha (2007), in an essay on the occasion of India's 60th Republic Day, points to the widespread neglect of tribals and quotes Jaipal Singh Munda, a spokesman for tribal interests, in a moving speech to the Constituent Assembly of India : "Sir, if there is any group of Indian people that has been shabbily treated, it is my people. They have been disgracefully treated, neglected for the last 6,000 years. This history of the Indus Valley civilization, a child of which I am, shows quite clearly that it is the newcomers—most of you here are intruders as far as I am concerned—it is the newcomers who have driven away my people from the Indus Valley to the jungle fastness. . . . The whole history of my people is one of continuous exploitation and dispossession by the non -aboriginals of India punctuated by rebellions and disorder..., I take you all at your word that now we are going to start a new chapter, a new chapter of independent India where there is equality of opportunity, where no one would be neglected". (Guha 2007). Six decades, since this speech was made at the Constituent Assembly, the tribal development still remains a mirage with no remarkable difference.

Tribal Development in India: Broken Promises

In India, the tribals form a significant section of the population because of two factors. They constitute 8.6 per cent of the total population (2011 census); and they have distinct cultures, customary practices, dialects and economic pursuits in different ecological settings. The Government of India's list of Scheduled Tribes included 212 tribes in 1950 which rose to 458 by 2000. The Indian Constitution does not define the word 'tribe', rather, it only mentions about identifying a group of communities as Scheduled Tribes

(STs). The President of India, through public notification can specify any tribe as Scheduled Tribe (Article 342). Further, a tribe can also be included in the list of Scheduled Tribes (Article 341). This indicates that the government uses the traditional notion of a tribe as being forest dwellers or those who are socio-economically backward.

D. N. Majumdar's (1958) definition of a tribe is still relevant in the anthropological understanding of a tribe. In anthropological literature, a tribe has been understood as having the following characteristics:

- a relatively isolated or semi-isolated community living mainly in forest, hill or hill clad settings;
- an autonomous cultural system;
- economically self-sufficient by exploiting natural resources in a primitive or crude mode, involving a low level of technology;
- distributed within a well-demarcated territory distinct world-view or belief system, folklore, deities and its own dialect.

Nineteenth century land laws turned the Indian economy into a supplier of capital and raw material and a captive market for products to suit vested colonial interests. The effort to turn the livelihood of the local communities into a commodity began with the Permanent Settlement Act of 1793. It continued in the Calcutta Law of 1824 and the Assam Land Rules 1838, and others meant to make land available for purposes like salt pans and culminated in the Land Acquisition Act 1894 that remains in force even today (Upadhyay and Raman, 1998).

Lord Dalhousie was the first ruler to understand the need for a forest policy. There were primarily two reasons for his thinking. After the railway was introduced in India in 1853, its expansion needed timber, and the Royal Navy needed good quality teak. The first Forest Act was passed in 1865. It extended the British colonial rights over the forests in India. The Forest Act of 1878 curtailed the traditional use of forest by villagers and tribals. The Indian Forest Act 1927 retained the spirit of the earlier Acts and categorized the forest area as Reserve Forest, Protected Forest, and Village Forest. It is important to note that all these Acts took away the rights of tribals over the places they were living and, instead, made it a privilege that could be withdrawn at will.

The process of designating or 'scheduling' tribes in India began during the British rule, which acquired a systematic character since the 1931 census. The Government of India Act of 1935 introduced a special provision for tribal people and a list of backward tribes was promulgated in 1936. The separatist movement of the British was a diabolical policy to create cleavages between the tribal and the non-tribals. The concept of 'excluded' and/or 'partially' excluded areas', thwarted the development of natural relationships between the different communities. The British policy was colonial and political and by designating tribals as primitive, it caused fissiparous tendencies in the socially stratified Indian society over which it ruled.

'The history of primitive society is the history of an illusion,' says Kuper (1988) and he rightly points out that the myth of the 'primitive' was created by the Europeans of the nineteenth century in order to understand their own selves because industrialization had shaken the foundation of their belief in the feudal order as being the natural unchangeable order of things. The 'primitive' were 'they' not 'us' and does not attempt to understand 'oneself' because that is what it is, it is not a matter of discourse (S. Channa, 2008). The concept, 'tribe' emerged from a political situation, which involved the dominance of the white man, of colonial power, and industrialization.

During the British period, administrators discarded the prevailing concepts of social utility and social welfare, including those that ensured a fair distribution of returns from forest resources. The sole purpose of forest management was to channelize economic gains in favour of the empire. This was achieved by large-scale deforestation, commercialisation of timber, and through restrictions imposed on the rights of tribals. Restrictions on people's access to forest were accompanied by an increase in reserve forest areas, which reduced the extent of forestland for common use (Guha and Gadgil, 1989).

The formal land laws of the State founded on the principle of the State's eminent domain, based on its American version, view land only as a commodity for cultivation and construction, while for tribals, it is an ecosystem with the local community at its centre. The first facet of the eminent domain is that land without an individual *patta* (deed) is State property. The second is that the State alone has the right to decide a public purpose and deprive even individual owners of their assets (Ramanathan, 1999). Both these were detrimental to the way in which tribals viewed land and forest.

The British period, a landmark in the history of forest management, marked the beginning of the breakdown of a symbiotic relationship between tribals and forest. In the process, traditional communal systems of forest management began to disintegrate (Shah, 1996). Thus, forest management was converted from a community-based regime to one of centralised control for commercialisation. This began with the Forest Act of 1865, passed by the British government, imposing the crown's control over India's forests. With one legislative change, tribals became trespassers in their own land, victimised by externally motivated systems of forest management that directly violated various facets of their economic and cultural survival (Singh, 1994). Their forest and other resources were increasingly seen as commodities and their lands expropriated as private property.

In independent India, the policy concerning the tribes has changed from colonial to that of welfare, from isolation to integration, and the focus is on national integration. Elwin (1941) supported the establishment of a sort of 'National Park' of tribals and advised that their contact with the outside world should be reduced to the minimum. After the Constitution of India was adopted in 1950, the President promulgated (in the same year) a list of Scheduled Tribes which was based substantially on the list of Backward Tribes announced in 1936 by the colonial government. As India's own 'Scheduled Area', it resists exclusion; while as the 'Scheduled Area' it resists inclusion in the mainstream pan-national identity.

Located within the nation space, tribals as social groups mark a space of 'otherness' and difference. Nationalist discourses intended to provide a space for the re-articulation of the tribals and to give rise to a cultural politics of representation as against the colonialist misrepresentation. The approach that has found favour over time is the one propounded by Nehru, who argued that 'the avenues for development should… 'be pursued within the tribal framework of the five fundamental principles', the *Panchsheel* approach. Jawaharlal Nehru's articulation of this cultural politics, embedded in his principles of *Panchsheel* construed the nation as a space for living together with dignity.

The assimilation of tribal people with the rest of the population is another approach. Mazumdar (1947), Dube (1960) and Ghurye (1963) opine that this culture contact has created a set of different types of tribes on the acculturation level. Ghurye (1963) characterised the tribals as backward Hindus (1963) and argued that any attempt to isolate them from the mainstream of Indian life would be meaningless. In the present context, the 'assimilation' view is not shared by many as it tends to be hegemonistic and deprives the tribals of their cultural 'identity', besides placing them on the lower rungs of the caste-system of Hindu society. Single line administration and an area development approach in the Fourth Plan, and drawing sub-plans from the Fifth Five Year Plan onwards reflect the policy of integration or mainstreaming with the regional and national setting.

The concept, 'mainstream' came into Indian Anthropology in the post-independence era, specifically in relation to the integration of tribes. Another term used was 'national culture' which denoted an industrialised, democratic, secular, and universalistic post-colonial culture. The term 'tribe' has its genesis in colonisation, and 'mainstream' is the product of post-colonial attempts at nation-building by multi-ethnic countries (S. Channa, 2008). Nirmal Kumar Bose (1972), speaking at the 1969 Seminar on the Tribal Situation in India said, "It was right and proper for Miss Marion Pugh (The *Khasi* from Assam) and Mrs. Khrielena Terhiya (The *Naga* from Nagaland), to raise the question as to what was meant by the term 'Mainstream of Indian Life'. Did it mean the Hindu way of life?" Especially for those who were categorised as 'others,' such questions were relevant to their culture and identity.

The Government of India tried to redefine the social-utility and social-welfare functions. The characteristics that distinguish tribals include their strong attachment to land, dependence on renewable natural resources, subsistence practices, distinct languages, culture, historical identities as a distinct people, and, often, mistrust towards outsiders. For development institutions and Indian planners, the challenge was how to incorporate such diversities into the development planning (Singh, 1994).

Continuation of forest regimes based on commercialisation and exclusion of local people led to the alteration of forest ecosystems and to denudation of vast tracts of forestland (Biswas 1988; Palit 1996; Poffenberger et al. 1996). The emphasis of forest management regimes continued to be on commercial timber exploitation and exclusion of tribals from forest. Growing dependence on ruthless moneylenders, linked with powerful feudal landlords and local politicians, led to massive land alienation and permanent or seasonal migration. These Acts which legitimized the systemic violence on a largely unsuspecting population was the imposition of an alien judicial system and the law and order machinery that subjugated them further compounding their vulnerability and subservience. Result of all these processes was erosion of their dignity, devaluation of their identities and disrespect of their ways of living (Bodley, 1988).

In the mid-1980s, the then Commissioner of Scheduled Castes and Scheduled Tribes, B. D. Sharma, used his constitutional office to highlight the plight of tribals and the constitutional responsibility of the State towards them. Subsequently, the Parliament set up a committee headed by Dileep Singh Bhuria, Member of Parliament and a tribal, to study the problems of tribals. His report argued that the grama sabha should be legally recognised as the primary centre of tribal governance. Released in 1995, the report also argued that the long-standing demand of tribals for control over productive land and forests should be conceded to and that administrative interference in the affairs of tribals should be minimised.

The assertions of tribals were powerfully summed up in one of their central motif slogans, 'Our Rule in Our Villages.' This declaration did not imply secession from India but meant the affirmation of relative autonomy from what was experienced as an intrusive and exploitative state apparatus and the unjust social and economic order that it legitimated at the expense of their livelihoods, identities and systems of self-governance. In December 1996, the Parliament passed the Provisions of the Panchayats (Extension to the Scheduled Areas) Act, (PESA), recognising the tribal's right to self-rule.

Even when development policies and programmes have been designed specifically to improve the welfare of tribals, the approach had usually been paternalistic, ignoring the strength of indigenous institutions and knowledge. This, in turn, contributed to worsening their poverty and social marginalisation and weakened their ethnic resistance (Jazairy, 1992). Dispossessed by modernisation's development strategy, millions of tribals have been pushed to the fringes of national and international life (Ghai, 1994).

Tribal Development through Five Year Plans-Pros and Cons

The Five Year Plans aimed at tribal development through emphasis on general welfare activities. The First Five-Year Plan (1951-56) laid down the principle that the general development programmes should be so designed as to cater adequately to the backward classes, and the special provision should be used for securing additional and more intensified development. The Second Five-Year Plan (1956-61) promised the trickling down effect of economic development. An important landmark during this Plan was the opening of 43 Special Multipurpose Tribal Blocks (SMPTBs), later called Tribal Development Blocks (TDBs).

The Third Five-Year Plan (1961-66) advocated creating greater equality of opportunity, bringing about reduction of disparities in income and wealth, and establishing a more even distribution of economic power. An important step during the Fourth Five-Year Plan (1969-74) was setting up six pilot projects in Andhra Pradesh, Bihar, Madhya Pradesh and Orissa in 1971-72, as a Central Sector Scheme with the primary objective of combating political unrest and Left Wing extremism. A separate Tribal Development Agency was established for each project. These agencies were later merged with Integrated Tribal Development Projects (ITDPs) during the Fifth Plan.

The Fifth Five-Year Plan (1974-78) marked a shift in approach, reflected in the launching of the Tribal Sub-Plan (TSP) for the direct benefit of the development of tribals. The TSP stipulated that funds of the state and centre be quantified on the population proportion basis with budgetary mechanisms and utilisation for welfare and development of STs. The TSP strategy was implemented in 194 Integrated Tribal Development Projects, 259 pockets of tribal concentration under Modified Area Development Approach (MADA), 82 clusters, and habitations of 75 Primitive Tribal Groups. There was substantial increase in the flow of funds for the development of STs under this arrangement.

The Sixth Five-Year Plan (1980-85) sought to ensure a higher degree of devolution of funds so that at least 50 percent of tribal families were provided assistance to cross the poverty line. Emphasis was on family-oriented economic activities rather than on infrastructure development schemes. In the Seventh Five Year Plan, for the economic development of SCs and Scheduled Tribes, two national level institutions were set up viz., (i) Tribal Cooperative Marketing Development Federation (TRIFED) in 1987 as an apex body for State Tribal Development Cooperative Corporations; and (ii) National Scheduled Castes and Scheduled Tribes Finance and Development Corporation (NSFDC) in 1989. The former was envisaged to provide remunerative price for the forest and agriculture produce of tribal while the latter was intended to provide credit support for employment generation. In the Eighth Five-Year Plan (1992-97), efforts were intensified to bridge the gap between the levels of development of the STs.

The Ninth Plan (1997-2002) approach envisaged advancement of STs through a process of empowerment wherein efforts were made to create an enabling environment conducive for the free exercise of their rights, enjoyment of their privileges and leading a life of self-confidence and dignity at par with the other citizens of the country. This essentially encompassed social empowerment, economic advancement and social justice. Percentage flow to TSP from the State plan outlay showed a steady increase from 4.2 in the fifth plan to 9.3 in the ninth plan. From the Tenth Five year Plan strategies were adopted to eradicate deprivation/ exploitation that focused more to enhance the self -the governance of the tribals. These interventions from the central and state governments did bring noticeable changes in the life world of the tribal communities. Improvement in the literacy rate is one such remarkable change.

Figure 5.1
Literacy Rate: A Comparison (1981- 2001)

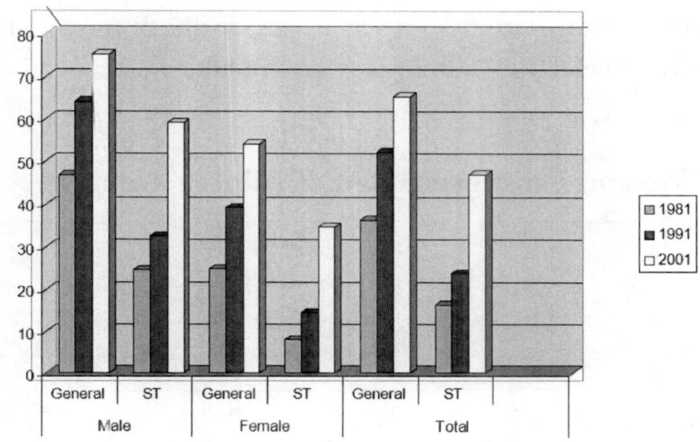

Source: Census Reports, Various Issues

Although, there has been a substantial increase in the literacy rate of STs during the last three development decades, the gap between the literacy rate of STs and that of the general population is not only persisting, but also found to be widening. In addition, there are the problems of intra-and inter-state/ district variations in the literacy rates amongst STs. The enrolment ratio has increased for the better. The dropout rate, another indicator in the field of educational development, also shows a steady decline.

Though the Constitution of India envisages protection and development of tribals, successive Central Governments have failed on both fronts to a large extent. Evaluation studies did not give a positive picture of the tribal development programmes. Reasons cited were many. Funds earmarked were insufficient, programmes did not have an integrated approach, schemes did not synchronise with the tribal needs, tribals were kept out of general development programmes and finally, development initiatives were designed without giving due consideration to the heritage and tradition of tribals.

The tribal developmental interventions in Kerala were also not a different story.

The Kerala Context

(This chapter is primarily used to analyse the ways in which the intervention of the PPC impacted the life- world and standard of living of the tribal community in Kerala. Hence all the data sets in this section are confined to the 90s so as to enable the analysis to juxtapose it with the PPC interventions in the same period.)

Tribal population in Kerala, according to the 1991 census, is 3,20967, which is 1.335% of the Kerala population. The socio-economic condition of tribals is much lower compared to that of the general population, though the Working Participation Rate (WPR) of tribals, for both men and women, is higher than the general population, as shown in table (5.1).

Table 5.1
Working Participation Rate of Tribals in Kerala (%)

Year		Scheduled Tribe	General
1961		47.0	33.3
1971		42.9	29.1
1981		45.2	30.5
1991	Total	46.0	31.4
	Men	55.1	47.6
	Women	36.9	15.9

Source: Development of Scheduled Caste and Scheduled Tribe, Training book, Kerala State Planning Board.

The high working participation rate in the case of tribals, however, is an indication of their abject poverty. Table (5.1) shows that the WPR of women in Kerala is just 15.9%, while the corresponding figure for tribal women is 36.9%. This implies that both tribal men and women have to work to earn their daily bread.

Literacy rate of both men and women in Kerala is higher than the national average. In Kerala, though the literacy rate among tribals is much lower than that of the general population, their literacy rate, when compared with the national average, is higher, as shown in table (5.2).

Table 5.2
Literacy Rate of Scheduled Tribes India- Kerala: A Comparison

YEAR	INDIA		KERALA	
	General	Scheduled Tribe	General	Scheduled Tribe
1971	29.45	11.30	60.42	25.72
1981	36.03	16.35	70.42	31.79
1991	52.21	------	89.81	57.22

Source: Development of Scheduled Caste and Scheduled Tribe, Training book, Kerala State Planning Board.

Tribals depend mostly on agriculture for their livelihood. Decline in agriculture in the past decade due to various factors made it not cost effective, resulting in a shift in the occupational pattern of tribals. The corresponding figures are shown in table (5.3). This shift had an adverse impact on the tribals, who were mostly dependent on the primary sector for their living. An increasing percentage of tribals, therefore, had to work in other sectors, like service and industry, where their earnings were lower than what they had earned from agriculture, which deteriorated their living conditions, further.

Table 5.3
Changing Occupational Structure of Scheduled Tribes in Kerala (1981-1991)

Occupation	1981 (%)	1991 (%)
Farmers	20.54	16.66
Agricultural Labourers	57.47	53.47
Others	21.99	29.87
Total	100	100

Source: Development of Scheduled Caste and Scheduled Tribe, Training book, Kerala State Planning Board.

The Process of Exclusion

In Kerala also, one could trace the exclusion patterns operating at all levels, which made the tribal population the most marginalised, exploited, and disadvantaged group in the State. This is clearly reflected in Wayanadu, the most tribal populated district in the State. Panamaram, the panchayat selected for the analysis on the impact of Tribal Sub Plan on triblas, is in Wayanadu district.

In spite of the fact that tribal development programmes have definite guidelines, including binding provisions to ensure full participation of the user groups in various stages of each scheme, the levels of participation by tribals are very low and effectively non-existent. It is pertinent to note that the Government of Kerala intervened in the first instance in the firm belief that tribals have remained excluded from the development process and that deliberate effort would be necessary to carry these underprivileged sections along with the mainstream of socio-economic progress. However, it appeared from the ground realities that the government interventions had only increased the exclusion of tribals. To understand this paradox, it is necessary to analyse the process of exclusion, which affected the tribal way of life since the active intervention of the government.

The exclusion process included historical, demographic, economic, environmental, politico-legal and social and policy induced factors. The tribal economy is often referred to as primitive and subsistence based. Marked by the absence of profit motive and accumulation, the means of production in the tribal economy is mainly land and labour.

With the formation of Kerala in 1956 and with the implementation of the Land Reform laws, the feudal landlords knew that their surplus land would be taken away by the government sooner or later. Consequently, they started leasing out land liberally to outsiders. Due to the absence of land records and clear specification of boundaries, the non-tribals took possession of larger areas than they were entitled to, most of them from tribal belts.

A more direct form of land alienation took place since the mid-1960s. With the forest law becoming stringent in the second half of the 1970s, the tribals lost access to their ancestral place of refuge, and became literally marginalised as far as land holding was concerned (Mathur, 1977).

The history of land alienation among the ST in Kerala is the history of selective blindness and calculated operations of the State policies that paved the way for the mega onslaught on the micro-society, even in a place like Wayanadu that had a cent percent ST population till 1930s. The government-sponsored migration of the non-tribals brought the ST population in Wayanadu to 60.4 percent by 1950 and to 27.3 percent by 1991.

The Dabur Commission constituted by the Union Government to study the land-related problems of the ST population in India recommended that the ST land alienated after January 26, 1950 be restored. But the Government sat on the recommendation till 1975 and then the question of land alienation was brought under the 20 point programme of the government. Accordingly, in 1975, the Kerala Assembly unanimously passed the Kerala Scheduled Tribes (Restriction on transfer of Lands and Restoration of Alienated Lands) Act. It was included in Schedule 9 of the Constitution of India to prevent the possibility of being questioned in any court of law. The provision in the Act that prevented land alienation after 1960, in fact, diluted the Dabur Commission report and supported the migrants to regularize the occupations till 1960.

Besides, the Act said that those STs who had documents to support their claim over the alienated land could get it restored. But the fact is that the majority of the ST population never had or even now has such legal documents.

Though the Act was passed in 1975, the Rules to implement the Act were formulated only in 1986. Even after that, the Act was not moved into action, following which Dr. Nallathampi Thera, a social activist, moved a petition in the Kerala High Court. The court, in 1993, ordered the restoration of alienated land within six months.

Though the government had got applications from 8553 persons, demanding restoration of 11,000 hectares of land, the decision was made only in the case of 100 applications. The government then stopped the process of restoration of alienated lands citing the lame excuse that there would be fight between the ST and non-ST people. The court extended the deadline by two and a half years. It ended in April 1996. The government filed an affidavit before the court and stated that the government was unable to cross the resistance move by the migrants. But the court ordered that all the alienated land of the ST should be restored within the next six months.

Instead of implementing the court order, the Kerala Assembly, on September 23, 1996, unanimously passed an amendment to the Act, which, in effect neutralized the crucial provisions of the original Act. The amendment that legalized all illegal occupation till 1986 got the President's assent in 1999. The ST population in Kerala stood as mute spectators when a legislation passed to benefit them was being neutralized through another act of the State assembly. Like the ST, the legislation intended to help them was also marginalized and the struggles for their land were scattered.

The Department of Economics and Statistics, Government of Kerala, conducted a survey in 1977 and identified the land alienated by tribals during the decade 1966-76. The study found out that 546 tribal families lost 9859 acres of land; 27.41 % of the area being transferred by means of lease; 42.1 % by sale; 18.8 % by mortgage, and the remaining area by oral transfer and other means.

The introduction of new cash crops, which required agricultural labour beyond family labour and alienation of tribal land, had a combined adverse impact on the tribal economy. Consequently, they were further pushed to work as agricultural labourers for meeting cash requirements. Thus, both pull and push factors operated in this respect.

Non-tribal settlers affected the tribal economy both by reducing the land availability and by introducing the cash economy. The sudden introduction of a monetised market economy and the unequal exchange process resulted in increased demand for cash, which made the tribals borrow money from moneylenders. This accelerated the process of alienation of assets, particularly land and cattle ((KFRI, 1991).

Unlike other communities, tribals have an organic link with the forest environment. From the ecological point of view, the magnitude and rapidity of the adverse changes were very significant. Right from the first Forest Act passed during the British rule; the tribals never got justice from the lawmakers. Lawmakers did not see them, and when they were seen, they were treated either as intruders or as barriers. Even the Forest Act of 1980 failed to view tribals as an integral part of forest.

One could trace the marginalisation of tribals in the political sphere also. In the 1950s, the Wayanadu tribals lived in an apolitical environment. From the early 1960s, there was a period of single party dominance with the Communists holding sway over tribals. This continued till the beginning of 1970s. That was the time when naxalite leaders used the tribals to give expression to the theoretical premise of their political statement. The tribals who had reached the nadir of impoverishment and exploitation, could easily be lured by the high sounding promises offered by naxalite leaders, who used tribals as tools to wage war against the State. With the State machinery unleashing its brutal force to quell the armed struggle, the tribals found themselves thrown from the frying pan to the burning fire.

Police surveillance in the belts of Wayanadu saw the emergence of a new phenomenon of unwed mothers among tribal girls. A phase of manipulative participation in political activity began soon. Local leadership and deeper political awareness were not encouraged. Leaders from outside used them as part of their larger political agenda, especially in the fight for land rights. Tribal development came to be seen as flow of funds from the State and not in terms of improvement of the quality of life of the tribals.

In this process, the most crucial factor that affected their lives was rapid destruction of the traditional forms of leadership. Along with the declining status of *Mooppan*, the tribal chieftain, one could trace the gradual loosening up cohesion of the tribal hamlet. Because of the influx of settlers and the alienation of land, there was physical scattering of households; tribal families moved away after selling their prime land and established new nuclear hamlets.

The loss of status of women was much felt in Wayanadu. With the break-up of traditional economy, women began to shoulder the bulk of the responsibility in raising the family. Finally, abject poverty pushed several women to sell their bodies and the empirical studies show the signs of organised flesh trade in the district (Manjula, B. 2012). Marginalisation of tribal women removed a potentially active and aggressive group from playing the socially constructive role as a pull factor in development.

Similarly, the plight of tribal youth was also of concern. They were caught between two worlds. With the introduction of formal education, the tribal youth got cut off from their traditional moorings. The onslaught of the mega culture on the micro-culture left the tribal youth with nothing of their own, neither the mega nor the micro culture (Luiz, 1962).

The essence of tribal development strategy in Wayanadu had been the development of infrastructure, particularly roads and housing. There were no consultations with people to find out their needs and identify their capabilities. In short, it was work-centred development strategy, as opposed to people-centred one, and money-driven and not demand-driven. Education and health schemes, focused on modern methods, ignored the traditional systems, completely. The land reforms policy was implemented without understanding the tribal land tenure system. This worked to the advantage of non-tribal settlers.

Another aspect of development strategy, which affected real participation, was the welfarism implicit in most schemes. Heavy subsidisation and liberal granting of discretionary doles created a sense of dependence among tribals. It was noticed that 95 percent of tribals who approached the Integrated Tribal Development Programme (ITDP) came there in search of free grants. The doles pushed them into a thankful faith in the benevolence of government and made them forgetful of the larger issues of misuse of funds meant for long term local development (KIRTADS, 1982).

All these worked in tandem. They reinforced each other and led to a vicious circle of cause-effect alternation, often resulting in marginalisation. All these processes brought about a direct form of exploitation. Thus, exogenous and endogenous factors caused the exclusion and marginalisation of tribals in all walks of life. The flow chart to show the process of exclusion among the tribals is given in Figure (5.2).

The Tribal Sub Plan (TSP)

The post-independence period saw tribal development activities under different programmes, which showed the change with respect to their names only, with the content of programmes remaining the same. Successive legislations on forest, commercialisation of forest, and the inflow of migrants turned the tribal economy upside down.

Figure 5.2
Exclusion of the Tribals in Kerala: Various Processes At Work

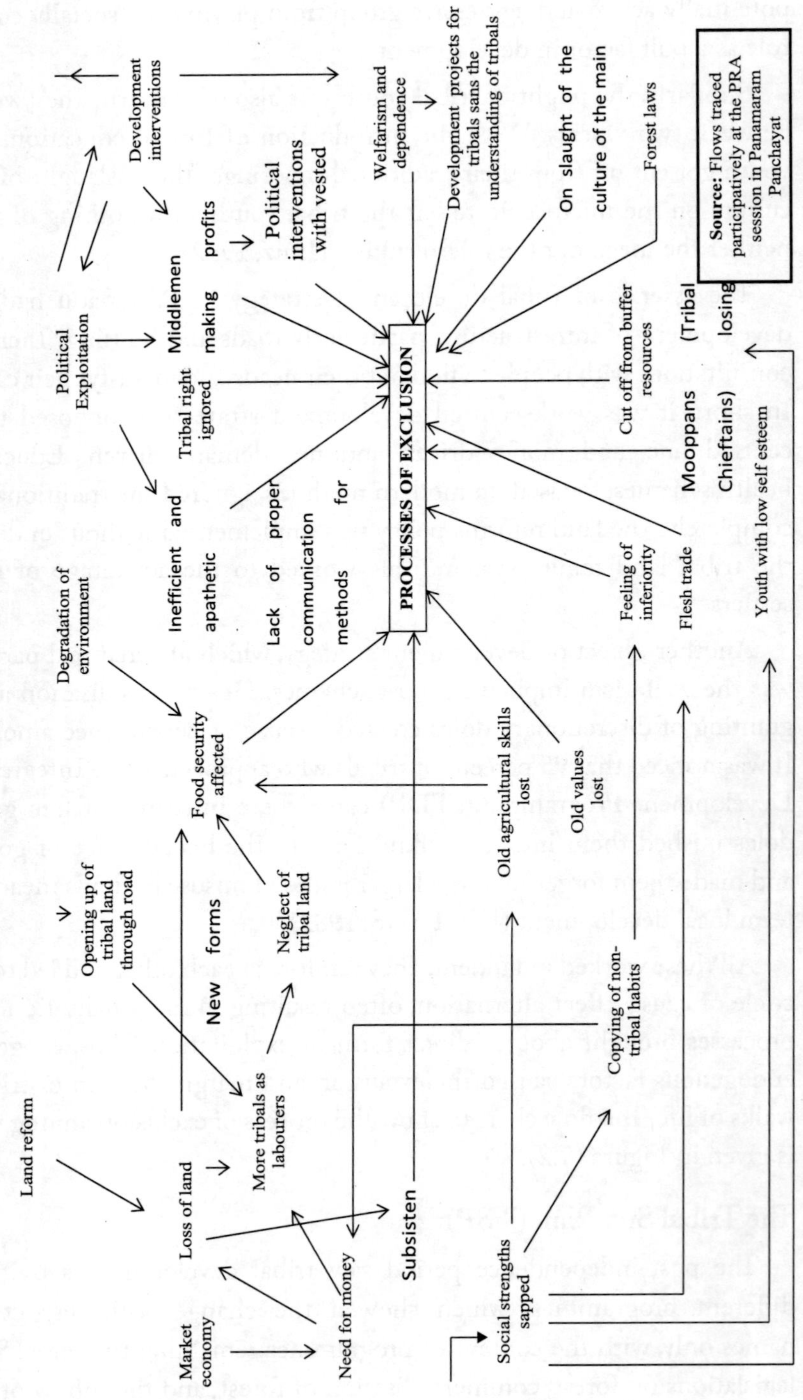

Source: Flows traced participatively at the PRA session in Panamaram Panchayat

Though the Constitution of India envisages protection and development of tribals, the successive State governments failed on both fronts. A survey conducted by the Department of Rural Development in 1992, revealed that 48.47% of tribals were below the poverty line. More than 72% depended on agriculture. Stagnation in the agricultural sector, obviously, hit tribals most. The first five-year plan aimed tribal development through emphasis on general welfare activities. Multi-purpose tribal development blocks, later renamed as tribal blocks, were started in tribal areas during the second plan, which also allowed tribal blocks outside the scheduled areas. The Attappady Tribal Development Block, formed in 1962, was modeled in line with this new perspective. However, evaluation studies conducted at the end of the fourth five-year plan had not given a positive picture of the tribal development programmes. The fifth plan had brought in the Tribal Sub Plan (TSP), designed exclusively for tribals. The TSP approach, adopted in the fifth five year plan, had a two-pronged strategy: promotion of development activities to raise the level of living standard of Scheduled Tribes; and protection of their interest through legal and administrative support. These changes in approach were reflected in Kerala too. A separate government department for tribal welfare was formed in 1975. Five-TSP areas were formed. Lacunae in the earlier programmes were rectified and seven ITDPs, in the place of the earlier five, started functioning. Still, they failed to achieve targets for many reasons; lack of interaction among the line departments, which prevented convergence of different programmes towards tribal development, being the most important.

Chart 5.1

Criteria for the TSP Allocation

Sectors	**Criteria**
Rural development (Centre-sponsored projects)	The criterion issued by the Central Government
Agriculture, Irrigation and Soil conservation	Number of tribal agricultural farmers.
Dairy development, Animal husbandry and Land reforms	Number of agricultural farmers in the particular sector.
Electricity/ Road/ Health / Drinking water supply	Number of tribal hamlets
Community development/ Forest/ Industry/ House construction / Social welfare	Tribal population
Education/ Co-operation	Number of Institutions at the district level/ its need

Source: Development of Scheduled Caste and Scheduled Tribe, Training book, Kerala State Planning Board.

Criteria used for the TSP selection in the State are shown in chart (5.1). Every year, the TSP was made at the district level. Based on this, officials at the line departments drafted the project plan and the programmes were implemented after it got sanction from the district level working group. Pooling system was introduced in 1996- 97 for full utilisation of the tribal funds. Tribal development programmes were categorised into two; programmes of the Tribal Development Department and programmes of other departments. Programmes of the Tribal Development Department were sub-divided into four; Programmes on education, health and house construction, economic development, and other development programmes.

Following were the main lapses in the implementation of the TSP:

Regional development, rather than economic and welfare development of tribals, was given priority;

Regional development programmes benefited the non-tribals more than the tribals;

The ITDP was reduced merely to an implementing agency in tribal planning, because planning and convergence of the TSP were vested with the district planning office;

There was only a convergence of different programmes at the district level, and it lacked planning in a holistic integrated approach;

The funds earmarked for ITDP were not fully spent. Only 87.21% of the total plan fund earmarked for tribals was spent during the eighth plan (1992-97); and

More importantly, there was rampant corruption and misutilisation of the tribal plan fund.

These failures in the tribal implementation programmes were mainly due to the non-participation of tribals in their welfare programmes, ignorance and indifference of the planning officials towards their needs and priorities, and the centralised nature of programmes. These development initiatives made them only passive and more dependent on the financial aid of the government. The result was the faminisation of tribals.

It was at this stage that the PPC tried to make an intentional development intervention. Panamaram Panchayat in Wayanadu district is taken for understanding the intervention of PPC among the tribal communities in Kerala.

Historical timeline, drawn with the participation of the tribals given in chart (5.2), gives an understanding of the important landmarks in the history of the Panamaram panchayat.

Chart 5.2
Historical Time Line: Important Landmarks in the History of Panamaram Panchayat

Year	Event
1802	Attacking the British military post in Panamaram under the leadership of Thallakal Chandu
1865	Forest Act. Forest management from community based regime to one of centralised control
1957	First Communist ministry in the State
1962	Multi-purpose tribal development blocks were formed. Panamaram grama panchayat was formulated.
1964	Recording of land rights and land agitations began.
1967	Naxalite interventions in the tribal belts of Wayanadu.
1971	Vesting of forests
1975	Integrated Tribal Development Programme was formed. Act abolishing bonded labour was passed.
1986	Tribal Land Alienation (Prevention) of Act was brought into force. Political parties of the State openly supported non-tribals in the land agitation fights of the tribals.
1988	Panchayat elections
1991	IAS officer ceases to be project officer.
1995	Encroaching the forest land in Panavalli under C.K. Janu, the tribal leader, and declaring that as their own land and the tribal agitations for the land

Tribal Development in the PPC

In principle, the PPC sought to intervene to disrupt the complex and interacting forces that were worsening the lives and livelihoods of the tribal population in Kerala. The Tribal Sub Plan (TSP) included special efforts to decentralize beyond districts to the regional level to facilitate incorporation of the local tribals in planning processes and their needs and demands in the tribal plan. The PPC included tribal development as a separate subject for discussion at all levels of training.

Following were the main changes incorporated in the PPC to address the development problems of tribals:

- Planning of the TSP was decentralised from the district to the regional level. This facilitated incorporation of the local tribals' needs and demands into the tribal plan, thereby rectifying the lack of convergence and integration found in earlier plans, besides introducing participation and transparency into the TSP;
- Tribal development was incorporated as a separate subject for discussion at all levels of training in the PPC;
- Special direction was given to ensure participation of tribals in the grama sabha;
- A separate *oorusabha* (the tribal gram sabha) was made mandatory, so that tribals could air their problems without hesitation;
- Separate discussion groups for tribals at development seminar and a separate chapter on tribals in the development report were made mandatory;
- Separate task force was formed for the TSP;
- Special review mechanism for redress of grievances of tribals; and
- Special conscientization classes on tribal issues for the elected representatives.

Though special and focused development strategies to address tribal issues were designed in the PPC, it was found that they were not effective in the field, especially in the Panamaram panchayat.

Panamaram is a panchayat in Wayanadu where the tribal population is the second highest. 25 tribal colonies of Panamaram panchayat, which comprised 334 households, 469 families and 3447 tribal inhabitants, were studied for one year for the study purpose. Out of 3447 tribals, 554 were interviewed. Out of the 25 tribal colonies, ten belonged to Adiyars, nine to Paniyars, four Kurichiars and two Kattunaikars. Details are shown in table (5.4).

Table 5.4

Details of the Tribal Population Taken for the Study

1	Total number of colonies visited	25
2	Total number of households in the colonies	334
3	Total number of families in the colonies	469
4	Total number of people in the colonies	3447
5	Total people interviewed	554
6	Total men interviewed	230
7	Total women interviewed	324

Source: Survey on Panamaram Panchayat, 2000.

Questions of general nature, like age, community and educational level, were asked to know their social background. Specific questions, like their attendance in the oorusabha, reasons for attendance and abstinence, their evaluations of the failure of the TSP, their perceptions of the Tribal Extension Officer (TEO), Social Activists (SA), and elected representatives were asked to know their understanding of the TSP. Study used PRA methods to elicit the response; there was no specific pattern of questions or uniform questionnaire. The Focused Group Discussions (FGDs) were informal in nature and the questions were posed extempore, considering the heterogeneous nature of tribals and the context of discussion.

Table 5.5
Community-wise classification of tribals in Panamaram

Name of The tribe	No. of Colonies	No. of House holds	No. of Families	No. of People
Adiyar	10	125	163	1428
Paniyar	9	141	228	1628
Kurichiar	4	61	70	360
Kattunaikkar	2	7	8	31

Source: Survey on Panamram Panchayat, 2000.

The general principle, with respect to the tribal economy, is that more the number of working hands, lesser the poverty, since the tribal economy is the subsistence economy. It was found that the situation in Panamaram was quite different. Density of population in the households of Adiyars and Paniyars was very high, going up to 25-30, comprising 5-6 families. But there was abject poverty in these cluster families, disproving the general notion about the tribal economy. Reason for this was found to be underemployment and unemployment of a very high magnitude.

Table 5.6
Sex-wise Break up of Respondents

Name of the Tribe	No. of Men Interviewed	No. of Women Interviewed
Adiyar	101 (43.9 %)	132 (40.7%)
Paniyar	74 (32.2 %)	148 (45.8%)
Kurichiar	51 (22.2 %)	42 (12.9%)
Kattunaikkar	4 (1.7%)	2 (0.60%)

Source: Survey on Panamaram Panchayat, 2000.

Table 5.7
Educational Qualification of the Respondents

Name of the Tribe	Illiterate	L.P.	Primary	U.P.	High school	PDC	Degree
Adiyar	36%	51%	13%	0%	0%	0%	0%
Paniyar	41%	57%	2%	0%	0%	0%	0%
Kurichiar	13%	32%	23%	11%	9%	7%	5%
Kattunaikkar	100%	0%	0%	0%	0%	0%	0%

Source: PRA with the tribals of the Panamaram Panchayat, 2000.

Most respondents were either illiterate or had only lower primary education as shown in table (5.7). As expected, the education level of Adiyar and Paniyar was very low compared to Kurichiar. It was surprising to notice that tribals with higher levels of education among them, especially with pre-degree and degree holders, showed a negative attitude towards the PPC during the informal discussions. They considered the PPC as a political process and expressed their disinterest in politics. Ironically, Kurichiars, who had a higher level of education than Adiyars and Paniyars, showed greater interest in activities of the PPC.

The table (5.8) shows that the percentage of attendance of both men and women belonging to Paniyar and Adiyar communities was high at the initial meetings of the ooru sabha. There was no marked difference between the male- female participation. This was because women in these communities moved out for work without gender discrimination. Also, the abject poverty in which they lived made the women feel that they would get financial benefits, if they participated in the ooru sabha. Ooru sabha was viewed as a mere forum to air grievances and to avail financial benefits.

Kurichiars, comparatively economically well off and who consider themselves up in the social ladder among other tribal communities, reflected the socially conditioned gender norms, seen normally in the mega society. That was evident in the low-turnout of Kurichiar women in the ooru sabha. Kattunaikars, who were completely cut off from the mainstream and, to an extent, from other tribal communities, were totally ignorant of the PPC or ooru sabha. Their attendance in the ooru sabha was zero. Even the verbal communication with them was difficult, since they were using a language of their own.

Table 5.8
Attendance in Ooru Sabha: Sector-wise & Sex-wise

Name of the Tribe	No. of men attended ooru sabha	No. of women attended ooru sabha	No. of men attended ooru sabha more than once	No. of women attended ooru sabha more than once
Adiyar	56 (55%)	82 (62%)	14 (13%)	32 (24%)
Paniyar	32 (43%)	63 (42%)	5 (6%)	25 (17%)
Kurichiar	33 (65%)	14 (33%)	24 (47%)	6 (14%)
Kattunaikkar	0 (0%)	0 (0%)	0 (0%)	0 (0%)

Source: PRA with the tribals in Panamaram, 2000.

Declining trend in the participation of the tribals in ooru sabha showed their marked disinterest in the campaign process. When 56% and 43% of Adiyar and Paniyar, respectively, attended ooru sabha once, only 13 and 6% of these communities, respectively, chose to attend it for the second time. Percentage of female population that participated in more than one ooru sabha was more than that of their male counterparts. While the overall decline in the attendance showed disillusionment among these tribal communities with respect to their wrongly perceived notion of ooru sabha, higher percentage of female participation showed that women still had hopes against odds. The participation of Kurichiar, though showed a decline, was not that steep. While the percentage of Kurichiar, who attended ooru sabha only once was 65%, the percentage that attended ooru sabha more than once declined by 18% only. This was because Kurichiar, both men and women, had a better and realistic understanding of ooru sabha and the PPC.

Table 5.9
Motivation of Tribals in Attending the Ooru Sabha

Name of the Tribe	Getting financial aid	Getting goat/ cow	Getting / repairing houses	Getting pension	Discussing Dvt. Needs
Adiyar	59%	22%	17%	2%	0%
Paniyar	36%	37%	16%	11%	0%
Kurichiar	24%	27%	17%	6%	26%
Kattunaikkar	0%	0%	0	0%	0%

Source: PRA with tribals of the Panamaram Panchayat, 2000.

Table (5.9) quantifies the attitude of tribals towards attending ooru sabha, a forum originally conceived to be the pivot of the PPC with respect to the planning process for tribals.

The very concept of ooru sabha, which was specially designed to make tribals participate in the planning process, got defeated at the first stage itself when tribals chose to view the ooru sabha as a forum in line with the earlier tribal development programmes. The tribals were not aware of the potential of ooru sabha even when it was conceived as the principal forum to discuss and decide their local needs and demands, which were to be reflected in the final plan. Absence of a well-designed communication strategy to disseminate the significance of ooru sabha among tribals in the whole process of decentralised planning proved detrimental to the effective implementation of the PPC. Response of different tribal groups towards the ooru sabha also showed marked differences among the different tribal communities, when age was taken as a variable. Among those who attended ooru sabha for the first time, Adiyar and Paniyar youth in the age group 20- 30 topped, whereas Kurichiar community was represented more by senior members in the age group 30- 40, reflecting their mature approach towards ooru sabha.

The drop-out percentage also indicated this attitudinal difference between Paniyar and Adiyar group on one side and Kurichiar on the other side. Wrong perception of ooru sabha by the Paniyar and Adiyar caused sudden disillusionment among them, resulting in steep decline in their attendance. Kurichiars, on the other hand, followed a steady trend with minimal dropouts. It was ignorance, rather than information, which made Adiyar and Paniyar attend ooru sabha in large numbers. Once they came to know that what they had perceived about the ooru sabha (as a forum for getting benefits) was wrong, they stayed away from it. This was why most of them chose not to attend the ooru sabha more than once. Like in any other community, it was the youth who jumped into the fray first and moved out of it first when their perceived notions about the PPC were proved wrong. While the Kurichiar took a reasonably sensible attitude towards the ooru sabha, and the Kattunaikkar completely ignored the PPC, the Paniyars and Adiyars just flowed in and flowed out of the PPC. It underlines the point that the developmental intervention strategy for the tribal communities should be designed considering the ethnic and perceptual differences of each of the communities.

Social mobilisation demanded conscientisation and training was very much a part of this process. But most tribals complained about the absence of training as one of the major reasons for their non-participation in the whole process of the PPC. Information dissemination on the objectives of the PPC was poor and most tribals perceived ooru sabha as a forum to receive concessions/ subsidies from the government rather than as a platform to air and discuss their problems.

Introduction of the Social Activists

Once the Kerala State Planning Board (KSPB) realised that the ooru sabha was not convened as it was envisaged, it planned strategies to help enhance the tribal participation in ooru sabha. The concept of Social Activists (SAs) evolved from the feedback on the failure of proper functioning of ooru sabha.

SAs were a group of tribal youth, matriculate or above, selected by the KSPB to work in the tribal hamlets and to report back the real local needs/ demands of each of the tribal communities, so that the KSPB could re-design the TSP, incorporating more tribal participation. A consolidated monthly salary of Rs. 1000 was given to the SAs. A five day orientation workshop was conducted for the SAs to conscientise them on the PPC, TSP, ooru sabha and their role in the TSP.

In Panamaram, however, the SAs were found to have defeated the very purpose for which they were formed in the PPC. Once the SAs identified themselves as part of bureaucracy, they started behaving the same way the bureaucrats would normally behave towards tribals. The very same SAs, who were matriculate tribals, started blaming their own fellow tribes as the causative factor for the failure of the PPC.

It was found that the SAs were trying their best to be identified as part of bureaucracy. Quite often, it was observed that the SAs addressed the tribals as 'they' and intentionally disassociated themselves from tribals. Moreover, instead of working in tribal hamlets, the SAs preferred to work in the office of the Tribal Extension Officer (TEO), helping him in his clerical jobs, thus defeating the very purpose for which they were introduced into the tribal planning process.

Table 5.10

Reasons for the Failure of the PPC: Perceptions of the Social Activists

Reasons	First reason	Second reason
Tribals are ignorant	41%	26%
Social condition	23%	30%
Economic condition	11%	15%
The policy decisions	8%	13%
The apathy of the officials	6%	7%
Corruption	11%	9%

Source: PRA with the Social Activists of Panamaram Panchayat, 2000.

The table (5.10) shows that the SAs held ignorance among tribals as the most important reason for the failure of the PPC. At the same time, the tribals who were interviewed gave a different picture about the SAs.

Table 5.11
Evaluation of Respondents about Social Activists and the Tribal Extension Officer

Variables	S.A.	T. E. O.
Rarely visit the tribal hamlets	83%	91%
Never listen to the tribals	73%	94%
Treat tribals as inferior	68%	93%
Blame the tribals for the failure of TSP	81%	95%
Corrupt	61%	92%
Inaccessible	21%	97%

Source: PRA with the tribals of Panamaram Panchayat, 2000.

Table (5.11) reveals that there was only a marginal difference in the evaluation by the tribals about the TEO and SAs, reflecting the poor performance of the SAs in the tribal community. SAs were hardly seen in the tribal hamlets.

The TEO was not accessible, except once, during the entire study period. The TEO excused himself to be too busy, though he was rarely seen either in the office or in the tribal hamlets.

Table 5.12
Attitude of the Respondents Towards the Tribal Extension Officer

Name of the Tribe	Apathetic Towards Tribal issues	Inefficiency	Bossy	Corrupt
Adiyar	61%	8%	15%	16%
Paniyar	57%	4%	12%	27%
Kurichiar	63%	11%	9%	17%
Kattunaikkar	100%	0%	0%	0%

Source: PRA with the tribals of Panamaram Panchayat, 2000.

All the tribal communities found the apathy towards tribal issues as the predominant attitude of the TEO, as shown in table (5.12). Corruption ranked second with bossy attitude and inefficiency coming next.

Though there were marked differences between the different communities studied for the purpose, all of them were unanimous in concluding that the TEO was apathetic towards tribal issues and that he was corrupt. There were certain specific things, the meaning of which could reach people the same way, cutting across all known barriers in the society.

Perception of the tribals about the SAs was not much different from their perception of the TEO. Though the SAs were from the tribal people and for the tribal people, it made no significant impact on the TSP. They made even the corrective steps go wrong. Efforts to remake the SAs to do their jobs correctly and to make them convene ooru sabha at their instance were being contemplated when the LDF government was voted out of power.

The elected representatives, though were fully supportive of the PPC, on long and continued interactions, were found to be not clear about the concepts of the PPC and its objectives. Though they were quite vocal about the 73rd and 74th Amendments, 60% of them did not have proper understanding of the Amendments. Their knowledge about ooru sabha was also vague and confusing. This level of ignorance among the elected representatives about the PPC was detrimental in the tribal belts, especially when the tribals mainly depended on them for information on the PPC. Dissemination of vague and wrong ideas was worse than lack of information dissemination.

Table 5.13

Knowledge Level of the Elected Representatives about the PPC

Knowledge Level on PPC	**Decentralised Planning**	**73rd and 74th Amendments**	**Ooru Sabha**	**Develop-ment Seminar**	**TSP**
Vague and Confused	51%	67%	44%	52%	61%
Average	44%	31%	49%	45%	29%
Good	5%	2%	7%	3%	10%

Source: FGDs with the Elected Representatives of Panamaram Panchayat, 2000.

The wrong/ low level of understanding of the elected representatives about the ooru sabha, its special features and objectives, as shown in table (5.13), had an adverse impact on tribals. Conversation with tribals revealed that the elected representatives asked tribals to attend ooru sabha to avail benefits. Proper training or sessions on the PPC were not held for tribals before ooru sabha, so as to equip them to discuss their problems. Their idea about the TSP was still very much confined to the early models of tribal development plans. Another interesting feature was their evaluation of the failure of the PPC, as shown in table (5.14).

Though it is often said that tribals have to be conscientised about the planning process, the idea, when it was actually implemented, was imposed on them without understanding their real needs. For instance, the ways in which ooru sabha was conducted in Panamaram panchayat was totally against the very spirit of convening it.

It was mandatory to convene ooru sabha with only tribals as its participants, to ensure their active participation in discussions. This rule was decided specially to prevent pseudo-participation of tribals. But in most wards, this ooru sabha was convened along with the other grama sabhas, where non-tribals also participated. This made tribals mere spectators and passive listeners of the discussions where their problems were discussed by non-tribals. In some wards in Panamaram panchayat, opinions of tribals on their issues were neglected or ridiculed, reflecting the perceived notion of the non-tribals that tribals were ignorant about their own issues. This defeated the very spirit of the PPC, since it was initiated to give voices to the marginalised groups in deciding or analysing their issues and problems.

Table 5.14

Reasons for the Failure of the PPC: Perspectives of the Elected Representatives

Reasons	**First reason**	**Second reason**
Party Politics	46%	39%
Social & Economic Condition	12%	15%
Inefficiency & non-co-operation of the councillor	12%	17%
Ignorance & Apathy of Tribals	21%	19%
Corruption	9%	10%

Source: FGDs with the Elected Representatives of the Panamaram Panchayat, 2000.

The dynamics of party politics was very strong in Panamaram panchayat. This was because the LDF, with the help of independent members, was ruling the panchayat. But with the withdrawal of support by the independents, the LDF lost power. During the study period, the UDF was ruling the panchayat and there was strong non- co-operation and often antagonistic stand from the LDF to the development projects of the panchayat. During the discussions with the LDF panchayat members, it was observed that most of them were indulging in petty party politics and evaded questions on development issues. Instead, they were very eager to know the political stand of the researcher. The ruling coalition (UDF) attributed the retardation in the process of the PPC to the non-co-operation of the opposition (LDF), while the opposition criticised the ruling coalition for its inefficiency and corruption, and cited it as one of the main reasons for the failure of the PPC in the panchayat. It was found that in Panamaram panchayat it was the party politics, which took its sway over the development politics and the panchayat and tribals had to pay dearly for that.

Certain unique characteristics among tribals, which were not addressed by the participative development strategy evolved for tribals, had their share in the failure of the PPC among tribals. They are mentioned below.

Blaming the Victims Theory

The TEO was of the opinion that tribals were too ignorant and inexperienced to handle the complexities of the planning process, and he had no regard for the indigenous and traditional knowledge of tribals. The elected representatives as shown in table (5.15) expressed almost similar opinion, who even blamed ignorance, inexperience, and lack of unity among tribals as causes for the failure of the PPC.

Table 5.15
Reasons for the Failure of the PPC among Tribals: Perspectives of the TEO and Elected Representatives

Evaluation	First Reason	Second Reason
Ignorance & Inexperience of Tribals	48%	21%
Lack of Training	24%	28%
Party Politics	28%	51%

Source: PRA with the TEO and elected representatives of the Panamaram Panchayat, 2000.

The culture of silence, in which tribals live, due to social, economic, political, and cultural marginalisation is not easy to be broken in a short span of time. The social and economic environments confronting the contemporary tribals are products of the past oppression and practice of prevalent exploitation inflicted on them. Persons in positions of influence and power continue to shape the society through hegemony to protect their vested interests at the community level. These practices have dispossessed and disadvantaged tribals where they continue to be marginalised. The failure to achieve sustainable economic, social, and community developments was wrongly attributed to the inability of tribals to manage their own affairs.

The conclusion then drawn by policy-makers was that tribals were dysfunctional. There was no confession that the past and continuing practices and policies imposed on tribals were the causes for the breakdown in their community order. In other words, tribals were blamed for failing to thrive and develop in a society that was not of their making.

Standards were being applied from an alien culture to test their standing in community life. They often failed that test because wrong standards were being applied. One cannot deny that sections of tribal community were vulnerable and remained trapped in a vicious circle. The Tribal community remained in a state of perpetual grief and loss caused by land alienation, high incarceration rates for juveniles and adults, and high mortality and morbidity rates. Domestic violence, drunkenness, addictive behavioural patterns, anti-social behaviour, and lawlessness were all symptoms of the underlying problems. One should take notice of these socio–cultural and political and structural realities while analysing the problems of tribals and designing the messages for their development.

The subculture of tribals (synonymous to subculture of the peasantry) indicated that their ideas and behaviour towards the PPC were irrational and constituted a formidable obstacle to the implementation of the PPC. From table (5.15) it was clear that people's representatives and the TEO made tribals the locus of blame for the poor pace of progress and changes in the areas.

The TEO and councillors narrated a number of examples, like not bringing proper certificates, not attending ooru sabha, not attending training classes, and general apathy towards the government, to illustrate the ignorance and behaviour of tribals. One could see that these analyses were made at a very micro level. But a macro analysis looking at the entire tribal society, its history, tribulation, social structure, power relationship etc. would definitely place the blame elsewhere. For example, socio-psychological variables, like dependence and apathy towards government programme, limited aspiration, lack of innovation, familism and fatalism, while appear irrational at the individual level, would seem perfectly logical when one considers the long history of oppression and exploitation tribal people had suffered. It is more logical to argue that these behavioural and attitudinal variables of tribals towards the PPC, which the representatives and the government official pointed against tribals, were really the consequences of the tribal-blind policies. Hence, non-participation of tribals in the PPC was the consequence of the long trajectory of underdevelopment and exploitation in their lives; and was not the cause for the failure of the PPC.

Many scholars had done exclusive research on the precarious existence of tribals in the developing countries. In the study area it was observed there was a similar pattern of the fear of daily bread, which had given rise to a 'subsistence ethics' (Davis and Soeftestad, 1985). More than 90% of the respondents, especially among Paniyars and Adiyars, did not have even one square meal a day, leave alone assured food for the next day. This ethics was the consequence of living dangerously close to the margin, where one day's abstinence from the daily work would mean starvation. Tribals live this living on the edge as their way of keeping alive.

So, it was the safety- first- principle that really anchored many of the social, moral, and planning schedules of tribals. Given the imminent possibility of facing starvation every day, it was quite reasonable to assume that tribals had different perspectives and reasons for not attending programmes of the PPC.

Tribals, especially Adiyar and Paniyar of Panamaram panchayat, were desperately trying to earn a minimum income for their daily bread. So it was logical to conclude that it was the absence of the safety net in the tribal societies, which formed the major reason for tribals to react passively towards this development initiative of the government, which demanded their presence at the various phases of the PPC.

The government's goal – achieving self-sustaining development that would improve the material well-being of tribals within a context of decentralisation was particularly difficult, and contained some unresolved contradictory tensions. Success required a highly sophisticated coordination of people's participation, local leadership and effective administration (Cernea, 1991). As shown in the figure (5.4), this coordination was not achieved.

Figure 5.3
Communication Gaps in the Tribal Sub Plan

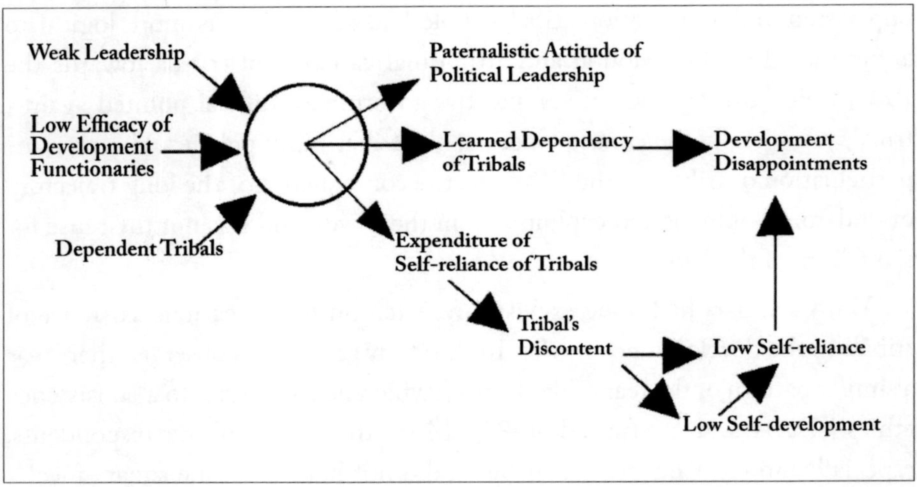

The inertia of the social system resulted in weak local leadership, ineffective functionaries in development bureaucracy, and dependent tribals. In fact, the use of development strategies that did not suit the needs of the local communities is a source of discontent. This was specifically true in the case of tribals since the development interventions adopted among tribals were not effective in ensuring their participation in the development plans of the PPC.

Perceived helplessness and discontent were observed in tribal hamlets of Panamaram panchayat that were detrimental to the effective functioning of the PPC. Majority of tribals in the research area expressed their helplessness to achieve the objectives of development. Discontentment and a feeling of personal inefficacy were serious concerns for development. They made people blame each other and withdrew from commitment to democratic participation, the PPC demanded. In Panamaram, Kurichiars were blaming the Adiyars and Paniyars for not participating in ooru sabha and making it a failure. The TEO and SAs blamed the tribals as such. Planners thought of them as helpless to participate effectively in planning and implementing development projects; administrators feared they were becoming too dependent on government handouts, and elected representatives found them too demanding but unwilling to take the initiative. On the other hand, tribals blamed the government and its functionaries. Some of tribals even criticised the PPC as a new ploy of the government for new ways of exploitation. Tribals perceived the SAs as partisans with vested interests. The SAs were found inadequate to communicate upwards in the development hierarchy, for which they were appointed.

These patterns of blame and counter-blame wrecked the kind of co-ordination necessary to achieve participation for the development objectives of the PPC.

A persistent complaint among participants in development was that the administrators were indifferent, that they did not take the time to investigate and redress problems, and so forth. The TEO perceived himself as having too many responsibilities; he was not trained properly to handle the tools of the PPC, effectively.

The message given to tribals in the PPC, with respect to the reason for its failure, was found to be contradictory. For example, when planners said they would take the responsibility, administrators and SAs conveyed the message that it was because of the lack of responsibility of tribals that the PPC had not worked. Learned dependency was more the result of this incompatibility between the statements made – probably unintentionally – by various government personnel. In the eyes of TEOs, most tribals in the hamlets had taken the fatalistic position of 'never can be good'. Tribals, mainly Adiyars and Paniyars of the seventh ward, conveyed that they were illiterate and too incompetent to understand the nuances and complexities of the process and could never become partners in the development initiatives of the government programmes. Studies showed that the primary setting for participative development was face-to-face interaction between tribals and the contact agents, and that the meaning of development was closely related to the reciprocal perceptions those persons had of each other (Ahlback, 1996; Arnold, 1992; Bradley, 1995). Data of these studies also indicated that bureaucracy lacked the specific knowledge and training about the development projects they were handling for tribals. The notion that any generalist administrator could administer any special development project was largely at fault. As a result of this notion, people were assigned projects about which they had little specific knowledge. This constrained their ability to function effectively.

One recurring complaint posed by tribals of Panamaram panchayat about the tribal development office was that there were too many levels of administration through which any message should pass before any action could be taken. Almost all tribals found these long procedural delays in the panchayat offices/tribal development office as impediments for them in getting benefits or as blocks preventing them from participating in the PPC. It was the usual custom of tribals to go in-groups to fill up forms in a panchayat office to avail benefits. But being illiterate, they were not well accustomed with the procedures of filling up standard application forms, which were necessary for processing their requirements. Obviously, tribals had to go to the panchayat office more than once, which, in effect, prevented them from going for their daily jobs, thereby denying their daily bread.

Table 5.16

Reasons of the Tribals for not Taking Part in the Projects of the PPC

Reasons	No: of persons (%)
Long procedures at the panchayat office	314 (56.67%)
Corruption of the Officers	107 (19.31%)
Party politics	57 (10.29%)
Apathy of bureaucrats	76 (13.73%)

Source: PRA with tribals of the Panamaram Panchayat, 2000.

While 56% of the respondents held long procedures as the main block preventing active participation in the development projects, 20% opined corruption as the main block, and 14% attributed apathy of bureaucrats as the cause for low participation, as shown in table (5.16).

Problems Faced by Tribals in Panamaram Panchayat

It was observed that the existing dissemination of communication strategies and networking neither efficiently nor adequately served the needs of tribals. Procedures of the PPC, especially the special features of ooru sabha and other components of the Tribal Sub Plan, had been tenuous, vague and confusing. This resulted in a very low understanding of the PPC among tribals, as shown in table (5.17).

Table 5.17

Level of Knowledge Among Tribals About People's Planning Campaign

Name of the Tribe	Knowledge of the P.C (%)			Knowledge of the ooru sabha (%)			Knowledge of the T.S.P (%)		
	VP	P	A	VP	P	A	VP	P	A
Adiyar	75%	19%	6%	56%	33%	11%	91%	8%	1%
Paniyar	78%	13%	9%	49%	38%	13%	84%	9%	7%
Kurichiar	36%	41%	33%	18%	21%	61%	26%	49%	25%
Kattunaikkar	98%	2%	0%	100%	0%	0%	100%	0%	0%

Note: VP- very poor, P- poor, A- average

Source: PRA with tribals of the Panamaram Panchayat, 2000.

Tribals viewed the SAs and the TEO as propaganda agents of the government. As a result, their cooperation and participation in the planning process – the principle force and sanction behind planning – remained a wish, and the objective of getting the administration and people to feel and act together remained unachieved. Bureaucracy was ill-equipped to let the tribal-oriented planning programmes emerge. They did not share the philosophy of organising people to assume initiative and did not accept the role of change agents attributed to tribals, who traditionally were expected to obey them only. They did not treat tribals as intelligent and capable of acting effectively. They were accustomed to set targets and press tribal people to achieve them. But such use of authority did not lead to self-reliance and active participation, which were vital for the success of the PPC.

Figure 5.4
Constraints, Development Orientation and Reaction of Bureaucrats & Tribals on the PPC

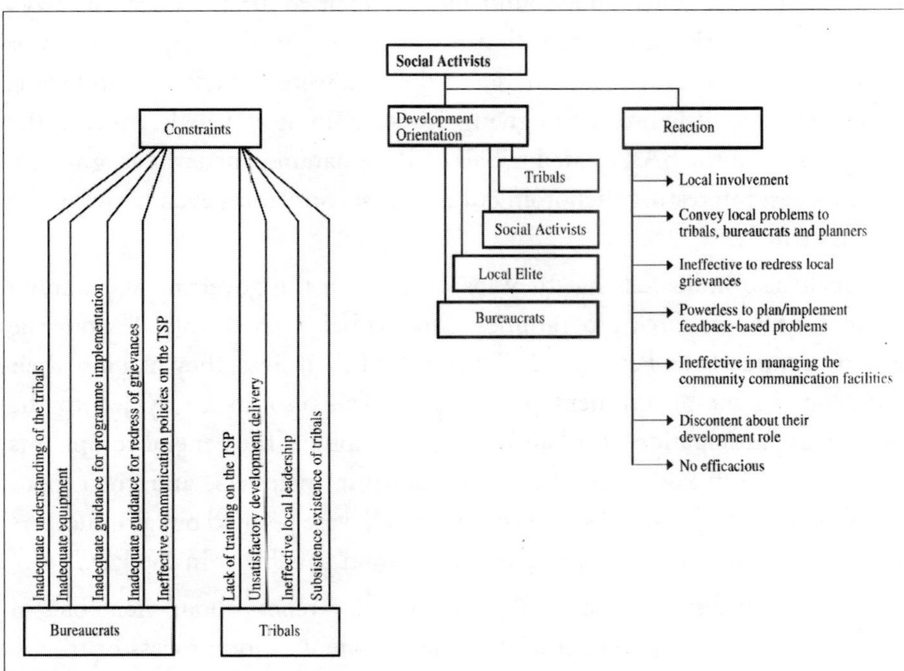

On the part of tribals, they listed a number of variables for their abstinence from the PPC as shown in table (5.18).

Table 5.18
Reasons for non-Participation in People's Planning Campaign: The Tribal Perspective

Reasons for non-participation in the planning process	First reason	Second reason	Third reason
Lack of training	54%	49%	16%
Lack of empathy towards the tribal situation among the planners	21%	6%	22%
Non-interest of tribals	9%	7%	15%
Lack of good volunteers	16%	38%	47%

Source: PRA with tribals of the Panamaram Panchayat, 2000.

Most tribals were interested in participating in the planning process provided they were given training for it. The training classes were given on working days, which they found inconvenient to attend since one day's absence from work meant starvation to the family on that day. Also, it was pointed out that volunteers in charge of the area were not efficient and some of them showed little interest in giving proper training to tribals. Most of the volunteers, even the SAs, treated tribals of Panamaram panchayat as ignorant. There was an interesting dichotomy of *us- them* correlation even between the SAs and tribals.

Tribals also indicated that they lost interest in the government planning due to continuous farce programmes. Most tribals were skeptical about the genuine nature of the PPC, for in the course of their lives, they had lost their confidence in the government programmes. This also, in a way, led to the decrease in participation of tribals in the programmes. The general complaints of apathy of officials, corruption of panchayat members, and their poor economic and marginalised social conditions all were pointed out as indicators for the low participation of tribals of Panamaram panchayat in the PPC.

Information dissemination and subsequent awareness about their roles in moulding their destiny were crucial in the conscientisation process of tribals. In the PPC, however, tribals were ignorant about the very concept of the PPC, even at its final stage. Most tribals were ignorant about the different phases of the PPC. [This was shown earlier in table (5.17)]. This ignorance was one of the main reasons for the low turnout of tribals for the activities of the PPC at all stages.

Table 5.19
Participation of Tribals in the Different Phases of the People's Planning Campaign

Name of the Tribe	Ooru Sabha	Dev. Seminar	Task Force	Plan Document
Adiyar	74%	3%	0%	0%
Paniyar	83%	0%	0%	0%
Kurichiar	76%	28%	4%	1%
Kattunaikkar	0%	0%	0%	0%

Source: PRA with tribals of the Panamaram Panchayat, 2000.

Table (5.19) makes it amply clear that participation of tribals in development seminar and task force was very minimal. Only Kurichiars had followed it up with 28% attendance in the development seminar, 4% in the task force and 1% in the formation of a plan document. Lack of conscientisation was the main factor in the poor attendance of tribals in different phases of the PPC. It can be seen that lack of understanding about the concepts of the PPC, as mentioned in table (5.19), played a crucial role in the non- participation of tribals in the activities of the PPC.

Among the tribals, Kattunaikkars had a highly secluded way of living. They were completely cut off even from other tribal groups. Unlike other tribal communities, there was not even a single Kattunaikkan with whom the researcher could communicate because her/his interaction with the world outside was practically zero. This explains the zero percentage of response from Kattunaikkar in the informal discussions and interviews. Among the different phases of the PPC, participation of tribals was most in ooru sabha for reasons discussed earlier.

There was no adequate and planned development- interventions from the government side to conscientise or mobilise tribal communities. One way of achieving the agenda of changing the learned dependency was to include Meta communication as part of development communication. In this process of Meta communication, every aspect of the development interaction should have functioned as a message, whether intended that way or not, about the relationship between the participants. For this, a development communication programme directed for tribals should have been designed as tribal- specific. It should have directly addressed the context in which the PPC had occurred. This required educating tribals to see development as an interaction leading to partnership with the government, which was lacking in the PPC.

The PPC should have acknowledged the contradictory messages tribals had received in the past and provided a way for interpreting them in the right perspective to help them come out of their learned dependency. This was crucial because there was every possibility that tribals would get confused over conflicting and contradictory messages. Even when they were invited to be crucial participants in development, they had little reason to believe that their participatory acts would be heard or considered. They were given conflicting messages to the effect that on the one hand they were termed incapable of making any contribution to development, and on the other, they were blamed for the failure of the PPC because of their non- active participation.

The PPC should not have hesitated to mention the mistakes the government had made in the past and should have expressed that clearly. That would have enabled various agents in the interaction to understand why they found themselves in confusing or frustrating situations.

This approach would have ensured active involvement of tribals in planning. Rather than being told they were helpless or technically incompetent, tribals should have been told that they alone could decide their future. The task of making the decision, or even of thinking in those terms, would have helped tribals to be more active participants in the PPC.

Field experiences at Panamaram panchayat indicated that development interaction had taken some unfortunate patterns because of the deficiencies in the communication infrastructure. These deficiencies had substituted infrequent and inadequate feedback for the dialogue that should have occurred.

Series of interaction with tribal activists and educated tribals in Wayanadu revealed that they were not at all sure whether they had been heard; and if heard, understood; and if understood, taken seriously; and if taken seriously, acknowledged as the cause of government action. The most frequent responses to their feedback were disclaimers from the SAs and the elected representatives (who said they passed the message through proper channels and did not know what had happened to them) and inferences from public pronouncements on mass media by the government, which were general messages not specifically related to the complaint or suggestion. Seeing one's message vanish into the bureaucratic system, without a trace, was an insurmountable obstacle to the development strategy.

The message for implementation of the TSP in the PPC was not tribal - specific, unlike the message for the implementation of the WCP (detailed in chapter 1V). Even those messages, which addressed the tribals, did not take into consideration the heterogeneous nature of tribal communities.

The PPC did not exploit the organic leadership, local representatives, and existing communication networks among each tribal community- like communication links between tribal chieftain and tribals and social gatherings in the tribal context.

Dialogue Action Strategies (DAS) should have created dialogue on the PPC in the tribal belts. The main requirement of DAS is that it should adapt itself to the specific characteristics of the communities in which it occurs. Tribal communities, due to their hamlet structure and kinship relations, do have strong interpersonal links and proper informal places for communication. A participative initiative like the PPC, should have first tried to locate such communication points and used those points as nodal centres for information dissemination. Most tribals, on interaction, complained that they were not aware of the programmes of the PPC.

Two considerations were particularly important in planning a communication channel mix. First, the channels must be easily accessible to tribals. Mere existence of a communication channel does not necessarily imply that it will have any value for development. The channels should be interactive in nature, permitting not only a two-way flow of messages but some way for both sides to know that their messages are heard.

The development experiences in the tribal areas revealed that greater use of mass communication may be unproductive for various reasons. First, mass communication channels were not necessarily effective means of reaching the poor and the marginalised, like tribals. For various physical, technological, economic and social reasons, an increase in messages on these channels may not result in any improvement in the pattern of interaction among development agents. Second, the available technological capacities of these channels were under-utilised. Third, when utilised, these channels were for most part, non-interactive. Fourth, tribals perceived some mass communication channels as not very credible. Fifth, repetition of messages in the mass communication channels soon led to satiation.

In the case of the Panamaram panchayat, for various reasons, the TEO and local elite tended to block the vertical flow of information between tribals and administrators. Horizontal networks of communication among friends and family were more open, but were poor in information about the PPC.

A process should be initiated to involve administrative and field-work officers and tribals in focused, problem-solving, face-to-face communication. The overall purpose should be to provide a forum in which each group would involve with the other in a task-oriented context. These should emphasise three dimensions of the participatory paradigm: self-development, self-reliance, and active participation. They insist that the communities plan their own need-based programmes; that they use their own resources, and they act on their own plans.

The PPC, in the tribal context, failed in its objective, though the development strategy was designed, and later redesigned, as an act of intentional intervention to facilitate effective communication among tribals vis-a-vis the concept of decentralised planning. Reasons for failure in the development strategy could be traced not to lack of interest in the cause of tribals, but to lack of proper understanding and application of the interplay of various socio-political and ethnic variables that make the tribal life and culture.

Further, the development interventions were based on inadequate research, and were implemented with insufficient co-ordination. Mass media, both print and electronic, hardly showed any interest in the development needs of tribals. Low literacy, pervasive poor education, and lack of adequate technology posed additional problems. Inadequate funds allocated to the media also resulted in low quality programmes, which again went against the interest of the whole process. Persons who made the productions of the media content could not empathise with the problems of tribals.

It was observed that the TEO relied too heavily on the SAs. The SAs were given multiple and conflicting roles. Most often the envisaged roles of the SAs and the training orientation given to them by the KSPB were quite conflicting with the practices followed in the field. On the one hand, they were to mobilise, motivate, and conscientise tribals but on the other hand, they were pressurised to do the routine official work. SAs were attached to the TEOs, who, in general, were antagonistic to the PPC. This practice which gave them the image of administrative functionaries, not as educators, thwarted them from fulfilling their task-communication link between tribals and planners.

Tribals, PPC, and Power

Main objective of any planned structural change in a society is to attack the status-quo, i.e., to attack the institution of power, or rather a technique or form of power in the Foucauldian sense. While positioning tribals in the context of power, the PPC assumes significance on two counts; one arising from the central ideology of the PPC- power to people- and the other, due to the explicit and implicit power structures in which tribals live.

Most theoretical constructs on power emerge from the continuing intellectual exchange of social and political ideas located within the Marxist perspective, which has emerged within the specific historical context. The positions of effect research and functionalism assume that power is visible, while the Critical Approach assumes that power is multidimensional and exercised at several levels, including opaque and unconscious levels of ideas, producing and reproducing relations of material and symbolic production (Wichhart and Thomas, 1995). Despite variations in different theoretical models adopted by the Critical Approach, common to all is the implicit conception of power as located not on the surface of society's structure but deeply woven into a complex contextual social web. It is in this theoretical context that the analysis of the power and its equations with tribals in the PPC become relevant.

While applying the categorisation of power-compensatory, condign and conditioned- by Galbraith (year) in the critical theory perspective in the context of tribals, it could be noticed that though the condign and compensatory forms of power were operating at various levels on tribals, it was the conditioned power that was more embedded into their social psyche. With the devolution of power to people, the PPC had to address this conditioned power, which was invisible, subtle, internalized, and deeply rooted in the cognition of the tribal society which, along with many other reasons, made them passive, dependent, helpless and dysfunctional.

Experience is not something pre-given. It is inherently implicated within the structures of power. Power is no longer outside culture (the social), but within the very structures of signifying practices. It was the cultural practices themselves that defined identities for their producers and consumers by weaving them into the fabric of their discursive spaces. The meaning planners connoted and denoted for tribals in the PPC was found to have a negative homophile with tribals, for the messages never addressed the complex power structures of their inter-and intra-kinship patterns.

The inherent subordination and subservience of tribals, resulting from the age-old oppression and exploitation, involved the colonisation of tribal consciousness or commonsense through the articulation of specific social practices and positions. Such effects were determined by a multiplicity of power relations that could only be identified within the particular context of tribal identity and power. This internalised and inherent subordination was visible even in the non-verbal gestures and postures of tribals in Panamaram panchayat.

For instance, it was observed that, without exception, all tribals, men and women, were sitting in a definite posture. This posture is the one that occupies the minimum space that a human being needs. The modern man is very much concerned about his personal space, so much so that he would shrink his body to protect his personal space if he happens to be in a crowd. For the tribal, it was not the crowd around him that made him shrunk his body. He would shrink it even when he is alone in his surroundings because the social, political, and cultural subjugation have squeezed him, leaving their long lasting impact on him that makes him internalise the shrinkage (Manjula, B., 2001).

From the outset, the PPC emphasized that the democratic participation envisioned in the plan presupposed conscientization; thus, intensive training was very much a part of this process. In programme evaluations, most tribals complained about the absence of training, citing it as one of the major reasons for their non-participation in the whole process of the PPC. This shared emphasis on training, however, fails to grapple with notable tensions integral to efforts to democratize technocratic processes of planning and budgeting. Commitments to democratic participation presuppose respect for the local knowledge and values of all participants. Yet the instrumental reasoning central to the rational, comprehensive decision-making model underlying the PPC, conflicts in fundamental ways with the epistemic commitments embedded in the spiritual values and the communal modes of the tribal living. Any systematic training then was bound to collide with the respect for indigenous knowledge.

Scheduled Tribes are not a monolithic bloc; their epistemic commitments are neither universal nor invariant, but the PPC did not take into consideration the heterogeneous nature of tribal communities. It made no effort to engage organic leadership, local representatives or existing communication networks within each tribal community. It did not probe substantive local knowledge for ideas about participation; instead relied on nested processes assumed to be neutral and inclusive.

Nor did the PPC consider the prolonged effects of colonization, oppression, and subordination on scheduled tribes. Long-standing practices of marginalization have affected self-understandings, aspirations, and modes of embodiment of the tribals. Tribal identities are structured by power relations that are evident in self-presentation, posture, and willingness to claim social space. Training programs designed to empower target such invisibilizing gestures and postures as they seek to enable individuals to claim space, articulate demands, and hold governments to account. Training to think instrumentally attacks the holistic approaches, spiritual investments in the natural world, and central tenets of cosmological ways of knowing. The individualism that underlies democratic claims-making and technocratic rationality subverts communalism. Thus, there is a gulf between Freire's conceptualization of conscientization and PPC's training practices to cultivate skills requisite to strategic planning and budgeting. Where conscientization requires respect for the world-views of all participants, training modules mandate cultivation of modernized mentalities: they seek to change traditional world-views.

In the tribal context, the PPC failed to attain its objectives. Although the planning strategy was designed, and later redesigned, as an intentional intervention to facilitate effective communication among tribals, its concept of decentralised planning turned on modernist pre-suppositions, were at odds with the tribal life. Rather than attributing this failure to deficiencies of tribals themselves, more could be learned from an analysis of the consequences—of lack of proper understanding of the interplay of local knowledge and various socio-political forces constitutive of tribal life and culture. Insufficient knowledge of tribal cultures may transform good intentions into bureaucratic callousness.

The PPC, it was thought, would break this power cocoon into which the mega society had squeezed in the tribal, long back. Unfortunately, the development strategy of the PPC could not strike empathy with tribals, causing the whole strategy to fall flat. While the PPC could, to an extent, help break the spiral of silence of one of the marginalised sections, women, it was unsuccessful in the case of tribals, the most marginalised section in Kerala society.

Post -PPC

The Cartesian-instrumental idea of development that derives its objective value from reducing the observed subject into a separable, quantifiable, and disjointed means for attaining certain rational ends cannot really take into account the non-measurable, invisible and subjective aspects of historically and culturally embedded ways of living of the tribals, specified by their sense of place and belonging. At an ontological and epistemological plane, the culturally embedded practices of the tribal community are still un-appropriable in many ways – in terms of customary practices, language, music, and spiritual value. Post-PPC interventions among the tribal belts in Kerala are far more dismissive and disheartening, making the life-world of tribals more vulnerable and deeply marginal.

The ST population in Kerala exists as 36 heterogeneous groups, and is connected by a single homogenous variable—shrinking space of land. A study conducted by KUSAT (2015) found that their land availability in Kerala has shrunk from an average 2.77 acres per family to 0.66 acre in just three generations. Besides land, the educational system and the service delivery of the health systems are not fine-tuned to cater to the specific life situations and cultural ethos of the tribal community. For instance, the philosophical underpinnings of education and its pedagogy exemplify this apathy towards the tribal development questions. Tribals in Kerala speak different dialects and have different cultures and traditions. But the public education system addresses their education problem in a monolithic and uniform manner as if they are a homogenous people. In the schools, where they share the physical space with the non-ST children, the medium of instruction is Malayalam, which most of the ST children do not understand. This results in a situation where the subjects that are taught and the medium used to teach the subjects both become alien to the ST, keeping them away from any debate or discussion over what has been taught, resulting in the ST children groping in the dark in the classroom that is supposed to light up the world around. They are branded as 'laggards' and subsequently, they withdraw or are pushed to the unseen fringes in the classroom, though they share the same physical space with the non-ST children. Who on earth wants to remain long in the periphery as non-entities? The ST children then make a physical withdrawal to the known spaces in their socially marginalized spaces, thereby increasing the school-dropout to alarming rate and making the spirit of the right to education and compulsory education a tragic tale of repeated mockeries.

The wide literacy gap between total population and STs continues even after six decades of Indian Independence. Among Scheduled Tribes of Kerala, there is a wide gender gap with regard to literacy attainments where the male literacy is far higher than that of the females. Moreover, the educational attainment of Scheduled Tribes also remains poor compared to that of other social groups.

A mere cosmetic surgery that changed the Right to education from the Directive Principles to the Fundamental rights will not bring about the desired social change. The spirit of the change needs to be materialized through tribal specific interventions in the ST hamlets. The Scheduled Tribes are overwhelmingly rural as 96.1 per cent of them reside in villages. The socio-economic condition of tribals is much lower compared to that of the general population, though the Working Participation Rate (WPR) of tribals, for both men and women, is higher than the general population. Excess mortality and morbidity among tribal children continues to be the starkest marker of tribal disadvantage. It has roots in a number of complex processes involving the general exclusion of STs. The politics of presence of tribals in the key decision-making structures and process of governance and the alienation of tribals from land and forests are central to their continued exclusion from progress and development.

Mostly invisible even in the statist archives, tribals are definitionally the constitutive other of historical temporality and politics. The dominant globalisation projects and the privileging of the 'consumer' over the 'citizen' in matters of rights have far-reaching implications in the life-world of tribals. While equal rights of all citizens give way to the rights of those who can afford the privilege of becoming consumers, the tribals are doubly victimised – one for their inability to become consumers, and the other, for their failure to enjoy rights because of being non-consumers. The concerns of the non-consuming public are thereby dismissed in the name of consumer rights. This is really problematic for the socially and economically fragile tribals, especially when their basic rights to health and education are at risk.

It is exactly, here the everyday practice and lives of tribals in Kerala are discussed as these are imposed from above in the globalised economy, and most often, dislodging, dislocating, and challenging the local identity, which are very important in constructing their collective identities in a defined cultural space. Hence, knowingly or unknowingly, condigned and compensatory power of the monetized market work together on the conditioned psyche of the individuals here,who accept the hegemonic and imperialist modes of functioning of the Corporate World as Gramscian commonsense, thereby depriving themselves of the traditional cultures and social networks.

The severing of organic bonds among tribal communities also, in a way, results in over-dependence on government for their livelihood and day-to-day activities. As mutual aid is replaced by dependence on faraway forces, tribals begin to feel powerless to make decisions over their own lives. It has always been an accepted dictum that cultural spaces are fluid and overlapping, particularly among the tribal communities where individuals engage in a higher number of social networks and social institutions. The activity of local and boundary construction allows for the cohesive operation of the components of cultural space, as long as the basis of their activity remains embedded in stable agreement with the wider cultural context. Any dislocation of function would subsequently dislodge the spatial arrangements that define it. Conversely, any dislocation of spatial arrangements could also disrupt the functioning of those relationships, every day practices and/or values that mark out that cultural space. It is this spatial dislocation of the tribals in Kerala from their natural abode- the forest- still is the most important reason for the present deplorable conditions of the tribals.

Another important reason for the breakdown of the tribal ways of life in Kerala along with the socio-economic variables is the psychological pressure to modernize. The profound onslaught of the mega-culture with its glamorized western images is making its impact on the most remote corners of this part of the world, with disastrous results on the community living and ethnic culture of the society. Continuous bombardment of one dimensional development images of the rich on the psyche of tribal youth make them feel the traditional way of life is inferior and absurd. Youngsters in Wayanadu who are asked by their parents to choose a way of life that involves working in the fields and getting their hands dirty feel ashamed of their own culture and agriculture. This has developed a feeling of inferiority among the youth, who reject their own ways of living and eagerly embrace the new one. What was once an element of their way of life becomes a product, rather than something unique they had made to suit their own specific needs and circumstances. Local culture's role as a spontaneous and integral part of people's life is eroded and it ceases to serve as the means of constructing societal values, reproducing group identity and building social cohesion. In the past, individuals in tribal communities had real power, since political and economic units were small and each person was able to deal directly with other members of the community. Today, 'development' is hooking people into ever-larger units. The very powerful monetized economy is making them less powerful and defenceless in an increasing trend of anonymity in the global cultural space.

The tribals, the original citizens without exercising or even realizing their citizenship, are now passing through a critical phase of history both at the national and state levels. The continuous relegation of the tribes and their day to day life to the periphery have resulted in various forms of collectives and resistances and has generated the language of the voices that retraced and redefined the oral narratives of the underclass, and have initiated the process of reimagining the development of tribes. The archaeology of history needs to be contested in this context, where unraveling the phenomenology of the absence of local tribal narratives becomes critical and crucial.

In the long list of the failed tribal developmental interventions is the flagship programme of Kudumbashree- the Sustainable Tribal Development Programme (STDP). Kudumbashree, the Sate Poverty Eradication Mission of Kerala, that was designed to eradicate poverty from the rights-based perspective, could not make any dents in the age-old structural and systemic exploitation of the tribal community tells volumes about the apathy of the system towards the development problems of the tribals.

In a state like Kerala, which is always recognised for its progressive interventions in the social development sectors, much reflected in the human development reports, the abysmal, negligent, and apathetic attitude towards the most marginalized section of the society – the tribals – is indefensible.

Chapter 6

Media and the PPC: Mediated Development - A Counter-hegemony (?)

Communication and Democratic Decentralisation

The study of communication can be traced back to Plato and Aristotle. Plato's theory of knowledge and Aristotle's story of rhetoric have provided modern communication studies with its identical anchors. The semiotic school in communication essentially pursues Plato's preoccupation with epistemology by offering theories of signs and meanings. The process school of the Shannon-Weaver models of information processing, focuses less on meaning and more on the transmission of message and its persuasive power.

This problem has become highly complex in the modern world dominated by the mass media, especially when there is evidence that military and economic power have important roles in shaping the role of media and information systems (Armand Mattelart, 2002). As in any other field of politics, the media governance is also decided by two conflicting systems—the state owned media, reflecting the Soviet model, and the privately owned commercial media systems, reflecting the US model—echoing the thoughts of the freedom of national security and the right to freedom of information, respectively.

The conflicting schools of thought on media governance had their impact on the third world nations, as they became sites of political wars over the question, which school suited each nation the best. The question became more relevant with the emergence of development and the discourses over development that found development had to be carried out through multilateral institutions and 'communication and its technologies being prescribed to occupy a key position in the battle for development'.

Theories of development-centered around two schools of thought: modernization and dependency-world systems. While the modernization theories that emphasize on individual freedom assume a consensus model of social change, place the State at the pivot of development processes, and depend on empirical methods in research and market solutions to economic problems; the dependent theories criticize the modernization theories for their failure to account for the structural factors at the national and international level and point to the increasing trend of incorporating the periphery economies into a dependent relationship with the world capitalist system, especially after the economic breakdown in socialist countries.

The world system theory, an offshoot of the dependency school, recognizes the possibility of autonomous capitalist development and shows examples of the East Asian countries like Japan, Taiwan, South Korea, Hong Kong, and Singapore. It is materialistic in orientation, emphasizes social equality, assumes a conflict model of society, and focuses on the world capitalist system as its chief unit of analysis with the center-periphery dynamics of development.

The liberal-modernisation and development policies of the Nazi, Fascist, Stalinist, and other totalitarian states form a third development paradigm. But World War II saw the end of both Nazism and Fascism. It took many more years for Stalinism to be thrown into the dustbin of political history. The totalitarian theories have lost their intellectual respectability and have resurrected in some countries, of course, in disguised ideological forms. However, the totalitarian political theory—both its original and disguised forms-offers a great opportunity for academic research, since it treats history as an arena for the exercise of human will; a concept rooted in Nietzsche's philosophy of Superman.

The fourth perspective on communication, the communitarian perspective, emerges from a long theoretical tradition of critical analysis of the processes of modernisation and industrialisation. Jean Jacques Rousseau, Emile Durkheim, John Ruskin, Mahatma Gandhi, Leo Tolstoy, and the environmentalists could be considered as the leading theorists of this school. According to this school, the community is constantly engaged in the process of actively negotiating with visible and invisible bonds of meaning that tie it together. Society's verbal and non-verbal modes of communication are the tools through which these negotiations take place; and ideologies constitute those competing world-views and hegemonic projects that attempt to unify a society towards a set of common sentiments, beliefs, values, norms, and behavioral objectives. The aforesaid analysis was primarily drawn from the writings of Majid Tehranian (2009) on the communitarian perspective of the communication process.[3]

---

3 The aforesaid analysis was primarily drawn from the writings of Majid Tehranian (2009)

Discourse theory provides useful tools for unraveling the mysteries of ideology, to some extent. If we view the processes of human communication as a series of multiple, interlocking layers of discourses, the communication genre can be correlated with the discursive practices and narratives. Communicative consciousness is closely associated with the social and interactive nature of human beings. 'Interacting' is, therefore, the central feature of the discursive practice in this mode of consciousness. As Habermas (1983) has argued, this mode of interaction requires a high degree of equality and communicative competence among the participants. Habermas's 'power-free communication' may be impossible in the real world. But to the degree that its conditions are met, negotiations of meaning can take place on an equal footing; truly communicative action becomes possible.

Communication can play a decisive role in promoting human development in today's climate of social change. As the world moves towards greater democracy and decentralisation, conditions are becoming more favourable for people to start steering their own course of change. But it is vital to stimulate their awareness, participation, and capabilities. Communication skills and technology are central to this task. Policies are needed to encourage effective planning and implementation of communication programmes.

This perspective is somewhat akin to the ritualistic dominant paradigm of communication, especially in the modernisation theories that prioritise the Latin roots of the word (as in making common through the exchange of meaning). Studies and experiences in development communication, over the past forty years, revealed this shift in the role of communication in development. The point of departure for development communication is not the dissemination of an innovation or a new idea that is full of promises, but the grassroots expressing their needs.

Participation, by putting emphasis on the needs and the viewpoints of individuals and groups, is the key concept of development communication. Today, development communication is understood as communities and individuals engaging in meaning making, which is a horizontal and deinstitutionalized multiple processes, in which senders and receivers have interchangeable roles. The difference lies in the fact that while the dominant paradigm continues to think of communication as a process that contributes to behavioural change, participatory models are concerned with transforming social conditions. Development communication, therefore, is making people aware of the various facets of the real development problems in their region; organising to react, collectively and effectively, to these problems; bringing to

---

on the communitarian perspective of the communication process.

light the conflicts that divide the various interest groups; becoming politicised and learning to provide alternatives to problem-situations and finding solutions to various problems; and becoming technicised by obtaining the necessary tools to put to concrete use the solutions provided by the community. It has allowed people to be subjects of their own development and not simply objects of technology or processes.

People's Plan, with its motto, *power to people*, demanded a brief analysis of the relation that co-existed among power, people's plan, and communication. Power is a strong concept in the democratic decentralisation as it is a process of devolution of power. There are a number of positions, which are based on a complex conceptualisation of social power operating as invisible forms of domination. In this web, the structures of social and power relations determine modes of communication and cultural expression. The underlying power structure and its impact on communication media, and the production of power within communication are relevant in the context of decentralisation.

Social power identifies the determining moment of social life with economic forces and relations, and establishes a correspondence between production and power. Such analysis assumes that the receivers are passive and unaware of the ways in which messages act upon them. Thus, communication becomes a process of self-colonisation of the individual. The participatory governance tries to change this approach through its interactive and dialogical approach towards communication. This mode of communication determined the modes of self-help groups and communes, formed in the PPC.

The following sections in this chapter would also throw light on the various debates and discussions on the role of communication in development and, more specifically, its position in the five year plans. This would provide us to locate our study in a historical perspective, as the study tries to understand the ways in which the local governance institutions of Kerala tried to address and intervene in the development issues of their locality.

Local Self Governance in India and Communication Approaches in the Five-Year Plans

In the initial plans, communication was conceptualised as a linear, top-down process with feedback from people. The first five-year plan document included a chapter referring to *plan publicity*, which specified the use of all communicative channels: interpersonal; mass media (radio, film, print); and traditional media (song and drama). Feedback from people was seen as an important factor in setting development goals. The role of communication was thought of in three ways.

The first function was to develop communication channels, and to incorporate upward information and feedback from people to planners. The planning document stressed that the plan has to be carried into every home in the language and symbols of people and expressed in terms of their common needs and problems (Desai, 1977). The technological infrastructure for a nation-wide mass communication system was developed, and informational programming was prepared for it. Interpersonal channels were developed through intensive training programmes for extension agents. Local leadership was recruited in an attempt to create indigenous enthusiasm for innovations among people.

The second role of communication was to disseminate development information through extension education methods. Ad-hoc committees, project advisory committees, and official and unofficial agencies were assigned the task of publicising the plan and dispelling people's suspicions about development and development functionaries.

The third role was to let the development functionaries recognise the value of the knowledge, wisdom, and experience of the common man (Desai, 1977). Evaluation of the success of community development programmes indicated that the forms of communication in practice differed from those envisioned by the planners. They were most successful in establishing channels by which information could be disseminated from the top to the bottom (Jain, 1967). They were least successful in implementing aspects of the plan that involved educating and motivating people for development.

Emphasis in the second five-year plan was on rural participation and democratic decentralisation. In order to circumvent traditional social structures, they formed inter-village co-operative organisations and imposed the Panchayat Raj system of government by local councils (Khan, 1978). The purpose of the Panchayat Raj was not fully achieved. The elites were disproportionately involved in the process, intensifying a communication gap or development benefit gap between the haves and the have-nots in the villages. As part of economic policy, two land reforms were enacted (Malhan and Uma, 1969). The Land Ceiling Act fixed an upper limit on the area of cultivated land that could be owned by an individual. The lands confiscated under this Act were to be distributed to the landless farmers. The second Act abolished the Zamindari system.

The planners continued to perceive communication in terms of plan publicity through multiple channels. The extension agencies, technical departments, and administration were seen as supporters for the Panchayat Raj, not as the primary structures for development (Raghavan, 1976). Information on agricultural innovations was disseminated by extension agents, through the mass media, and by means of demonstrations supported by the technical staff. Interpersonal channels were used to inform and motivate farmers to adopt innovations. For the first time, the press was identified as a component of plan publicity.

Communication as a concept of plan publicity continued during the third plan period also. Both mass media and interpersonal channels were used to publicise the plan, but there was special emphasis on radio. In 1966, Farm and Home programme, which discussed solutions to particular farm problems and other aspects of rural life for both men and women, was introduced. Its objective was to give rural people a vision of the future and enable them to become active participants in development projects. By becoming a forum expressing a variety of views, radio gained some measure of credibility, making people feel that their perspectives were being heard (Kishore, 1968). Television was introduced in 1959 through an UNESCO aided project. In 1961, Delhi School Television Projects were started for science education, and in 1965, the Krishi-Darshan, a special agriculture programme, was introduced for the Delhi audience (Manjula, B., 1992).

Sahai Committee Report on Public Participation, 1964, was asked to explain the reasons for the inadequacies of the developmental programmes. The Committee found that the masses had little understanding of development as a whole; viewing it simply as something the government was doing for its own benefit. The masses accepted innovations that met their felt needs, or gave immediate results, but did not see themselves as partners with the government in a common endeavour of national reconstruction. The rural elites exploited the less educated and less powerful members of their communities rather than helping them, and the poor continued to be preoccupied with survival rather than development. This characterization of the masses is, of course, a description of 'passive participation' (Narula and W.B. Pearce, 1986). The plans were made without local participation and were unsuccessful in achieving widespread public co-operation. The committee concluded that steps must be initiated to develop a new social faith among people that would enable them to subordinate their personal interests to the common good.

On communication, the committee found that plan publicity – the communication strategy in the earlier five-year plans- had failed. The report stated 'the needs of the society we are seeking to establish are neither efficiently nor adequately being served by the existing publicity programmes. The impact on the public has been tenuous, vague and confused. In an unplanned attempt to achieve too much with too few resources, plan publicity has failed to touch any section of the society in a forceful manner' (Sahai Committee, 1964).

The Sahai Committee report cited four reasons for the failure of plan publicity. First, the public viewed the publicity personnel as propaganda agents. As a result, public co-operation and favourable public opinion – the principle force and sanction behind planning – remained a wish, and the objective of getting the administration and people to feel and act together remained unachieved. Second, plan publicity was based on inadequate research and implemented with insufficient coordination. Third, the mass communication media were judged poorly adapted to cater to the needs of plan publicity, and the media institutions showed little interest, familiarity, or sympathy with development objectives. Fourth, inadequate funds were allocated for plan publicity. The report noted that low literacy, pervasive poor education, and the lack of adequate technology posed additional problems (Narula and W.B. Pearce, 1986).

Ensminger's Evaluation of Community Development Programmes and Panchayati Raj, 1972 noted that community development had been introduced in the first development decade as a dynamic force that would revolutionise the village India. In the second decade, the political leaders and development planners and administrators became disillusioned about community development, and these programmes were blamed for India's failure to solve the problem of insufficient food. Ensminger argued that both the administration and people were responsible for the disillusionment, which led to a de-emphasis on community development, particularly the Panchayati Raj system. The administrative bureaucracy was ill-equipped and did not share the philosophy of organising people to assume initiative; and they did not comfortably take to the role of change agent to villagers, who traditionally were expected to obey them. They often did not treat people as intelligent and capable of acting effectively. They felt comfortable in setting targets and pressing people to meet them. But such use of authority did not lead to self-reliance and active participation. Further, targeted programmes displaced more general goals of social education, which were less immediate and less conspicuously effective but nonetheless essential for achieving self-perpetuating development. Ensminger argued that the real problem was that the panchayats were becoming a source of power in the villages, and reflected deeply embedded caste and factional structures in Indian life.

Iqbal Narain (1970) found the Panchayati Raj ineffective from two perspectives. From the vantage of people, the panchayat was seen as the extension of the government into the village. This made any efforts by the panchayat viewed as part of the government-guided development, and not an aspect of local initiative. To the extent that the panchayat was active, it increased the dependency of people on the government. From the vantage of the administration, the panchayat was the lowest, the least educated, and the least-effective tier in the organisational structure, and not a vital or important part of planning or implementation.

Norman Nicholson (1973), in his report, concluded that the Panchayati Raj had not been a successful means of generating community efforts to solve local problems. Rather, it intensified political conflicts within the village and this inhibited co-operative action. Partly, this occurred because the local elites made disproportionate use of the co-operatives and the panchayats, which increased the gap between the elites and the poor. A second problem noted by Nicholson was the extent to which community development programmes, designed to foster local self-reliance and initiative, ironically, led to dependency. Finally, he observed, the way the development contributions to communities were administered often created a conflict between the needs and interests of individuals and the needs and interests of the community.

Akther Khan (1978) found four crucial imperfections in the community development programmes. First, they were more effective as welfare programmes than in eliciting productive activities by the masses. Second, they did not succeed in forming harmonious communities; the poor remained, as they were, apathetic and skeptical. Third, by relying on their own agents and by collaborating with established leaders, the community development programmes enhanced the traditional elitist and paternalistic bias, inhibiting the growth of local initiative. Fourth, experts were unwilling to work with the untrained community development functionaries.

The fourth five-year plan showed a greater sophistication about the use of communication media for plan publicity. Information imbalance was identified as the problem. The plan document stated: "In the spread of information facilities, the imbalance in favour of urban concentration and prosperous areas continues. There is a need for a deliberate attempt to inform people in the rural areas and particularly those in backward regions about the development activities so that the benefits of these development programmes are more widespread".

During this and the subsequent fifth plan, extensive campaigns were undertaken for development programmes in family planning, health, nutrition, adult education, and agriculture. In addition to using virtually every available public channel, this was the first time that the interpersonal channels of communication among friends, family, and opinion leaders were identified and utilised. These channels came to the attention of the planners for two reasons. First, the extension agencies and government's development personnel were not sufficiently effective, they realised. Second, since family planning is an intimate aspect of life, more personal channels were appropriated.

The emphasis shifted from informing and educating the masses to motivating them to adopt development practices. For the first time, motivators-groups of voluntary workers – were used as a communication channel (in the family planning programme). Both the motivators and the adopters were given incentives in cash and commodities, like transistor radio, for adopting the practice or technology advocated by the development programmes. Other communication channels included group discussions, mass meetings, mobile demonstrations, family planning camps for mass sterilisation operations, and interpersonal contact on a house-to-house basis. Rural opinion leaders were taken to motivational camps to increase their effectiveness (Mulay and Narula, 1972).

The fifth five-year plan had to cope up with disastrous rates of inflation. In 1975, the Government of India imposed a state of emergency and announced a 20-point development strategy, designed to achieve certain short-term objectives that would bring direct relief to the masses. Films were used to create audience's awareness on the 20- point programmes. Short films were shown in cinema houses and were screened in the villages, using mobile vans. Official communication in that period, however, was mainly used as a propaganda tool to disseminate the official version of the government.

The new government, elected in 1977, replaced the concept of periodic five-year plans with rolling five-year plans reformulated every year. Plans for this period were referred to as the sixth draft, because they were never implemented, for the new government was voted out of power before the five-year plan was completed.

During this period, explicit attention was given to communication. This emphasis led to a flurry of sophisticated but depressing lists of all that was erroneous with development communication. For instance, the report of the Asian Regional Seminar in Rural Communication (1977) faulted the media, the message, the audience, and the communicators. Audiences were seen as having insufficient access to media, lack of aspirations, poor motivation, inability to formulate and articulate their needs and grievances, vested interests opposed to change and progress, and problems stemming from illiteracy. Media was seen as an ineffective channel for communication, partly because there were too few of them and partly because the existing ones were too little utilised, too costly, and without sufficient inter-media coordination. Messages were evaluated as not addressed to the neediest people, not in the language or idiom of the audience, incompatible with the values and traditions of people, contradictory, and repetitive. Communicators were described as having low credibility and little knowledge of rural areas, poorly motivated, unskilled, too few, and inattentive to feedback from the masses.

A disappointing pattern was found in special development programmes that included massive information campaigns. Their initial effect on awareness, knowledge, and adoptions was quite high, but this was quickly reversed when many abandoned the innovations. Continuing the campaigns was relatively ineffective; those who had not adopted the innovation early were not likely to do so later. Some development planners attributed this pattern to the satiation effect produced by an information glut, particularly in family planning and agriculture. Field studies, however, showed that people were not satiated with information per se but with poorly devised messages (Mulay and Narula, 1972). What they needed was more relevant and timely information.

This period, for the first time, marked that besides the urban and rural people, there was a predominant section of the population who had the traits of the urban and the rural, the rurban. In fact, rurban development programmes were sometimes administered using the infrastructure of urban and sometimes rural programmes, though they differed from both and required special structures (Malhan and Narula, 1969).

The assigned role of communication in this period was to inform, educate, and motivate people. Based on research and experience, three distinctive areas were highlighted. First, the disappointing results of target-oriented persuasion in development campaigns led to an emphasis on promoting general pro-development attitudes. Second, the notion of a satiation effect led to a concern with the content of messages. Planners envisioned communication strategies with more variation that would sustain the interest of people. Third, specified groups were identified as not being reached by development communication. Strategies were developed to enable communication media to reach these groups (Muthayya, 1981).

The sixth plan was based on an unprecedented amount of research evidence about the nature and importance of communication in development. Previous plans referred to communication only as the publicity of government plans. Even within the limits of this concept, no overall conceptualisation or policy coordination was developed for the use of various media. The sixth plan was the first to articulate a programme of development communication.

The plan responded to the dissatisfaction with the previous development programmes with some modifications, some of which were based on a series of research studies conducted in 1975 to assess the need and status of development communication and communication policies in India. The most significant of these studies was done by Dubey (1976), who argued that development programmes would fail to produce desired results if they are not supported by adequate and effective development communication programmes. The pre-requisites of such programmes include adequate communication networks, conducive communication situations, and appropriate communication policies.Dubey (1976) suggested that the time-bound, unsystematic series of development plans that included communication only as publicity did not constitute an effective programme for development.

In February 1979, the Indian Institute of Mass Communication and the International Institute of Communication (London) organised a conference on rural development and communication policies. The participants noted several problems in development communication. In the top-down pattern, development messages do not reach those for whom they are meant; and when they reach the target audience, they are often not utilised. In horizontal patterns, there is an inordinate amount of information loss between the development agencies. The conference proposed a series of recommendations designed to rectify the imbalances in the flow of information. One of its suggestions was the establishment of communication resource centers for every village or group of villages to provide access to media and to serve as a clearinghouse for information. Another recommendation urged densification of communication.

In March 1979, an international conference on communication and development was held in Delhi. In the light of three decades of development experience, the question asked was: Is it possible to leave communication to the existing structures, or is it necessary to have a public policy regarding development communication? The question was answered at the conference of communication specialists and administrators from South Asia, in 1980. The agenda was the MacBride Commission Report, and the conference reached a consensus that each country should evolve a national communication policy. India endorsed this view, partly.

In the milieu of these studies and conferences that gave unprecedented attention to the sophisticated analysis of communication, writers of the seventh five-year plan assigned communication the role of involving people from all walks of life in development. This was to be accomplished by greater use of media to motivate people rather than to disseminate information through greater emphasis on interpersonal communication and by monitoring and evaluating programmes in a continuous manner so as to provide adequate feedback to improve programme performance (Narula and Pearce, 1986).

The plan and related policy decision imposed new criteria at many parts of the communication process. The major thrust of the plan was based on the concept that people must be brought into a more active participation with development efforts. The plan was synchronised with a new model of Indian development aimed at the same goal with which the nation began: a just, social, and economic order based on the principles of socialism, secularism and self-reliance.

The eighth plan approach was to aim at the maximisation of employment. Special focus was on the development of women, their education, health and nutrition, work opportunities for ensuring a minimum level of income, and maternity and child care, all of which were expected to curb population growth and to raise the quality of life.

The first step in this direction was decentralisation of the planning process, involving reorientation of priorities in the processes and mechanisms of plan formulation and implementation. Such reorientation requires democratic decentralisation of the body politic. This called for a fundamental change in policy and restructuring in the decision-making and planning process. Seventh and eight five-year plans also gave prominence to development- support communication in the plan documents. The plans estimated and evaluated the inadequacy of existing infrastructure facilities in the communication networking of the country and recommended proper strengthening or restructuring of the facilities for effective implementation of the development programmes.

In spite of these findings, squeeze in the budgetary allocation for the information sector, following structural adjustment programmes, affected the financial autonomy of the public media. In the 90s, both the print and the electronic media started to play an important role in deciding the agenda of the everyday lives of the Indians and soap operas and epic serials like Ramayana and Mahabharata started changing and even shaping the religious fabric of the Indian polity.

Decentralisation, Development Communication, and Media

In the post-independence period, the Gandhian suspicion towards modern media deprived broadcasting funds (Robin Jeffrey, 2010). The task of the media, once the national independence was achieved, was understood as fulfilling the mission of education and information in terms defined by the Indian state. 'Development' comprised a phased state-led approach to modernisation that involved cultural and institutional changes and the introduction of carefully selected catalysts that could promote such change leading to modernisation.

The dominant paradigm, the modernisation approach, emphasised and reiterated the role of communication in development activities. Development communication is often associated with Daniel Lerner (1958), Wilbur Schramm (1964) and Everett Rogers (1962). They viewed modern means of communications essential for development of pre-modern societies. As a result of the spread of the mass media, they argued, old habits would die, modern beliefs and attitudes would become widespread, and society would develop naturally.

In the "Passing of Traditional Society: Modernising the Middle East", Lerner (1958) viewed mass media as an important and ideally placed tool reaching the individual, directly, by-passing the cultural institutions of traditional society and providing examples of rewards that a commitment to change could bring. The mass media was regarded as the mobility multiplier. Wilbur Schramm and Everett Rogers' approach had so much in common with Lerner's model. However, their emphasis was rather different. Roger's Diffusion of Innovations (1962) was very much concerned with the effects of communication and their role and impact on creating new ideas and practices, which are essential for the modernisation process, and also their role in persuading people to accept and adopt the exogenously introduced innovation. Wilbur Schramm (1964) emphasised on high correlation between the indices of modernity and availability of mass media. He extended the argument of Lerner and Rogers and termed mass media, *the magic multiplier*.

A qualitative evaluation of the modernisation raises serious doubts about its positive contribution, especially the contribution of mass media, to improve the quality of life in the third world. Mass media in the third world has been criticised for emphasising values such as commercialism, consumerism and materialism, inconsistent with the needs of these countries. Moreover, these values, along with elite or government ownership of the media, did create a lack of the media credibility. (Melkote, 1991; Tehranian, 1978). Indeed by the early 60s, it was clear that the media did not produce national development and it was accepted that the revolution of rising expectation has been a major casualty of the past decade (Lerner and Schramm, 1967).

Criticisms against the modernisation theories began to be heard among the third world countries, particularly in Latin America, in the 1960s. The best known critic of the modernisation theory is Gunder Frank (1969). His criticism is fundamental and threefold: the progress paradigm is empirically untenable; has an inadequate theoretical foundation; and is, in practice, incapable of generating a development process in the third world. Therefore, referring to the uni-linear and evolutive perspectives and the endogenous character of the development solutions, these critics argue that the modernisation concept is a veiled synonym for westernisation in a third world context. (Frank, 1969).

Modernisation theories, as Fair (1989) has pointed out, were very much informed by the Powerful Effects Model. Of the 224 studies of communication and development published between 1958 and 1986, 132 (62.8%) treated media as an independent variable, where the media was seen to act as a powerful force in the creation of social changes or influence on audience members' attitudes, behaviours, or knowledge (Fair, 1989). What is striking is that despite the fact that the focus of such research and studies was on the impact of media, only in less than half of such studies researchers came face to face with recipients of media messages in the developing countries.

Another related problem with modernisation theories was that while obsession with media and their effects continued, only a little attention was paid to the content of the messages. The uni-dimensional modernisation theory also ignored the all-important institutional, class, and structural variables.

Dependency theories or cultural imperialism thesis came to the fore in the second half of the 60s. The main feature of these and the subsequent Marxist theories was that underdevelopment of much of the world is an integral part of the international system that polarised the world into the center and periphery. Cultural imperialism thesis extended this argument by looking at the nature and structure of media production in developing countries and how this contributed to another form of domination (cultural) in addition to economic and political domination of the periphery by the center. Cultural imperialism school argued that there is an international trade in media artefacts, particularly in television programmes, and in news reports, films, records, magazines and so on. Although there are a number of smaller cultural exporters, notably the UK, the trade in media artefacts, overwhelmingly, is from the USA to other countries (Schiller, 1976). Analysis of television programming in developing countries showed that they were, and are, dominated by imported, overwhelmingly, US materials. (Varis, 1974, 1984; Manjula B., 1992). This imported notion of the development manufactured mainly by the western media was deeply problematised in the 90's and was criticised for depoliticising the development discourses.

One of the key criticisms of development discourse has been that it de-politicises development by rendering it into a technically manageable problem (Escobar, 1995; Ferguson, 1994; Harriss, 2002). In the contemporary neo-liberal era, media has emerged as a key word in socio-political and cultural landscapes, effecting contested terrains and shifting boundaries in our debates and discourses. The recent focus on media is an important part of the neo-liberal transformations taking place around the world. Events are represented by media, which even make or mar the events for the public discourses at the national and international levels, making Baudrillard state that 'Gulf war did not take place'. (Baudrillard, 1994).

Since the onset of satellite television and the end of government monopoly over the airways in India in 1990 and 1995, respectively, there has been a transformation in media ownership and control. State agencies no longer dominate broadcasting; privately produced content dominates the scores of channels. The era of government monopoly often aimed for a far wider audience, while privately owned media has presented an upper middle class lifestyle (L.F Williams, 1985). This ubiquitous penetration of media into the private, political and social spaces of the everyday lives of Indians by the end of 90s had its own impact in forming public discourses on citizenship debates, which were very important in the democratic decentralisation process.

In the examination of public discourse and cultural citizenship, Murdock (1993) negotiates the complex territory of identity, media and consumerism, and defines the fundamental prerogative of citizenship as 'the right to participate fully in social life with dignity and without fear'. To Murdock, the right to participate in the formation of democratic societies includes the right of expression constituted by the rights of listening, as well as speaking.

Mediation is a social process that extends beyond 'media', and must be understood in larger and more dynamic terms. The terms public sphere refers to the space in which publicity is to operate, because it points to the definable effect. In his work on the 19th century, Habermas offered a historical argument about how novel reading and critical discussion make the ground for the individual participation in modern democracy. The questions posed by Habermas are more interesting than his arguments—like what is the relation between a communication form, such as print, and its socio-political context, and whose interest it represents best in a particular public sphere. His sociological account of political formation through communicative practices is important in its effort to locate the possibility of democratisation outside the realm of the state and potentially independent of it. The context of anti-colonial nationalism, with its deployment of colonial categories and the use of indigenous forms and practices show how communicational context cannot be reduced to technology but require an assessment of the relevant historical and political condition as well as the material and practices through which certain things are rendered as information.

Media is centrally implicated in discussions on the functioning of contemporary democracies. Most studies on the role of the media in democratic societies have focused on debates surrounding the notions of public sphere; media text as the site of contestation and conflict and ideals of public service broadcasting as opposed to commercial media (Keane, 1991). It is important to explore and unravel the link between both democratisation of the media and democratisation through the media. It is in these engaging debates that correlate the democratization and media that an analysis of the nature and role of media—print, electronic and folk—in the PPC become relevant and significant.

The innovative nature of People's Plan, coupled with its decentralised concept that demanded participation of people, made the role of media relevant, imperative and significant in the context of the planning process of the IX Plan of Kerala. Media had to conscientise people through information dissemination on the Plan, set its agenda to create an environment for the new development culture, interact with people so as to enable them to plan and organise the developmental activities of People's Planning Campaign (PPC) and to capacitate people through the forward and backward communication linkages.

Role of Media in Decentralised Planning

The opening for media in Decentralised Planning (DP) comes from the recognition that in participative development there are multiple stakeholders, all generating and exchanging information. There is, therefore, a need for building bridges, linking different viewpoints and creating a common language among different stakeholders (Cernea, 1991). The contrasting interpretations of reality between common people and policy makers, or between technocrats and elected representatives, are the challenges faced by the media in the DP. However, these are the exact entry points for strategically designed media messages aimed at linking different stakeholders. Media, for development, is about aiding different types of actors interested in understanding needs and assessing opportunities jointly; it is about providing them with the methods and modes to strike common meaning, and about enabling them to negotiate with other actors, who have contrasting perceptions and interests (Melkote, 1991).

In the DP, everyone is a user and a provider of information. That includes data, information, and appropriately packaged experience and knowledge. The need for information arises at all levels, from senior decision-makers at the national and international levels to the grassroots and individual level

(Casebiar and Janet, 1992). There is substantial evidence that without the two-way information flow, development efforts would fail (Schramm, 1964). This acknowledgement of the fundamental role of media is a significant pointer in the context of the DP. In the earlier development plans, media was understood merely as a mechanism to transfer knowledge and technology in a unidirectional mode and as a publicity tool to convey development messages of the government. Today, there is a growing recognition that the impact of such approaches is limited or short-lived and additional efforts are needed to give voice to the knowledge and perspectives of people at the grassroots, since they are no longer willing to be treated as passive recipients of information.

In a very broad sense, three roles can be assigned to media in the DP:

- The information dissemination role of media can be used to make things visible. This role assumes more significance in the context of the DP due to its heterogeneity, diversity, and mammoth nature. This can be done increasingly with the aim of creating new perspectives rather than transferring pre-packaged solutions;
- The advocacy role of media can be utilised in enacting and fostering policy decisions and to gain acceptance of people for it, rather than using it as a conventional propaganda tool; and
- The *vox populi* role of media can be exploited in facilitating and giving voice to people, especially the marginalised, providing them a platform to engage in dialogical communication and making them visible in the decision-making process of the State.

The third role constitutes a more promising dimension of media in the context of DP. Linear transmission of information is no longer the only focus; rather, the orchestration of platforms for dialogues and discussions among multiple actors is the most important component in a participative planning process. Media can be a facilitating force for the dialogic participation if its three roles in the DP— a meeting ground for information exchange, public awareness, and stakeholder dialogues—are utilised effectively (Khushu, 1993).

Success of the DP requires partnership and full participation of all citizens. The extent to which people participate in activities around them depends upon their knowledge of the issues at stake and an understanding of how these issues affect their lives and livelihoods.

Media has, therefore, emerged as one of the single most powerful mechanisms by which messages of critical importance can reach the widest cross-section of people. Media should engage people to discuss the meaning of DP and has to define its role in ensuring its continuity providing them with relevant and digestible information about what is going on around them in an interesting and creative way. Unless one makes these linkages in simple graphic form, there is a possibility of the messages failing to deliver. It is in this area of public education that there needs to be a partnership between media and planners involved in the DP (Smith, 1994). They have an obligation to explain the concept of DP in understandable terms. In turn, in delivering its messages, the media must avoid presenting the concept of DP as a generic term; rather it must explain the relationship between particular events and themes.

Linkages with the DP information networks to inform on new policies to initiate and stimulate dialogue on issues of importance must be taken up. The capacity to stimulate such debates on national priorities is an invaluable part of the processes of participatory development (Manaev, 1993).

It is paradoxical that while the role of media in the DP and in the participatory form of governance is proved beyond doubt, the structure of media is becoming more and more centralised with mergers, acquisitions, and conglomerisations. This conflicting trend—centralisation in the ownership of globalised media and the expected participatory nature of media in decentralised planning—makes the forces operating in the media more dynamic.

The entire world, during the 20th century, was brought into the market system and, in the process, the western capitalists pumped much of the surplus generated by the industrial revolution of the nineteenth century in the media sector. Media system reflected the patterns of this political economy. The crucial change for global capitalism, which laid the groundwork for the rise of global media, was the emergence and ascension of the Trans-National Corporations (TNCs). The increasing hegemony of the market is important today because the digital revolution and convergence are forcing a rethinking of media and communications regulations and policies everywhere in the late 1990s (White, 1997).

Globalisation and the growing power of the TNCs have made the containment of media concentration and centralisation more difficult. The centralising firms contend that they need greater size and vertical integration to compete in the global market, and their political power and the support of market forces have essentially removed anti-trust barriers to media concentration (Bagdikian, 1990). In short, the aim of media decentralisation is politically utopian in the developed countries today. At this historical juncture, it is extremely difficult to contain further centralisation.

Another point worthwhile to mention is the role of the globalised media in production of false consciousness in the interests of a dominant class, which owns and controls the media. This increasing monopolisation of the culture industry, through its concentration and diversification, caters to the demands of the elite and, most often, only voices their interests. Media in a participative decentralised economy, on the other hand, tries to become the *vox populi* of the most marginalised sections of the society, and acts as a facilitator to enable them to be decision-makers in the policies of the State. This conflict between the hegemonic interest of the centralised nature of the globalised media and the ideology of participation envisaged in the decentralised media was one of the real challenges before the planners of a participatory and decentralised form of governance. Governance structures and content of the global media and its ongoing debates and anxieties in the decentralization project need to be read along with the media history and culture in the Kerala context to understand the mediated readings of the PPC in the process of democratic decentralisation in Kerala.

Media History and Culture of Kerala

Anthropological studies reveal that civilization in Kerala dates back to the upper Paleolithic period. Stone tools excavated from the banks of Kanjirappuzha in Palakkad and Thenmala in Kollam testify this. The cave carvings at Edakkal and Thovari in Wayanadu and the cave paintings in Marayoor prove that a civilized society had lived in these places. The ritualistic dance forms, drawings of animals, geometric patterns, and cart with wheels can be seen as the first markers of communication in the Kerala society.

With the advent of metal technology, the Kerala society spread out to a larger land mass encompassing a portion of Tamil Nadu. During this time, people lived as separate ethnic groups. Sangham literature has mention of Kuravai koothu and Thunagai koothu in many places. Dr. K. N. Ganesh (1997), in his book, 'The Yesterdays of Keralam', says that the koothu, during the Sangham period, was the means of social communication. Kuthu was performed in connection with war, marriage, death, and birth. The period had a sound history of folk art as reflected in drama, chorus song, and group dance.

The Kerala society that went through a series of churning processes with the advent of Buddhism and Jainism, migration of Brahmins, caste system, feudal system, religious conversions, trade links with foreign countries, and colonial rule had adopted different modes of communication at different stages of its history. Temples became an important power centre with Brahminisation of the society; and that saw the relocation of many art forms of the common into the temple premises. One example is the transformation of Koothu as a temple art. "The Brahmins succeeded in uprooting koothu from the common man" (K.N. Ganesh,1997). It was during this period that art forms like Nangiar koothu, Prabandham koothu and Koodiyattom adopted the Hindu mythical stories that had nothing to do with the Kerala life. Drama, song and dance were the main art forms of the common outside the Brahminical society. Theyyam, Thira, Kuthiyottam, Thottampattu, Naganpattu, Thekkanpattu, Koithupattu, Kakkarassi natakam, Purattu nadakam, Kothamuri natakam, etc. are some among them.

Kadhakali that originated from Krishnanattom, and Thullal which adopted many features from Padayani were mainly based on mythical and mystical stories. While sculpture and painting were confined to temples, classical music blossomed at the feudal courts. Onam, Vishu, Thiruvathira, and temple festivals became the meeting places of the common. Oppana, Defmuttu, and Mappila pattu among the Muslims; and Margamkali and Chavittu natakam among the Christians became famous as modes of artistic expression in the respective communities.

It is the evolution of language that defines the growth and development of indigenous forms of communication. One can trace the influence of many other languages in Malayalam, which has evolved through the interaction with different communities, religions and cultures. Since Sanskrit was used for dissemination of knowledge and literature, it caused alienation of the vast majority from the world of knowledge. 15-18 centuries saw the growth of written language; different branches of literature evolved along with its growth. Literature in Manipravalam, a mix of Sanskrit and Malayalam, and Pattukavithakal, which had the influence of Tamil, were the initial artistic expressions through written language.

The influence of Tamil and Sanskrit could be traced during the shift from Vattezhuthu to Kolezhuthu. But written language was used only by a minority. This period saw the confinement of education, which was common to all during the Sangham period, to the Brahmins and the upper castes. A. Sreedhara Menon (2007) observes in his book, *Kerala Culture*, that the universal education, prevalent during the Sangham period, got weakened due to the impact of caste system. But the missionaries, who introduced the modern education system, helped the lower castes to access education and knowledge. The development of prose began with the introduction of the modern form of education. The *Roman Travelogue* by Paramakkel Thoma Kathanar in 1785 and *Canons of Udayamperor Sunnahadose* in 1599 are the important initial expressions in prose (Sreedhara Menon, 2008).

Printing freed literature and the educational system from the clutches of caste hierarchy. Educational institutions of the Christian missionaries that had the patronage of the colonial rule axed the root of monopolisation of the world of knowledge by Brahmins and the upper castes. It was during this period that the language of the common developed into a well-defined prose form. The newspapers and magazines, published in Malayalam, had an important role in defining the structure of Malayalam prose. Malayalam language was first printed in *Horthus Malabaricus* (1686), a Latin book published from Amsterdam. The declaration of Itti Achuthan Vaidyar, partner in data collection of medicinal plants, is given verbatim in the book. The first book in Malayalam is *Samkshepa Vedartham* (1772) published from Rome. In 1811, the *New Testament* was printed in Malayalam from Bombay. In 1821, Benjamin Bailey started the first Malayalam printing machine in Kottayam. The publication history of Malayalam language begins with the publishing of the Malayalam version of the *New Testament* in 1829 and the *Bible* in 1842, both at the Kottayam press. The first government press was started in Thiruvananthapuram in 1839.

Like in printing, the history of Malayalam newspapers in Kerala also owes its origin to the Christian missionaries. *Rajya Samacharam*, published by Dr. Hermann Gundert in 1847, from Thalasseri, is the first Malayalam newspaper. The paper, published on behalf of the Basal mission, aimed the spread of religion. In the meantime, Basal mission started publishing another monthly newspaper, *Paschimodayam*. Another contemporary publication during this time was *Jnananikshepam*, from CMS press. The history of independent journalism in Kerala starts with the publication of newspapers, like *Kerala Mitram* (1881), *Kerala Patrika* (1884) and *Malayala Manorama* (1890).

Kerala Mitram, started by Devji Bhimji, a *Gujarati businessman*, was started to expose corruption in different departments of law and justice in the Kochi province. Chengulathu Kunjurama Menon, who got inspiration from the Bengali newspaper, *Amritha Bazar Patrika*, started *Kerala Patrika* from Kozhikode. Kunjurama Menon was fined to the tune of Rs. 51 for criticising the colonial regime.

Malayalee, published from Thiruvananthapuram in 1886, had an important role in the political history of the erstwhile princely state of Travancore. It facilitated the cultural leaders of Travancore to submit the Malayalee Memorial to the king, demanding more job opportunities for the people of Travancore.

Nazrani Deepika, started by Nitharikkal Mani Kathanar from Kottayam in 1887, is the oldest surviving newspaper in Kerala. *Malayala Manorama* is the first newspaper registered (1888) under the Companies Act, 1866. In 1890, the company brought out its first publication, *The Malayala Manorama*, under the editorship of Kandathil Varghese Mappila. The editorial penned by Varghese

Mappila and titled Newspapers and Certain Objectives and Ethics, on Feb 14, 1891, reads, "It is the main duty of the newspaper to bring to light any corrupt activity of any individual, whatever high the position he may occupy." Malayala Manorama started publishing its copies thrice in a week in 1918, and became a daily on Jan 16, 1928. License of the paper was cancelled in 1938 by then Divan C.P. Ramaswami Iyer as a punitive measure for participating in the Utharavada Bharana Prakshobham (agitation for responsible rule), and the editor, K.C. Mammen Mappila, was jailed.

Kerala society witnessed the fight for freedom of the press with the starting of *Swadesabhimani* newspaper from Thiruvananthapuram by K. Ramakrishna Pillai in 1906. Divan brought new legislation to cancel the membership of Ramakrishna Pillai in the legislative assembly of Travancore. The incidents that followed resulted in the exile of Ramakrishna Pillai in 1911. Ramakrishna Pillai had made it clear in the introductory note carried in the first issue, dated Jan 17,1906, that the paper would do the real watchdog function of a newspaper.[4]

Kerala Kaumudi, started in 1911 from Mayyandu, was for the upliftment of the downtrodden. Since its owner C.V. Kunhiraman was a government employee, the name of the editor was shown as Mullor, a poet. *Kerala Kaumudi* was banned for some time for publishing an article favouring the responsible rule agitation. In 1940, *Kerala Kaumudi* became a daily, and started publication from Thiruvananthapuram.

Mathrubhoomi, started publication on March 18, 1923 from Kozhikode under the editorship of K.P. Kesava Menon, took a lead role in the Indian independence movement. It was formed as a public limited company, floating public shares. It became a daily in 1930. *Malayala Rajyam* (1929) published from Kollam, and *Chandrika* (1934) from Thalasseri, two prominent newspapers, started publication before Indian independence.

By the 1930s, the left movement occupied a prominent role in Kerala politics. In 1939 the Communist Party of India (CPI) was formed. On September 6, 1942, *Desabhimani*, the mouthpiece of the CPI, was started. Its publication had to be stopped in 1948, following a ban imposed on CPI. When the party split in 1964, *Desabhimani* became the official organ of the CPI (M).

4 Vidya Samgraham (1864), Keralam (1866), Sandishta Vadi (1867), Kerala Pathaka (1870). Keralopakari (1874), Sathyanada Kahalam (1876), Malayala Mitram (1876), Thiruvithancore Desabhimani (1876), Kerala Deepakam (1878), Kerala Chandrika (1879), Vidya Vilasini (1881), Keraleeya Suguna Bodhini (1886), Katha Vadhini (1887) and Keral Sanchari (1888) were the newspapers that had fairly good circulation in these days. Besides, there were many local newspapers that had to be folded up sooner or later.

Janayugom that started publishing from Kollam in 1947, is the mouthpiece of the CPI.

Kesari A. Balakrishna Pillai holds a unique position in the history of journalism in Kerala. He was the editor of *Samadarshi* and *Prabodhakan* before he started *Kesari*, in 1930. He had, in 1930, in an article penned in Prabodhakan, stated that newspapers in the west were owned by a handful of rich and powerful, whose vested interests the newspapers were protecting.

One cannot but refer to the editorial pieces by Kumaran Asan when one evaluates the role played by newspapers in the social reformation in Kerala. Ezhavas and Government Jobs, Theendal should be abolished, and Nair-Ezhava clash, are some of the pieces by Asan written in the language of the common.

Newspapers initiated the mission to take language to the ordinary people by freeing it from the literary style, and played an important role in setting the social tone for the reformist movement in Kerala led by leaders like Chattambi Swami, Narayana Guru, Ayyan Kali, Poikayil Yohannan and Vagbadanandan. The youth wing of Namboodiris under the auspices of Yogashema Sabha, which was formed to fight against the wrongs in the community, started a publication, Unni Namboodiri, which had a crucial role in the reformation process, initiated by leaders like V.T. Bhattathiripad. Towards the fag end of 19th century, many literary periodicals were started in Malayalam.[5]

In 1927, the Samastha Kerala Sahitya Parishad was formed at Edapalli thanks to the collective efforts of Appan Thampuran, Ullor S. Parameswara Iyer, Vallathol Narayana Menon, and G. Sankara Kurup. The official organ of the organisation- Parishad magazine- was published in 1932. Jeeval Sahitya Sangham, an organisation with the aim of writing and propagating books with progressive thoughts, was formed at the collective initiative of M.P. Paul, P.

---

5 *Vidya Vilasini, published in 1881 from Thiruvananthapuram, is the first Malayalam literary periodical. Abhijnana Sakunthalam by Kerala Varma Valiyakoi Thampuran was first printed in this magazine. Vidya Vinodini, published from Trissur with C.P. Achutha Menon as editor, was another literary magazine during this time. Vasana Vikrithi, the first short story that had all the necessary qualities of a short story, was published in this magazine. The editorial published when the magazine turned 12 years made it clear that the magazine would address political issues also. Bhashaposhini, started in 1892 under the editorship of Kandathil Varghese Mappila, is another magazine worth mentioning in this regard. This was started as the official organ of Bashaposhini sabha, formed in 1891. It was Bashaposhini that gave a common space for the literary persons in Travancore, Kochi and Malabar. It published serious articles on literature, linguistics, history, education, science & technology, and biography. Kavanodayam (1896),Rasika Ranjini (1903), Vivekodayam (1904) and Kavana kaumudi (1904), Mathrubhoomi weekly (1932) and Malayala Manorama (1937) were the other major literary magazines started before independence.*

Kesava Dev, Thakazhi, and Ponkunnam Varkey in 1937. This was renamed as Purogamana Sahitya Sangham.

The Changing Face of Newspapers

Though the early Malayalam newspapers were started for religious propaganda, they became politically and socially sensitive during the later years. Naturally, there were many attempts from the part of the government to restrain and restrict the press. Newspaper and Books Registration Act (1867), Press Act (1922) and the Indian Press Ordinance (1930) were some of the measures in this direction. When the colonial rule, through its education policy, fragmented the society on the basis of caste, the newspapers addressed all sections of the society from a secular perspective. The Mathrubhoomi, dated September 13, 1942, reported the first widow marriage among Namboodiris thus: "It was interesting to watch those who assembled at the Namboodiri village sitting shoulder to shoulder at the function, irrespective of caste and class distinctions." E.V. Ramakrishnan, a writer and thinker, observed that widow marriage became news because of the presence of many invisible readers.

The period of 1900-1950 forms a critical period in the formation of modern Kerala. It was during this period that people who were divided on lines of caste and small kingdoms got the common Malayalee identity. Newspapers, publishing houses, cultural and literary institutions, and the spread of libraries all had their roles in building a public space and making the society more political and democratic.

Malayalam newspapers faced the challenge of approach vis-à-vis the newly elected democratic government of India. The newspapers had to address a state of turmoil following a series of political developments like the unification of Travancore and Kochi kingdoms as Thiru-Kochi, elections in the Thiru- Kochi and Praja Socialist Party led by Pattpm Thanu Pillai forming government with the support of Congress party, collapse of the ministry following withdrawal of Congress support, formation of the state of Kerala, the first communist government under the leadership of E.M.S., and dismissal of the government following the liberation struggle.

But what we saw after the formation of Kerala was commercialisation of newspapers, especially the front line papers like *Mathrubhoomi* and *Malayala Manorama*. Both the papers had around 7000 copies in 1937. In the next 20 years, they could take it only to 50,000 copies. Absence of modern machinery and financial crisis weakened the growth of newspapers. Meanwhile, newspaper owners realised the imperativeness to bring in more professionalism.

Advertisement became the main source of revenue because it became difficult to run newspaper with the revenue from sales only. It led to increasing the number of editions because to earn more advertisement revenue, it was necessary that the papers reach more readers. *Mathrubhoomi* started its second edition, from Kochi, in 1962, which helped the paper take the lead in circulation with 1,70,000 copies. " That marked the beginning of the change in identity of the language newspapers in India; from nationalistic identity to that of business centers that strive for existence and increased profit" (Robin Jeffrey, 2003). Malayala Manorama, realising that leading corporate houses would give advertisement only to leading newspapers, started its second edition from Kozhikode, in 1966. There were six newspapers in Kerala at that time with circulation ranging between 20,000 to 30,000 copies.

The public and the political leadership looked askance at the competition in the newspaper world. "Journalism too became a business like any other business. It is this commercialisation that became the hallmark of post-independence journalism". (E.M.S., 1984)[6]

With the declaration of national emergency on June 26, 1975, independent journalism became impossible in India. Three ordinances were promulgated to control newspapers. 208 newspapers and 1434 periodicals were banned across India. Newspapers had to work hard to bypass the censorship and to fight against the government notion that the business of newspapers was to give publicity to government activities. The growth of newspapers was badly affected during this time.

Newspaper owners started initiatives for reaching out to more places and more people after the emergency was lifted. It was by carrying sensational reports on the naxalite action on Pulpalli police station and on the combing operations on naxalites by the police that *Malayala Manorama* stole the show in the circulation game. "That news had all the ingredients—murder, local flavour, mystery, international linkages— to ignite public interest. Besides, the incident happened in Malabar, where *Malayala Manorama* was hunting for more readers." (Robin Jeffrey, 2003)[7]

---

6 *Malayala Manorama reached the number one position in circulation in 1970 by printing 1,90,000 copies, and became the second largest circulated language newspaper in India. There were 50 newspapers in Malayalam during this time with Malayala Manorama, Mathrubhoomi, Desabhimani and Janayugom; each having two editions.*

7 *Mathrubhoomi and Malayala Manorama captured more than half of newspaper readers in Kerala by the end of 1980s. By 2000, Malayala Manorama started printing around ten lakh copies, while Mathrubhoomi had seven lakh print order. Both Mathrubhoomi and Malayala Manorama had ten editions each in Kerala. While Malayala Manorama has five editions in*

Periodicals like Kala Kaumudi (1951), Kumkumam (1966), Malayala Nadu (1968), Madhyamam (1987) and Samakalika Malayalam (1997) caught the public attention.[8] Both *Mathrubhoomi* and *Malayala Manorama* started periodicals, focusing on different target groups, during this period.[9]

Parallel to the commercialisation of mainstream media, there were many off beat initiatives, including little magazines and inland magazines. Pathumma's Goat, by Vaikom Mohammed Basheer, was first published in *Gopuram*, a little magazine.[10]

The growth of printing technology was very much visible in the history of Malayalam newspaper industry.[11] By 2000, the newspaper houses started journalism institutes to mould journalists to suit their companies.

It was commonly believed that TV would push the newspaper industry down. In fact, television industry had rattled the newspaper industry in many foreign countries. In India, TV and newspapers took off to growth almost the same time. It was during this time that newspapers started giving more emphasis to its visual appeal, through photographs, to counter the visual dynamics of TV.

---

different states in India and two foreign editions, Mathrubhoomi has four editions in other states. Other major newspapers are: Desabhimani (nine editions), Madhyamam (10 editions) and Kerala Kaumudi (10 editions). Janmabhoomi (1977), Veekshanam (1978), Siraj (1984), and Mangalam (1980) are the other newspapers worth mentioning. In 1992, Deepika brought out its eveninger-Rashtra Deepika- and Kerala Kaumudi brought out the mid-day paper- Flash. Many small newspapers that had started publication during the post- independence period left the scene unable to stand the financial crisis.

8 *As per the newspaper registrar of India, there were 1431 newspapers and periodicals--216, 175 weeklies, 776 magazines-- in Malayalam language in 2001.*

9 *When Manorama brought out Vanitha, Balarama, Kalikudukka, Karshakasree, Thozhil Veedhi, Paarpidam, and a health magazine, Mathrubhoomi brought out Grihalakshmy, Balabhoomi, Chitra bhoomi, Thozhil Vartha, sports, a health, and a travel magazine. Another significant development in the history of periodicals was the phenomenal growth of Malayala Manorama weekly and Mangalam weekly. Malayala Manorama, published in 1937 to discuss serious literary issues, started serialising popular novels by 1960s, and gained a quantum jump in circulation figures. Mangalam weekly that started publication in 1969 with a print order of 250 copies had 8 lakh copies print order in 15 years. It can be found that the high literacy rate in Kerala played a crucial role in the sudden increase in the circulation figures.*

10 *There were nearly 200 such small magazines in Kerala during 1990s. Ideological discussions done through periodicals like Navasahithi, Kerala Kavitha, Sameeksha, Jwala, Utharam, Anweshanam, Samkramanam, and Soochimukhi played a crucial role in strengthening the civil society in the 70s and 80s.*

11 *Mathrubhoomi was the first to introduce tele-printer, rotary press, and mono type composing machine. Manorama started tele-printer service in 1950. That Malayala Manorama had, in 1971, bagged the national award for best design and printing is proof that Malayalam newspaper had achieved quality in printing technology. Colour printing and offset were introduced in the 80s. With Malayala Manorama computerising their units in 1997, and other major newspapers following suit, Malayalam newspapers made a leap in technical advancement in production.*

Leading newspapers applied new design in form and content to cope up with the changed media face. Papers started focusing on melodramatic features and controversies. Interpretative news analysis too gained importance. Most of the newspapers gave one full page for obituary; started special sections and pull-outs to cater to different tastes of the reader. Local news started gaining more space. Moreover, newspapers started organising programmes of social relevance as part of their social responsibility. Sukrita Keralam (sanitation programme) and Palathulli Peruvellam (water conservation) by *Malayala Manorama* are two examples. Newspapers could increase their advertisement revenue through catering to the local readers through matrimonial, classifieds, and special pull outs in connection with the local festivals. Special offers like insurance for readers and gift schemes helped to increase circulation.[12]

Books, other than religious and government publications, were published with the starting of Vidyabhivardhini press (1886) by S.T. Reddiar, heralding a new era in the publication history of Malayalam literature. "It played a crucial role in taking Kilippattu, Thullal Kathakal and Attakathakal to the common" (M.V. Thomas, 2004).[13]

The library culture in Travancore began with the establishment of the Public Library in Thiruvananthapuram in 1829. Vanchiyoor Kunnumpurathu Sugunaposhini Library, started in 1894 at Thiruvananthapuram, was the first library established by the general public. During the same time, public libraries were started in Kochi at Chirai and Kodungaloor. Malabar region also showed immense interest in libraries by opening many libraries as part of the independence movement.[14]

---

12 *Information technology is another component that revolutionised the working of newspapers. It helped the papers to use new technology for collection and dissemination of news. The first internet edition was started in 1997 by Deepika, followed by Mathrubhoomi, Malayala Manorama, Desabhimani, and Kerala Kaumudi. It created online readers, cutting across the geographical boundaries.*

13 *Bhartahavilasom (1904), B.V. Book Depot (1903), Mangalodayam (1911), Sree Ramavilasom Book Depot (1926), Sahitya Pravarthaka Sahakarana Sangham (1945) and Current Books (1952) were the other major publishing houses*

14 *The Kerala Granthasala Sangham, formed in 1943, was the result of this library movement. On September 14, 1945, representatives from 47 libraries, under the leadership of P.N. Panicker, convened a meeting, and gave a unified structure to libraries and defined their activities, across the three princely states. "It can be observed that the concept of a unified Kerala, as reflected in the formation of the Sanghom, was there even before the formation of the state of Kerala." (Prof.S. Achutha Warrier, 2008). The motto of the sangham was that knowledge is for development. The night- school, initiated by the libraries in Malabar, in 1937, can be viewed as the genesis of the literacy movement in Kerala. In 1948, the Sanghom brought out its official organ, Granthalokam.*

Malayalam language theatre evolved from the tradition of Kakkarassi Natakam, Chavittu Natakam, and Vellari Natakam, and temple arts like Koothu and Kootiyattom.[15] The first social drama in Malayalam is Mariamma, penned by Kocheeppan Tharakan.[16] Kaumara Kusala Sangham, formed in 1885 at Perunna in Changanaseeri, is the first drama troupe in Kerala.[17] The main troupes in Malabar were Bhaktha Magaranthini Mala, under the leadership of poet Kuttamathu, and Sree Muthappan Devavilasom Nadana Sabha that staged the dramas of Vidvan P. Kelu Nair. Dramas were played on stages, plain grounds or in fields after the harvest.

Theatre gained the status of a tool for social change with Adukkalayil Ninnu Arangathekku by V.T. Bhattahthirippadu, a drama that focussed on the atrocities against women and other maladies in the Brahmin society. The play was staged mostly before the collectives of families than on public stages. This was followed by Marakkudakkullile Mahanarakom by M.R.B. and Rithumathi by M.P. Bhattathiri. "When the traditional art forms were confined to the caste-ridden outlook, the new theatre visualised the imaginations of the common. That fact that Navayugom, written by Abhayadev, was banned is testimonial that drama, by this time, had become a powerful weapon for social criticism.

Parallel to what was happening in Travancore, quality plays were produced and staged in Malabar region also. The movement was led by poet Kuttamathu and Vidvan P. Kelu Nair. Though Devayanicharitham by Kuttamathu was based on a myth, it portrayed the poverty and sufferings of the poor and also featured the ills of alcoholism. This play was staged when anti-liquor movement, led by Gandhi, was gaining momentum across the country. The plays by Kelu

---

15 *Chavittu natakam that gave prominence to dance and song is based on Christian mythology, used a mix of Malayalam and Tamil languages. The first Malayalam drama is Bhasha Sakunthalam, translated from Sanskrit by Kerala Varma Valiyakoi Thampuran. It was staged in many stages, following which many works from Sanskrit were translated into Malayalam. During this time, there was mass audience for Tamil music- dramas. Troupes like Kalyana Ramayyan set, Ramadu set, and Sami Iyer set had staged plays like Kovalan Charitham, Nalla Thangal Charitham and Parsi lalithangi in many places. In north Malabar, it was the troupes from Karnataka that staged plays. Sada Rama by K.C. Kesava Pillai and Sangeetha Naishadam by T.C. Achutha Menon were the independent Malayalam music- dance productions during this time.*

16 *The play that ridiculed the wife and mother-law-clashes in the Christian families was written in 1892. The coming together of the local language, slangs, local traditions, and the common things made Mariamma a landmark in the history of Malayalam drama. This was followed by Abrahikutty, authored by Kandathil Varghese Mappila. Chandrika, penned by Kodungaloor Kunjukuttan Thampuran, and Kalyani, authored by Kodungaloor Kochunni Thampuran were the other important social dramas during this period.*

17 *This was followed by troupes like Vinoda Chinthamani, Rasika Ranjini, Kayamkulam Nataka Sangham and Vanchiyoor Sree Vilasom Nataka Sangham.*

Nair helped to strengthen the agitation against the colonial rule. His plays had patriotic songs; he often gave the images of mythical characters to the contemporary political and social leaders. His Pakkanar Charitham voiced against the caste system, while *Vivekodayom* voiced against the social order that deprived women of their rights. *Pattabakki* portrayed the rise of peasants against the feudal practices. C.J. Thomas described *Pattabakki* as the first political drama in Malayalam. A new audience developed in Kerala thanks to Adukkaliyil ninnu Arangathekku, and Pattabakki, by K. Damodaran, and the translation of plays by Ibsen. (E.V. Ramakrishnan, 2017).

It was in this socio-cultural sphere created by Pattabakki that Kerala People's Arts Club (KPAC) was formed, in 1950. It was formed in line with India People Theatre Association (IPTA) in Mumbai. KPAC's first production was, My Son is Right. Ningalenne Communistakki (1952), the next production, created waves in the socio-cultural milieu of Kerala. Thoppil Bhasi, who authored the dramas, said that it was written with the specific objective of giving a fillip to the political movement of the common. KPAC's productions that propagated communist thoughts had an important role in making drama an art form of the common.[18]

During the same period, many adaptations and translations of world classics were staged in Kerala. Kesari A. Balakrishna Pillai translated Ghost, by Ibsen, into Malayalam and initiated the new trend. New experiments in production and form were tried during this period. While plays by Prof. N. Krishna Pillai and C.J. Thomas gave new fillip to this trend, libraries and art societies gave amateur theatre a cultural space to evolve and grow. Koottukrishi, penned by Edasseri Govindan Nair that addressed the rural people, marked the beginning of this trend. The Malabar Kendra Kalasamithi was formed after realising the potential of the plays based on rural issues.[19] Plays by P.J. Antony, S.L. Puram Sadanandan, C.L. Jose and N.N. Pillai gave power to professional theatres.

---

18 *Suveykallu, Aswamedhom, Sarasayya, Puthiya Akasom; Puthiya Bhoomi, Thulabharom and Mooladhanam are the other major plays of KPAC.*

19 *Thikkodiyan, K.T. Mohamed, Cherukadu, A.K. Puthiyangadi, Nilambur Ayisha, Santha Devi, Kunjandi and Nellikode Bhaskaran were the main artistes who either wrote plays or acted or did both. Many drama competitions and drama camps were organised under the auspices of Malabar Kendra Kala Samithi. Sangamam and Kalinga (in Kozhikkode) and Kalidasa Kalakendram (Kollam) were the major professional troupes. These dramas were staged at festival grounds, as part of the annual day celebrations of cultural organizations, or at the conference venue of political parties.*

Thanathu Nataka Prasthanam that applied the form and techniques of traditional folk and temple arts in drama also developed during this time. C.N. Sreekantan Nair, M. Govindan, G. Sankara Pillai, Dr. K. Ayyappa Panicker, Kavalam Narayana Panicker, and P.M. Taj led this movement. Many dramas that featured the anxiety and issues of the modern man were penned in the 70s.

However, it was the street-plays that most effectively used drama as a medium to propagate ideology. They could take their message to the people and trigger thoughts. The sastrakala jathas of Kerala Sasthra Sahitya Parishad popularised the street-plays. Silent valley agitation, Bhopal gas tragedy, commercialisation of education, corruption in government offices, and problems in the health sector all formed themes of street plays. Another group that used street plays, effectively, was the extreme left groups. The naxalites found street plays an effective tool to communicate with people. Padayani, Amma, and Spartacus by Ranachethana in Kozhikode, and Nattugadhika by Wayanadu Samskaravedi are the most popular among them.

Street plays were used by the Literacy Campaign and the People's Plan Campaign to take their message directly to people. Trade unions, students, political parties, and university unions all used street plays at different points of time.

Women's presence has been there right from the beginning of the language drama. Ajnathavasam (1890) by Kuttikunju Thankachi is the first drama written by a woman.[20] Women artistes had to cross many social hurdles, face public ridicule and, at times, even physical assault. The orthodox Muslims

20 *The story is based on Pandava's life in exile. It followed the theatre tradition of Sanskrit plays. Subhadrarjunam (1891) by Thottaikkattu Ikkavamma was the second woman to publish a drama, and it created waves at that time. It was translated to Sanskrit, and there were many write-ups on this drama in many contemporary periodicals. During the initial days of theatre, it was men who played women characters. Ochira Velukutty was the man who played many female characters during that time. It was the literacy and social reformation that helped women to come to theatre. The first woman who entered the Malayalam theatre was Varkala Ammukutty. Later, Palluruthy Lakshmy, C.K. Rajam, K. P. Kamalakshi, M. K. Kamalakshi, Pattom Saraswathi, Mavelikkara Ponnamma, P.N.Seethalakshmy, Thankam Vasudevan and Arammula Ponnamma came to theatre. Most of them had training in acting from Balanatana Sabha, an institute for learning theatre. Seetha Lakshmi, who started acting in Anjathamudra by Sebastian Kunjukunju Bagathavar was a prominent artiste during that time. She turned to theatre after learning music from Swathi Thirunal music academy. Famous plays of that time were Kovilan Charitham, Anarkali, Magdalana Mariam, Jnanasundari and Nalla Thangal. "Women's entry into theatre made the Malayalam drama inclined more towards social reality (Sajitha Madathil, 2010).*

pelted stones at Nilambur Ayisha and manhandled her for acting in Ijju Nalla Manisan Akan Nokku.[21]

During the same time, Vyazhavattathinu Sesham was staged in Thiruvananthapuram at the auspices of Sree Chithira Thirunal Library in which Anna Chandy, who later became the first woman judge in the High Court of Kerala, played the role of an educated social reformer. It was the period when women, under the leadership of Anna Chandy, were arguing for women's reservation in government offices and representation in the legislative assembly. Sree Chithira Thirunal library played an important role in bringing many women to theatre.[22] Manushi, a women group, staged their production, Stree, in 1986. It was a total women production- from the stage of conception of idea to the staging of the drama. Sara Joseph, a gender activist, played an important role in the formation of the women collective and production of the play.

The impact of television and cinema and the entertainment-oriented popular arts affected the growth and development of Malayalam theatre during the post-1990 period. There were many cultural organisations in the rural areas, across Kerala, which had staged plays. More than 1200 such groups have registered their names with the Kerala Sangeetha Nataka Academy.[23]

---

21 *The transformation of Malayalam theatre from music- drama to social reality witnessed the increasing and powerful participation of women. While Mariamma, written during the fag end of 19th century, portrayed the situation of women, realistically, Kuruppilla Kalari by C.V. Raman Pillai and Pennarasu Naadu by E.V. Krishna Pillai ridiculed women's intervention in the social sphere. But with the staging of Adukkaliyil ninnu Arangathekku, the society started discussing the issues faced by women within and outside their homes. Savitri alias Widow Marriage (1934) by lalithambika Antharjanam and Thozhil Kendrathilakke (1948), staged under the leadership of Arya Pallathu, are two prominent dramas staged exclusively by women. Lalithambika penned the drama well before the Namboodiri community witnessed the first widow remarriage. The reluctance of man to recognise the new economic and social position women had earned through doing job outside their homes was the theme of Thozhil Kendrathilakke. The play was set against the backdrop of the weaving training center for women in Lakkidi.*

22 *The socio-political environment in the late 1970s brought more women to theatre. The street plays staged across India at the auspices of different political parties had the effective participation of women. Women theatre became popular in the 1990s when the women groups started their activities in the socio- political milieu of Kerala. Women theatre was an offshoot of these activities. It began with the street plays and slowly became part of the mainstream theatre culture. Naxalite movement, Kerala Sasthrasahitya Parishad, School of Drama, and the drama camps, exclusively for women, all had their roles in developing the women theatre.*

23 *But the amateur drama culture in Kerala faded out, unable to cope up with the financial requirement the troupes demand. There was a time when plays were written for the amateur theatre, and the plays were published by important publishing houses. Today, there are more than 300 professional drama troupes in Kerala. But the reality is that none of their plays are published in the book form.*

Radio

There were six radio stations when India got freedom, besides five other stations in the princely states, including Travancore.[24] Radio became the most effective tool to take the message of development activities of the government during the post-Independence era. Radio clubs and village collectives were formed to discuss the development reports and programmes of AIR. The LSGs and developmental agencies of the government gave effective support to such forums. In 1964, the government, realizing the potential of radio, formed the A.K. Chanda Committee to suggest measures to improve the functioning of AIR.

Akasavani started giving more importance to programmes focusing on rural people, as part of the Community Development Programme initiated in 1952.[25]

The major change in radio in 2000 was the FM radio. Radio Mirchi, Club FM, Big FM, and Red FM are being broadcasts from Thiruvananthapuram, Kochi, Thrissur, Kozhikode, and Kannur. FM mainly broadcast music and chats. There has been no worth mentioning efforts in the field of community radio in Kerala, except for the narrow casting by Radio Alakal, being done in Vizhinjam among the fisher folk. Production of the programme, started in 2006, is done using the free software.

Kadhaprasangam

Kadhaprasangam, one of the most popular art forms in the beginning of the 20th century and the post-independence period, had its origin from the

---

Children's Theatre and Campus Theatre did not gain any momentum in Kerala. Perhaps, the only branch of theatre that is active is the one- act plays that are being penned to cater to competitions at the youth festivals at the district and state levels, annually.

24 *The first Malayalam broadcasting was in 1939. That was a message given by Kollamkode Vasudeva Raja, which was broadcast from the Madras radio station. On March 12, 1943, the first broadcasting station in Kerala was started at Thiruvananthapuram. It was known as Thiruvithancore Radio. Broadcasting was timed for three hours in the evening. Music, kadhakali verse, and drama were the main programmes. The Government of India, in 1950, brought all the radio stations under the princely states part of All India Radio (AIR). On April 14, 1950, a radio station was commissioned at Kozhikode. It was followed by a full-fledged station at Thrissur, in 1954, and a relay station at Alappuzha, in 1971, which was to transmit the programmes aired by the Thiruvananthapuram station. Today, there are seven radio stations in Kerala. Thiruvananthapuram and Kozhikode stations have the commercial broadcasting centers of vividhbharathi. Thiruvananthapuram has an FM station, by name Ananthapuri FM station*

25 *Agriculture, family planning, health, rural development, education, cooperation, home science, irrigation, and animal husbandry were the areas thus focused.*

Harikadha, a traditional Tamil art form. Kadhaprasangam was very effective in airing the reformist ideologies and for mobilising agricultural labourers.[26]

Soon, social issues and important literary works were presented through Kadhaprasangam, and the important literary works in Malayalam became the subjects for Kadhaprasangam.[27] In the 1950s, Kadhaprasangam played a vital role in popularising the communist ideology. Kedamangalam Sadananthan and V.Sambasivan were the leading exponents in Kadhaprasangam. Sambasivan, a known communist, exploited Kadhaprasangam to popularise the communist ideology.[28] He was arrested and jailed during the national emergency for presenting 20th Century by Bimal Mitra.

Television

The television programmes in Kerala started telecasting in 1982 with the technical support of KELTRON, which later withdrew from the scene after Doordarshan telecasted Asiad, directly. On April 2, 1984, Thiruvananthapuram Doordarshan started functioning from Kudappanakunnu.[29]

The first satellite television in the private sector- Asianet- started telecasting programmes in 1992[30]. Soorya, the second satellite channel in Malayalam that

---

26 *It was King Swathi Thirunal who popularised Harikadha in Kerala. He wrote Sanskrit works Ajavila Moksham and Kuchela Akhyanam, and made Meru Swami Bagathavar present them in the Harikadha format. This was the genesis of Kadhaprasangam. C.A.Sathyadevan, who got training in Harikadha from Tamil Nadu, presented the first Kadhaprasangam—Markandeya Charitham— at Neyyattinkara in Thiruvananthapuram for which Kumaran Asan wrote the Sanskrit lyrics, and later, presented Chandala Bikshuki of Kumaran Asan, for which Pandit K.P. Karuppayyan wrote the lyrics. Following this, Sekharan Vadhiar, brother of Kumaran Asan, presented Karuna, written by Kumaran Asan, and Swami Brahmavrithan presented Bharatha Sthreekal Than Bhavasudhi, written by Vallathol Narayana Menon.*

27 *This included Ramanan by Changapuzha Krishna Pillai and Ayisha by Vayalar Rama Varma.*

28 *He chose progressive works like Kudiyozhippikkal written by Vyloppalli, Puthan Kalavum Arivaalum by Edasseri, Vazhakkula by Changampuzha, Vilakku Vaangam by Bimal Mitra, Devalokam by Cherukadu, and his own works like Vyasanum Marxum for Kadhaprasangam. His contribution in popularising the Russian literature in Kerala is also commendable. He presented Crime and Punishment and Brothers Karamazov by Dostoevsky, And Quiet Flows the Don by Sholokhov, War and Peace and Resurrection by Leo Tolstoy, and Mother by Maxim Gorky, and made the works popular among even ordinary people in Kerala.*

29 *The first programme telecast by the center was a children's drama-Orukuuttom Urumbukal. High- power transmitter started operating from Kochi and Kozhikode in 1988. Today, there are 23 terrestrial transmission centers in Kerala. The satellite channel of Doordarshan started 24x7 programmes in January 2000.*

30 *Asianet Satellite Communication, the first cable TV company, was also started along with it. This company started a channel, Asianet Cable Vision, in 1997. In 1999, Mumbai-based Raheja group bought the shares of the cable company. In the same year, Asianet started Asianet News, a 24x7 news channel. Asianet has a significant role in moulding the visual culture of Malayalees*

used digital transmission right from the beginning, was started in 1998.[31] Jeevan TV that started in 2000 with Thrissur Archbishop Mar Jacob Thunkuzhi as its president initially focused on spirituality-related programmes but shifted its focus to popular programmes in 2003. Kairali TV, started in 2000 by the company, Malayalam Communications Ltd., is owned by 2 ½ lakh shareholders. The channel is backed by CPI (M), and it marked the beginning of political parties starting news channels.[32] India vision that focused on live news telecast was started in 2003. MM TV, the television channel of Malayala Manorama, and Mazhavil Manorama, its entertainment channel, started telecasting programmes in 2010 and 2011, respectively. Victors, the education channel as part of the IT @ School project, also started telecasting programmes during this time. Amritha TV under the Amrithanandamatom, JaiHind TV under KPCC, and Reporter, the 24x7 news channel, are the other major channels. Shalon, Darsana, Powervision and Atmiya Channel are spiritual channels. Besides, there are many local TV channels in the fray. Mathrubhoomi, Kerala Kaumudi, Flowers Channel, Madhyamam all started news channels.

Cinema

Vigatha Kumaran, released in 1928, is the first film in Malayalam. It was made by J.C. Daniel under the banner Travancore National Pictures.[33] The orthodox community in Kerala was not ready to accept the reality that a woman had acted in the film, and the first heroine, Rossy, had to leave Kerala. Balan, released in 1938, is the first talkie in Malayalam. The film, directed by

---

in Kerala. It produced and telecast many programmes, other than the run- of- the- mill ones, disregarding its financial and technical limitations. Programmes like Ente Keralam, Patra Vishesam, Nattarangu, Akathalam etc. are some of them. Asianet introduced the half-an-hour live newscast. It also introduced a forum—Can ask the Chief Minister— to help people raise their problems and concerns directly with the Chief Minister. The mega serial culture in Malayalam television began with ' Stree', the serial telecast by Asianet for over a year.

31 *It is the Malayalam unit of Sun TV network. It focused on serials and film-based programmes, and started a serial –war with Asianet eyeing on the TAM rating. Television prime time was earmarked for serials, sidelining the discussions on serious issues concerning the society. For Soorya, news was just one of its programmes.*

32 *Kairali followed the model set by Asianet in news and news-related programmes. It also telecast programmes like Penmalayalam, Madhyamavicharam and Veritta Kazhchakal, which are not run-of-the –mill ones. Though Kairali brought the one-week serial model as an alternative to the mega serial, it did not click either with the audience or with the advertisers. Later, Kairali started a news channel—People—and an entertainment channel—We. Of late, the reality shows on music, dance, and comedy sidelined even mega serials in TAM rating in almost all the major channels.*

33 *It was screened for nearly two weeks in the Capitol Theatre in Thiruvananthapuram, following which it was screened in Alappuzha, Kollam, and Thalasseri.*

S. Nottani, had its story and script done by Muthukulam Raghavan Pillai.[34] Prahladhan is the first film produced by Merry Land, the first film studio in Kerala. In 1949, Udaya studio was started in Alappuzha. The first film from Udaya was Vellinakshatram. Jeevitha Nauka, released in 1951, is the first box office hit in Malayalam.[35] Navalaokam (1951), scripted by Ponkunnam Varkey, for the first time, presented communist ideology on the screen. The central characters of the film were the socially and economically exploited.

Neelakuyil, penned by Urub and directed, jointly, by Ramau Kariat and P. Bhaskaran, is the first film to take the caste system as its central theme.[36] It bagged the award for the second best film at the national level. Newspaper Boy, scripted and directed by P. Rama Das, is better known as the first neo-realistic film. It was released in the same year Pather Panchali was released, and had poverty as its theme. All those who were part of the film were below 23 years old.

It was in the 1960s that cinema adopted themes like reformation and pro-left ideas, which had been successfully tested in literature well before.[37] Chemmeen (1966), directed by Ramu Katriat bagged the president's gold medal for the best film in India, gave a new direction to Malayalam film industry. It was in the 60s that eminent film personalities like A. Vincent, K.S. Sethumadhavan, and M.T. Vasudevan Nair became active in the Malayalam film industry.

Olavaum Theeravum is the first film that freed Malayalam film industry from the studio floors. P. A. Backer produced, M.T .Vasudevan Nair scripted, and P.N. Menon directed the film that changed the course of Malayalam film industry through its brilliant photography, creative use of new technology in production, and the progressive nature of the theme.

Swayamvaram (1973), directed by Adoor Gopalakrishnan, a product of the film institute, Pune, heralded the new wave in Malayalam film. The film that

---

34 *Jnanambika (1940) and Prahladhan (1941) were made after Balan.*

35 *Screened for 300 days, continuously, Jeevitha Nauka successfully tested the wife and mother- in-law conflicts and the issues between husband and wife.*

36 *Neelakkuyil (1954), Newspaper Boy (1955), Rarichan Enna Pauran (1956) and Randidangazhi (1958) are other early films that portrayed the real life of Malayalees.*

37 *Mudiyanaya Putran, Puthiya Akasam; Puthiya Bhoomi, Ninamaninja Kalpadukal, Bhargavi Nilayam, Oodayil Ninnu, Murappennu, Chemmen, Iruttinte Atmavu, Aswamedham, Asuravithu, and Kallichellmma are some of the films based on famous literary works. Besides commercially exploiting the popularity of famous novels and dramas, these films portrayed the social realities of life in the post-independence Kerala. These films were box office success and got recognition and accolades.*

deviated from the mainstream films marked the beginning of a film culture that could effectively communicate through visual dynamics.[38]

Nirmalyam, the debut film by M.T. Vasudevan Nair, tells the story of an oracle alienated at the onslaught of modern trends and the wastefulness he feels about his very existence as the messenger of god. The most powerful character of the Malayalam film industry, perhaps, is the protagonist of Nirmalyam, who spits on the idol of the god that he had been representing throughout his life. It is doubtful whether a film like Nirmalyam is now possible in Kerala, which has drifted much towards communal thoughts.

Though these films were snubbed as art films and award films by the mainstream industry, they had their presence in the 80s also.[39] Production cost of the film Amma Ariyan was met through money collected from the general public, and John Abraham was suggesting an alternative model to the highly expensive film production.

The film culture of the 70s was made possible thanks to a lot of factors varying from the mushrooming of film societies across Kerala following the formation of Chitralekha film society in Trivandrum. The film society movement in Kerala had the motto: to see the world, join the film society. The societies, besides screening films by masters, also provided the space for discussions on them. Association of Film Societies in Kerala (AFSK), an umbrella organisation of the film societies in Kerala, was formed at the initiative of Chitralekha.[40] It was around this time that Chitralekha started a film production unit, Chitralekha film cooperative ltd, and made its first film, the much acclaimed Swayamvaram. Jansakthi and Odessa also made films. Odessa made history in the release of films by organising parallel screenings,

---

38 *Nirmalyam (1973) by M.T. Vasudevan Nair, Utharayanam (1974), Kodiyeetam (1977) by Adoor Gopalakrishnan, Kanchana Sita (1977), Thampu (1978) and Esthappan (1979), all by G. Aravinadan, Athidhi (1974) by K.P. Kumaran, Swapnadanam (1975) by K. G. George, Kabani Nadi Chuvannappol (1975), Manimuzhakkom (1976), Chuvanna Vithukal (1977) and Sanghaganam (1979) all by P.A. Backer, Njaval Pazhanjal (1976) by Azzez, Agraharathile Kazutha (1977) by John Abraham, Yaro Oral (1978) by Pavithran, Aswathamavu (1978) by K. R. Mohan, and Eekakini (1978) by G.S. Paniker were the important films made in the 1970s.*

39 *Elipathayam (1982), Mukhamukhom (1984) and Anantharam (1987) all by Adoor, Pokkuveyil (1982), Chithambaram (1985) and Oridathu (1986) all by G. Aravindan, Cheriyaachante Krurakrithyangal (1983) and Amma Ariyan (1986) by John Abraham were important films in the 80s.*

40 *This organisation provided the space for screening good films, gave right advice to people who wanted to start film societies, and to bring to Kerala outstanding film personalities from other states. With the formation of the Kerala chapter of Federation of Film Societies of India (FFSI), the activities of AFSK were stopped. Aswani, a film society in Kozhikode, was very active like Chitralekha. It organised a two-week-long international film festival in 1980. 1970s and 80s saw many societies like Janasakthi, Odessa, Rashmi film society, and Kasaragodu film society organising film festivals.*

outside cinema theatres. However, this period also witnessed the withering of film society.[41]

Another important aspect of the films in the 80s was the presence of political films. Films like Angadi (1980), Eenadu (1982) and Vartha (1986) showed the ugly face of parliamentary democracy, trade union, underworld, and media. While the heroes fumed like volcanoes, heroines were reduced to the status of their shadows. The rise of Mammootty and Mohan Lal as superstars happened during this time.[42]

It became extremely difficult to make good cinema crossing the blocks laid by the commercial dictums of an industry that has become almost completely commercialised. Television was another major challenge the film industry had to face in the 90s. The increase in number of entertainment choices brought the number of film goers down. This period saw the restructuring of cinema theatres as shopping complexes and marriage halls. The onslaught of consumer culture, thanks to the increasing inflow of the Gulf money, and the improved financial position of the middle class, helped the free flow of electronic devices like TV, VCR, and VHS cassettes and CDs of Malayalam cinemas into the Malayalee homes. Cinema-viewing became an affair inside the home. Video cassette libraries mushroomed across the state.

By 2000, more satellite channels started telecasting programmes in Kerala. Films were made exclusively eying on the satellite rights. That marked the beginning of the end of video libraries. Many theatres relied on soft-porn films for survival, unable to stand the burden of loss caused by the box office failure of even films by super stars. With films like this, known as the Shakeela wave, capturing the theatres, the family audience moved away from cinema halls. Cinema viewing changed its mode from the secular context inside the theatre to a home-based private affair. The social impact of this shift was that

---

41 *The mainstream film industry underwent important changes, while the parallel cinema was doing experiments with the medium. Popular cinema started working on new and different themes, deviating from the repeatedly used family–based melodrama, under world stories, and stereotypical love stories. This stream that sprouted through the films of Ramu Kariat, P.N. Menon K.S. Sethumadhavan, and A.Vincent bloomed at the hands of Padmarajan, Bharathan, K.G. George, Lenin Rajendran, Hariharan, and Mohan. Their films came to be known as the middle- path films and turned out to be a strong face of Malayalam cinema. I.V. Sasi, the popular film director, made Avalude Ravukal, based on the life of a sex- worker. The film rattled the moral conscience of Kerala society.*

42 *While the 90s became a carnival of melodramas, good cinema touched the screen once in a blue moon. Vidheyan and Kathapurushan by Add or Gopalakrishnan, Piravi and Swam by Shaji N. Karun, Ponthanmada, Oormakal Undayirikkanam, Mankamma, and Susanna by T.V. Chandran, Aparahnam and Kazhakom by M.P. Sukumaran, and Daivathinte Vikrithikal by Lenin Rajendran were some of the films in the parallel cinema wing that touched the screen in the 90s.*

people, by and large, pulled out of social and political collectives and confined themselves to the inner shells of their homes. Cinema became a commercial product. It lost its sense of dialogy and political perception. The impact of Hollywood and Bollywood films on the visual culture of the audience made it difficult for the regional cinema to bloom as a medium of art. Added to this was the lack of concerted effort on the part of film makers to exploit the potential of digital revolution.

Malayalam documentaries, during the initial days, were mostly films division documentaries and biographies. Vallathol, directed by P. Bhaskaran, Thakazhi by M.T. Vasudevan Nair, and Kumarana Asan directed by Kerala State Film Development Corporation are some of the documentaries made during that time. But there were not many productions in this area, since the possibility of financial returns was very poor.[43]

The coming of satellite channels, institutes that teach video production, and comparatively lesser cost of production all attracted more and more young people to documentary production. Video festivals and social networking sites like Youtube provided space for video documentaries.

Kerala has had a socially sensitive and vibrant media culture. As detailed in the aforesaid session, the media grew with the nationalist movement and played a crucial role in the social remoulding of the State. Kerala has a bipolar political culture with either the Congress Party or the Communist Party taking the political leadership. While the print media helped the nationalist movement and the Congress Party, it was theatre and indigenous art forms, like kathaprasangam, that helped the communist movement to penetrate into the social psyche of Kerala.

In the history of communism, Kerala has a unique role. It was in Kerala that a Communist government was voted to power for the first time in the world. It is significant to note that the communist party grew while it was in the underground. At the same time, the communist ideology reached the common man, overtly, through the theatre productions of pro-communist troupes, like the Kerala People's Arts Club (KPAC). The theme and message

43 *Basheer: the Man, directed by M.A. Rahman, in 1987, is the first Malayalam documentary to bag national awards. Silent Screams: A Village Chronicle, directed by O.K. Johny, which portrayed the tragic life of unwed mothers in Wayanadu, is the first documentary to address a burning social issue. The introduction of video in the late 1980s, gave a new fillip to documentary production. Save the Western Ghats March: The Kerala Experience (1987), and No to Dams: A Pooyamkutty Tale (1988), both directed by C. Saratchandran, are the initial productions that used the video format. 18th Elephant directed by P.Balan, Ara Jeevithangalkku Oru Swargam by M.A. Rahman, Kanavu Malyilekku by M.G. Sasi, Kanam by Babu Kamrathu, Pestering Journey by K.R.Manoj, and Only An Axe Away, and Thousand Days and Dream, two documentaries jointly directed by C. Saratchandran and P. Babu Raj, are the significant documentaries.*

struck a common homophile with the common man, who formed the base of the communist movement. Media, in general, was sensitive to the social needs and problems of the society and played a crucial role in the trajectory of the development of the State.

This remained the trend, till the fag end of the 20th century. Since then, it is the luring world of consumerism that has been shaping the policy and agenda of the media itself. Circulation figures, not the social sensitivity, became the yardstick for rating newspapers. This, in fact, was only reflecting the changes in attitude and behavioral patterns of the Kerala society, which had accelerated its pace towards consumerism. The content of media was fine-tuned to cater to this new consumerist society.

It was in this consumerist society that the Kerala government, in an attempt to tide over the economic crises of the Kerala Model of Development much acclaimed for its development in the social indicators, launched the message of decentralisation, which demanded a hyper social sensitivity.

Media and People's Planning Campaign

The PPC had developed a media strategy to disseminate the new message of decentralised planning that demanded the participation of people. It was decided that the focus should be on print, electronic, and folk media, besides interpersonal and group communication, used extensively throughout the PPC.

Accordingly, a meeting of editors of all leading newspapers and newsmagazines was convened to brief them about the purpose of the PPC and to seek their editorial support. A media workshop was conducted at Kodungallor, as follow-up, to equip journalists to be sensitive to the local perspectives of development and to report the objectives and activities of the PPC. Yet another workshop, this time for the resource persons, was organised to train them to prepare press releases and handouts on the decentralised activities of the PPC at regional and local levels.

Centre for Development of Imaging Technology (C-DIT), a government agency, was assigned the task of producing video documentaries on various subjects and aspects of the PPC to be aired through public and private broadcasting channels and to be shown at training sessions for elected representatives and KRPs.

The Kerala Sastra Sahitya Parishad (KSSP) in the Total Literacy Programme had earlier successfully used the rich folk art tradition of Kerala. Hence, the expertise of KSSP was sought to exploit the potential of folk media to disseminate the message of the PPC among people, especially at the panchayat level.

Electronic Media in the People's Planning Campaign

Though the potentiality and power of electronic media in the campaign processes had been studied in the earlier researches (Lishan, 1995; Bruce, 1997), the use of electronic media in the PPC had been minimal. Both the public broadcasting (Doordarshan) and the then existing two private Channels (Asianet TV and Soorya TV) did not give the needed time slot for broadcasting one of the largest development projects of the State.

The Kerala State Planning Board (KSPB) had entrusted the Center for Development of Imaging Technology (C-DIT) with the task of making visual documentaries on the campaign. These documentaries were for telecasting through different channels and also for screening at training sessions of the PPC to sensitise and conscientise both the masses and elected representatives of the Panchayati Raj.

C-DIT formed a special video production unit to cater to the communication needs of the PPC. This unit was in constant touch with the planning cell of the KSPB, which functioned as the nodal centre for collecting information on development activities of the panchayats. Production team comprising trained professionals in the unit produced two types of visual documentaries: in- depth 15- 20 minutes long documentaries covering a unique development activity of any panchayat; and 4-5 minutes short films intended to give a glimpse of the unique and human interesting features of the PPC.

Table 6.1
C-DIT Productions on the People's Plan

Theme of Documentary	Number
Women	5
Tribal	5
Agriculture	7
Industry	4
Education	6
Health	8
Children	3
Grama Sabha	6
Training	19
Kalajatha	26
Water	3
Mini hydel project	4

Source: Video Production Unit, C- DIT

The C-DIT documentaries were on 13 different areas of development, included in the PPC. Only documentaries of 15-20 mts duration have been included in the table. Out of the 96 documentaries, 27% were on *Kalajathata*, the folk art form used to disseminate the message of the PPC; and 19.8% were on training. Remaining 53.2% was in 10 areas, including women and tribal, each had 5.2%. Besides these, C-DIT produced 26 spots of 3-5 mts duration highlighting certain specific instances of the successful aspects of the PPC.

The table (6.1) shows that the second highest priority was given to training, which was not meant for the general public, leading to the conclusion that dissemination of message to the trainees, elected representatives, and resource persons was one of the main thrust areas of the media strategy of the PPC, as applied to the electronic media. Besides documentaries, specifically on training, the trainees were shown other documentaries also, since screening of documentaries was included in the training modules.

General public, on the other hand, could see documentaries mainly through Doordarshan, which telecast 60 documentaries. But the time slot allotted in DD was not at peak hours, since the Fixed Point Chart (FPC) of DD was presumed to be too rigid to effect any alteration. That resulted in documentaries being telecast at non-peak hours, and the messages of the PPC not reaching the maximum audience. The spots designed for repeated telecast so as to reduce the entropy and semantic noise, and thereby, to enhance the effective communication of the PPC, did not achieve the objectives since DD was not ready to make changes in its FPC.

Among the private channels, Asianet TV had the maximum reach, and it did not stick to FPC. Its programme timings were flexible so as to accommodate documentaries or spots. Surprisingly, no serious effort was made by the KSPB to rope in the Asianet TV for the dissemination process of the PPC. Soorya TV, a new channel at the time when the PPC was launched, was almost completely ignored by the media planners of the KSPB.

The documentaries did not get a regular time slot in both public and private channels. Thus, the dissemination of documentaries was very minimal. Even training sessions did not fully utilise the screening time of the documentaries for further discussions and analysis of the issues featured in the documentaries. Communicative potential of the video was not exploited in the PPC. This adversely affected the overall information dissemination of the PPC through electronic media, both among people and elected representatives.

Print Media

The print media usually, with its editorial and business interests, set an agenda before its readers. One of the important findings of agenda-setting research is the positioning of an issue on a media agenda, which subsequently determines that issue's salience on the public agenda. Salience measures the perceived relative importance of an item in the agenda, i.e., amount and nature of coverage given to an issue within the media that determine how the public will treat that issue - and whether they will actually see it as worthy of being an issue (Chomsky, 1989).

Print media presents only a highly selective sample of newsworthy events from a continuous stream of occurrences. Events are identified as newsworthy when they satisfy certain rules, commonly understood as the criteria for determining news value (Stein, 1998). The necessity for such selection comes from the fact that there is only a limited amount of time and space available in the media agenda. Only parts of the criteria of news value are intrinsic to news events. Often the selection process/ gate keeping function are determined more strongly by journalistic worldviews and by media production routines.

Media has its own aims and rules that do not necessarily coincide with, and indeed often clash with, those of political communicators. Because of the power of media, political communicators are forced to respond to media's rules, aims, production logic and constraints (Mazzoleni and Schulz, 1999). They believe that not only the form, but also even content must be negotiated if politicians wish to address the public. If an issue is to climb the public agenda, it must push other issues down the agenda and eventually shove one of the earlier issues off the agenda.

In this context, framing can be important. Framing is the various selection patterns of certain aspects of an issue by the media (the page on which the news appears, the length of the news item, whether accompanied by photo etc.) to make them more prominent and thus to emphasise a particular cause of some phenomenon.

It is as a result of factors, such as framing, under certain conditions, media of mass communication tell people how to think about issues, and, therefore, what to think (Dearing and Rogers, 1996). This conclusion - stronger than the traditional agenda-setting outlook - indicates the importance of media agenda and, consequently, the power associated with those who influence this agenda. In a study conducted to evaluate the objectivity of newspapers, thirty three percent of newspaper editors, across the world, opined that they would not feel free to print an item damaging to the parent firm (Bagdikian, 1997).

This is not to imply that corporate-controlled media never carry stories critical of their interests, but the positioning of an issue on a media agenda importantly determines that issue's salience on the public agenda. Mere reporting in the media is not sufficient to allow an issue to move onto the public agenda. The amount of coverage, its prominence and format are also important. In agenda-setting terms, media production routines mentioned earlier, could lead to industry-wide biases on how issues tend to be framed and what stories are seen to be newsworthy by the editors.

The print media in Kerala, both vernacular and national, gave more detailed reportage of the PPC than the electronic media. Hence, a content analysis of articles/ reports on the PPC in four newspapers—three vernacular (the *Mathrubhoomi*, the *Malayala Manorama* and the *Deshabhimani*) and one English newspaper (*The New Indian Express*)— for a period of 18 months was done.

These four newspapers were selected for specific reasons. While the Deshabhimani is the CPI (M) official organ, [the People's Plan was introduced by the CPI (M)- led Left Democratic Front (LDF)], the *Malayala Manorama* is overtly anti-LDF. The Mathrubhoomi is neutral, to some extent, and The *New Indian Express* is the most popular newspaper among the English reading population in Kerala.

Reports on the PPC formed the data source for content analysis. The PPC was officially inaugurated on 17th August 1996. Reports on the PPC appeared in the newspapers, mentioned above, for 18 months, from July 1996 to December 1997, were selected for the study. The time frame of content analysis was chosen to reflect the attitudes and vested political interests of the newspapers in reporting the most important development initiative undertaken by the State Government, since the formation of the State in 1956.

For analysing the reports, three categories were used: the number of articles appeared in newspapers during the period of content analysis; whether the report was accompanied by photo; and the column length of the report.

Reports were subdivided into three categories:

- Events reporting (information oriented);
- Comments on the PPC; and
- Evaluation reports on the PPC.

Comments and Evaluation sections were further divided into two categories: positive and negative comments; and positive and negative evaluations.

As mentioned in the agenda setting function of media, newspapers set the agenda on the PPC-first in an information oriented mode and then, in an evaluation mode-reflecting the managerial and editorial interests of the newspapers.

The time period was split into three spans of six months each - the first period began one month prior to the inauguration of the PPC, July 1996-December 1996, the second span stretched from January 1997 to June 1997 and the third time period was from July 1997- December 1997.

Table 6.2
Content Analysis - July 1996 to December 1996

Framing Details	The New Indian Express	Mathrubhoomi	Malayala-Manorama	Deshabhimani	Total
No:of articles	43	97	108	194	442
Space	730 Cm.Column	1410 Cm.Column	2080 Cm.Column	3240 Cm. Column	7460 Cm.Column
Photo	16	42	68	167	293
Information Report	38 (88.37%)	64 (65.98%)	78 (72.22%)	104 (53.61%)	284 (64.25%)
Positive Evaluation Report	Nil	Nil	Nil	Nil	Nil
Negative Evaluation Report	Nil	Nil	Nil	Nil	Nil
Positive Comment	3 (6.98%)	21 (21.65%)	17 (15.74%)	90 (46.39%)	131 (29.64%)
Negative Comment	2 (4.65%)	12 (12.37%)	13 (12.04%)	Nil	27 (6.11%)

Note: Figures in parentheses represent the percentage of the total number of articles on the PPC in the respective newspapers.

Table (6.2) shows that during the initial phase of the PPC, all the newspapers, irrespective of their regional/national character, editorial policies, managerial interests, and party lineage, gave similar coverage. Most articles were information oriented, reporting the unique nature and characteristics of the PPC. None of the papers had given evaluation reports during this period. But as expected, Deshabhimani, the mouthpiece of the CPI (M) gave wide coverage to the PPC and, in fact, celebrated the event with lengthy reports accompanied with photographs. The table (6.2) shows that the dailies of Kerala were very sensitive to the reporting of the PPC. Well informed articles on decentralised planning, 73rd and 74th amendments, Panchayati Raj, special features of the PPC and its financial devolution were all subjects of reports.

Table 6.3
Content Analysis- January 1997 to June 1997

Framing Details	The New Indian Express	Mathrubhoomi	Malayala-Manorama	Deshabhimani	Total
No: of articles	46	82	93	197	418
Space	510 Cm. Column	1060 Cm. Column	1320 Cm. Column	3180 Cm. Column	6070 Cm. Column
Photo	6	23	20	133	182
Information Report	21 (45.65%)	43 (52.44%)	31 (33.51%)	89 (45.18%)	182 (43.54%)
Positive Evaluation Report	1 (2.17%)	5 (6.10%)	11 (10.85%)	10 (5.08%)	27 (6.46%)
Negative Evaluation Report	3 (6.52%)	4 (4.88%)	2 (2.95%)	Nil	9 (2.15%)
Positive Comment	8 (17.40%)	13 (15.85%)	36 (38.71%)	87 (44.16%)	146 (34.93%)
Negative Comment	13 (28.26%)	17 (20.73%)	13 (13.98%)	11 (5.58%)	54 (12.92%)

Note: Figures in parentheses represent the percentage of the total number of articles on the PPC in the respective newspapers.

Table (6.3) shows the content analysis of the reports in the newspapers, five months after the commencement of the PPC. A close scrutiny of the table revealed the changing and emerging trend in the reports. Percentage- share of the information-oriented reports in the newspapers showed a decreasing trend. Comments given by persons of eminence on the performance of the PPC got wide coverage. Politics of the newspapers started reflecting in this period. Newspapers, depending upon their vested interests, started selecting and framing the news- thus setting a clear agenda before its readers.

While the *Malayala Manorama*, with its anti- LDF stand, selected and gave prominence to negative comments, the Deshabhimani, with its gate- keeping function, filtered all negative comments and gave only positive comments in its reports. The *Mathrubhoomi* and The *New Indian Express* maintained almost a neutral stand in the treatment of news. But even then, these papers started giving importance to the political controversies regarding the PPC and neglected the development nature of the PPC.

Table 6.4

Content Analysis - June 1997 to December 1997

Framing Details	The New Indian Express	Mathrub-hoomi	Malayala-Manorama	De-shabhi-ma-ni	Total
No: of articles	52	113	121	212	498
Space	620 Cm.Column	1200 Cm.Column	1840 Cm.Column	3240 Cm.Col-umn	6900 Cm.Column
Photo	4	13	9	78	104
Informa-tion Report	13 (25%)	34 (30.39%)	21 (17.36%)	96 (45.28%)	165 (32.93%)
Positive Evaluation Report	7 (13.47%)	22 (19.47%)	13 (10.74%)	44 (20.75%)	86 (17.27%)
Negative Evaluation Report	9 (17.31%)	26 (23.01%)	34 (28.10%)	7 (3.30%)	76 (15.26%)
Positive Comment	10 (19.22%)	12 (10.59 %)	16 (13.22%)	57 (26.89%)	95 (19.08%)
Negative Comment	13 (25%)	19 (16.81%)	37 (30.58%)	8 (3.78%)	76 (15.46%)

Note: Figures in parentheses represent the percentage of the total number of articles on the PPC in the respective newspapers.

In the third time frame, the newspapers, especially the Malayala Manorama, the most circulated paper in Kerala, started showing an explicit anti-PPC stand. Reports became more evaluative in nature and in this evaluative analysis, various framing strategies mentioned in the table (6.4) were adopted. During this phase of the PPC, out of the total news, 30.67 % of the news was in an evaluative mode and there was a substantial increase in the percentage of comments and evaluation.

When people's representatives of the panchayat bodies were confronted with the implementation of development projects in the field, mostly arising because of their inexperience and ignorance in handling them, the print media in Kerala did not take an approach to understand those problems and to respond to them in a development-oriented way. Most reports on the PPC at that time were on trivial arguments between the political parties, which had nothing to do with the development initiative. The *Deshabhimani* had limited reach and that too to party cadres/ supporters. The Mathrubhoomi, though remained neutral to a great extent in covering the reports, too saw the PPC mainly through a political angle.

Role of Media and its Manufacturing Consent Role in the PPC

The status of media as an Ideological State Apparatus to maintain the interests of the elite minority who hold power was also used in reports against the PPC. The ideas of the ruling class are in every epoch the ruling ideas: i.e., the class, which is the ruling material force, is, at the same time, its ruling intellectual force (Althusser, 1971). The class, which has the means of material production at its disposal, has control over the means of mental production, so that, generally speaking, the ideas of those who lack the means of mental production are subject to it.

Gramscian notion of hegemony discusses the political power that flows from the dominant elite and maintains their power structure in civil society, i.e., by creating cultural and political consensus through unions, political parties, and media, where a ruling class exercises hegemony over allied classes and social groups. Gramsci (1971) argues in his Prison Notebooks that the way society is controlled and manipulated is of direct consequence of the practice of a false consciousness and the creation of values and life choices, which are to be followed. It is this process which Gramsci refers to when he tries to explain the way in which organisation of people, media and information controls the thought and actions to create a state of domination through the creation of dominant ideologies.

The role of media has to be taken into account within the context of the theory of hegemony due to the value of media and the public-imposed powers it yields. This theory of hegemony is relevant in the case of the PPC, for the print media, especially the Malayala Manorama, took a strong ideological stand against the PPC. The daily, the most circulated one in India, is known for its pro-Congress and anti-Communist stand. In the content analysis discussed above, the editorial stand of the Malayala Manorama was very clear. Being anti-left in its ideological stand, the paper focused only on those news items that tarnished the image of the PPC among its readers, or reported the politics of the PPC sans its development and set the agenda to discuss only the debates between the political parties on the PPC, which most of the time were on trivialities, and thus deviated the attention of people from the real development nature of the PPC. Through this continuous anti-PPC reporting by focusing only on the negative stories on the PPC, the Malayala Manorama was able to manufacture the consent of its readers, which comprises a considerable chunk of Kerala society, either against the PPC or passive towards it.

At this point, it is worthwhile to mention about the effective role media in Kerala played in another Campaign, some ten years ago, that time to disseminate the message of literacy, which helped Kerala to become the first total literate State in India. This may sound paradoxical given the negative and, at times, passive role played by the print media towards the PPC. Reasons for this different approach towards these two developmental initiatives could be due to the high voltage political and economic dimension in the PPC, as against the uni-linear and apolitical approach of the literacy campaign, which, in no way, affected the power structure of the dominant elites, whose interests the major newspapers, like the *Malayala Manorama* and the *Mathrubhoomi*, represent. Needless to say that the total restructuring of society and power structure, inherent in the concept of the PPC, was looked at with askance by the apostles of the status quo, always best exemplified in the attitudinal policy of the media. Which was why the *Malayala Manorama*, an anti-communist propaganda machine, and the *Mathrubhoomi*, the symbol of the Kerala Psyche which opposes any radical changes in social status-quo, played negative and passive roles, respectively, while the *Deshabhimani*, the CPI (M) organ, eulogised the PPC as the new dawn, and The New Indian Express, though similar to the Mathrubhoomi with respect to its attitudes, played neutral because the national daily had no well-defined political interests in the political and economic structure of Kerala.

At the same time, the print media was used effectively to announce the activities of the PPC, like convening of grama sabha and development seminars and selection of beneficiaries.

One of the most effective media strategies of the PPC was the advertisement it displayed in leading newspapers and television channels inviting retired technocrats to join the PPC in its crucial stage of assessing the technical feasibility and financial viability of the projects recommended by the grama panchayats. The idea to rope in retired technocrats was made against the backdrop of the reserve pool of retired hands in a State where the retirement age, 55, is the lowest in India, and the average life expectancy of an educated person is 80. The advertisements read like this: "*If you are a retired person, this advertisement could be the beginning of a new chapter in your life. The Planning Board invites you to give technical leadership to the developmental projects to be initiated by the people of Kerala, for the first time in its history .You can partake in the voluntary exercise to create a new social system. Besides, it would give a new meaning to your life".*

The advertisement had a tremendous impact. This was reflected in the composition of the Volunteer Technical Corps (VTC). More than 68% of the VTC members were retired hands.

Folk Media in People's Planning Campaign

Folk media, in decentralised planning, has spawned significant attention and praise. Since the early 90s, attention has been showered on the novelty and wisdom of using culturally appropriate channels in development communication (Melkote, 1991). They can convey relevant development information, stimulate critical analysis, elicit collective action, and facilitate popular participation. Because of their inherent characteristics, such as high credibility, richness in cultural symbols, local orientation, intimacy, low cost, and flexibility, indigenous media ensure cultural continuity and socio-psychological stability in the process of social, political, and economic changes. In the context of a variable paradigm shift from mechanistic, source-based communication models, indigenous media serve as vital elements in shaping an organic, and interactive, dialogical communication system and as viable alternatives to large-scale communications media (Wang and Dissanayake, 1994).

Though in a limited scale, the PPC exploited the potential of the traditional media. In the initial phase of the PPC, volunteers, especially the Kerala Sastra Sahitya Parishad, an NGO, which popularised it, used street theatre. Synopsis of one of the most popular folk drama, which had tremendous impact on the audience, especially at the grassroots, is as follows:

The drama titled *Anangapaprakal* (immovable stones) begins with five people reading out newspaper, a common village sight in Kerala. They read out headlines of the sensationalised news items and skip news items on the PPC as "boring". They make sarcastic comments about people who voice for developmental activities. All the time they are seen scratching their body. When the panchayat member approaches them seeking their co-operation to clear the waste disposed in their village, they counter him with the stand that it is his business to look into such matters of public concern, for they had elected him for that purpose only. Finally, he takes them then to an expert, who shows apathy towards the local problems and starts to conscientise them about the global threat caused by pollution. It takes time to convince the expert that the essence of globalisation is to think globally and to act locally. He then agrees to prepare the project for the disposal of waste; the panchayat member guarantees financial help from the panchayat; and, most importantly, the group decides to discuss the matter at the grama sabha.

The group symbolises the cynical psyche of common man in Kerala, his attitude towards development news, lack of sense of responsibility, and blaming-the-other nature; nature of the reports explains the sensationalising attitude of media; panchayat member is the messenger of the PPC; and the subject expert, as usual, turns a nelson's eye towards the immediate local issues while analysing the global issues. Since the context, characters and message typified the grassroots reality, ordinary people could strike a common frame of reference with the drama, making it very popular and effective in putting across the message of the need for participation of people for making the PPC a successful endeavour.

Though folk media proved effective in disseminating the concepts of the PPC, especially during the initial phase, it could not counter the negative propaganda aired by the print media, effectively, in the latter phases of the PPC. The campaign used this potential of folk media, particularly in the training sessions for women. Themes were chosen and scripts were written by the women elected representatives, reflecting the socio- cultural and political problems faced by them while administering the office of the panchayats. Most of the women representatives, who attended the training sessions could very well identify themselves with the chosen theme of the theatre and it really sparked a lot of serious discussions and debates on gender problems. Thus, these media formats were very well used as facilitative mechanisms for sensitising and conscientising gender issues and paved the way for an authentic dialogue among women on issues that directly affected their daily lives and had impact on their future.

Indigenous media used in the PPC was found to be effective for more than one reason:

- It sensitised the Kerala community in the initial phases of the PPC towards assessing its own needs and defining appropriate solutions to community problems and issues;
- It addressed the plurality and diversity of opinions and made possible the authentic and interactive exchange of information; and
- It facilitated the dissemination of contextual information and integrated learning with the social experiences of people.

The logo of the PPC was designed using five elements symbolising the Five -Year Plan, viewed from the economic angle of the DP, which is an aspiration for the material development of people. It also symbolises the five elements—

ether, water, earth, fire and sky— that constitute the human body at a micro level and the cosmos at a macro level. It also denotes the five senses through which human beings perceive and experience the world, and the McLuhanian extensions of senses in the communication context. Most importantly, the five denote the Panchayat.

The seven Peepal leaves, bordering the logo at the top, represent the seven days in a week, besides the Peepal tree under which the traditional panchayats had their sittings. It is quite natural that the Peepal tree reminds of the Buddha and his enlightenment which, in the communication context of the PPC, denotes a new conscientisation with respect to power.

The tapering end of the leaves gives a bleeding effect to the logo which creates the impression that the impact of the PPC would go beyond the social, political, and economic borders the PPC was expected to change. Just below the leaves are three semi- circular motifs, which give the impression of a rainbow, besides symbolising the trinity. It also stands for the three tiers of the Panchayati Raj system, and represents the headgear common to many traditional and ritualistic art forms of Kerala, like *Oottanthullal* and *Theyyam.* The leaves and the semi-circular motifs form the upper half of the logo, viewed horizontally. The upper half comprising the Peepal leaves and the semi-circular motifs give the image of the rising sun, signifying a new dawn in the planning history of Kerala.

The lower half has three elements, making the basement of the logo look stronger, giving expression to the message of the PPC that it is the grassroots that has to become the strongest. Five circular motifs denote the assemblage of men and women, with no scope for gender discrimination of any kind. Below that is five *Uddukku* (the indigenous drum), which stand for the messenger role of the *Paanans (the* traditional singers who popularised the hero image of the warriors in the northern Kerala through songs and *Uddukku),* symbolising *Thudipattu,* viewed as the harbinger of change and hope.

At the bottom most level is the central message of the PPC- Power to people - inscribed in Malayalam, the mother tongue of Kerala. This central message is so designed that it appears to hold all other elements in the logo in its spread out form implying the strength of devolution of power. The logo became very popular with all sections of the Kerala polity and even tribals could identify the PPC through the logo.

Lacunae in the Media Strategy of the PPC

The media strategy of the PPC could not counter the negative and passive reports on the PPC, churned out by the media, especially the print.

Even in the global context, the ownership pattern and the structure of media houses in Kerala remained regional. At the same time, the regional/ local development issues rarely received the attention it demanded, and that was true with respect to the PPC also. So, activities in the centre stage of the DP, the grama panchayats, seldom became newsy to be reported. That explains why results of the developmental activities did not reach the common man of Kerala.

The decentralised planning, sadly, did not have a decentralised media strategy. Moreover, the KSPB had not taken lessons from the past successful media experiences in decentralised planning projects, elsewhere. A notable example in Brazil had been TV Maxambomba, an experimental effort of the Popular Image Creation Centre (CECIP), dedicated to producing alternative educational materials. TV Maxambomba targeted Baixada, a large working-class district in Rio de Janeiro, and the project had involved local video training, alternative filming of working-class materials, and screenings. Baixada's 300 residential associations were polled on member needs, and since 1989 the project's video production crews had gone into the neighbourhoods on a nearly daily basis to make short videos of residents expressing their views on various topics (condom usage, clean water, sanitation etc.). Five nights a week, TV Maxambomba's crews set up moving exhibitions to show residents' comments along with other local station video programmes. A moderator tried to encourage people to discuss the issues. Maxambomba's videos often used the telenova format to attract audiences. TV Maxambomba has been a success avoiding partisanship and stimulating a real democratic dialogue.

The PPC could have taken a leaf out of such successful experiments, formed flexible and vibrant media unit at the panchayat level and designed a localised and decentralised media strategy to help the conceptualisation of a proper media mix, integrating the traditional and popular media to focus on the local developmental issues of the PPC from a non- partisan, development oriented, interactive, and participative angle. Media strategy of the PPC was focused, mainly, on elected representatives and resource persons. So, while the target audience received the right message at the right time in the right manner, the ultimate user groups- the common man- were, in general, groping in the dark in the midst of conflicting and confusing media reports that reached them directly. This resulted in a bi- focal effect of media strategy with the elected representatives and resource persons developing a positive attitude towards the PPC and the general public forming a totally different and negative perception, which defeated the very purpose of the PPC.

Media strategy of the PPC should have aimed to inform, conscientise, motivate, and activate people to participate in a dialogical and interactive communication mode so as to help the PPC sail smooth through the troubled waters it had confronted at the implementation stage and thus, to concretise the objectives for which it was started. Unfortunately, it did not happen. As mentioned earlier, what was expected of the popular media in the PPC was not materialised. At the same time, the PPC had not developed a decentralised media unit of its own, to disseminate the message of DP required at various phases. Media strategy of the PPC, therefore, failed to inform the Kerala polity on the development nature of the DP and thus, could not use the potential of media, which could have been used as a powerful tool in an information economy to counter the prevalent hegemonic norms and to manufacture the consent of the society, positively, towards this pro- development initiative.

It is a foregone conclusion that the media report what sells the best. In Kerala, politics is the most saleable commodity. It was natural that the media in Kerala got hooked to the political elements of the PPC. They did that in a way best suited to their political slant and vested interests. In the process, media turned Nelson's eye towards the development issues raised by the PPC. Through that act, the media failed to accomplish one of its primary and fundamental functions—catalyst for development—in a democratic system. That apart, the over politicised reports aired a wrong image about the very concept of this development initiative. In democracy, the media is expected to set the agenda for the overall betterment of the society. But in this case, the media hijacked the spirit of development breathed into the system by politicians. Not only the media hijacked, it attempted to hack what all positive elements the PPC had created in the socio- economic and political milieu of Kerala. On July 2, 2003, the Mathrubhoomi front-paged a half- toned box story report that the CIA was a party to the PPC. The Malayala Manorama made it the first news on the front page, next day, with photographs, framing it in a hyper sensational manner, setting the agenda for discussion on the very genesis of the PPC in a politically surcharged State. Through these reports, based on baseless and trivial allegations, the media once again reinforced its role as a strong ideological apparatus in the information economy, and showed how effectively it can set the agenda, jeopardising its role as a change agent in the development process, using even concocted reports.

Post-PPC

We live in a period when an event is said to have 'occurred' only when it gets 'reported' in the media. However, in the information economy, the media is becoming concentrated oligopolies through mergers, acquisitions, and conglomerisations and produces mainly false consciousness in the interests of a dominant class, which owns and controls the media. One could notice that even the much acclaimed public sphere tended to be male, urban based with disposable incomes, educated, and literate. Content of the media is increasingly being shaped by the demands of advertisers and sponsors who in turn cater only to the interests of the people with disposable income and purchasing potential that hardly reflect the heterogeneous interest of the public at large, making it oriented towards urban rich, and barely reports the concerns of people living in poverty. This shift in the focus of the media from a 'mass media' to a 'class media' and the change from 'broadcasting to narrowcasting' reflect the 'classigenisation' of the media (Manjula. B, 1998). The digital divide between information- haves and information have- nots being shaped by far more than access to technology; it is one shaped by access to content relevant to people's lives, and the capacity of people to have their voices heard in the public domain. In an information society, the values associated with media as the 'source of information for public interest, agent of development, and index of development' are deeply appropriated, concocted and seized by the powerful, and make media 'of the powerful, by the powerful and for the powerful'. This is a public catastrophe. In this context, it is important for the policy makers to come out with interventions, which could engage with the media as development agents.

Recognising the power of the media in activating the public sphere with developmental discussions and debates, Kerala Government initiated a unique developmental programme, titled Green Kerala Express, (GKE) in 2014, the first social reality show in Indian television history, to select the best panchayat in Kerala that has developed sustainable development models. Green Kerala Express is unique in that it re-designed a very popular television genre for social communication, where the elected representatives were subjected to a social/ expert auditing on a media platform. This programme attempted to integrate the popular traits of reality shows with the development- oriented content. This has also turned out to be a very valid experience in peer learning and show-cased replicable good practices and aired the message to develop sustainable development models in different sectors like agriculture, animal husbandry, watershed management, and service sector. By focusing on sustainable developmental models and bringing to light unnoticed initiatives at the grassroots level, the programme has opened up more creative ways to address the local issues in a media landscape, presently filled with sensationalised and exaggerated stories. It also tells us the importance of decentralisation and the 'principle of subsidiarity' in Indian planning, which suggests that many of the local level issues can be identified and solved at the local level itself.

There is no doubt that GKE is a bold and significant initiative in the landscape of governance in Kerala, which for the first time, dedicatedly and sincerely tried to bring in the mediated representations of the local governance in Kerala, a much discarded entity in the media framework of contemporary Kerala. Moreover, it has also, as discussed, brought out the importance of convergences and integration between and among departments for a meaningful and collaborative democracy. Doordarshan with its unique positionality as a channel with credibility, information oriented reporting, and pro- poor and pro-rural based coverage of the programmes, through telecasting GKE, has brought the relevance of PSB back into discourse. GKE, though was successful in bringing out the unnoticed and non- reported successful grassroots level interventions in the Kerala mediascape, was not effective in activating the debates on these movements in the public sphere. In today's space of the industrialisation of culture, the luring world of consumerism has been shaping the policy and agenda of the media itself. Circulation figure, and not social sensitivity, has become the yardstick for rating media. This, in fact, is only reflecting the changes in attitude and behavioural patterns of the Kerala society that has accelerated its pace towards consumerism. The content of the media is fine-tuned to cater to this new consumerist society. Public sphere today, as Habermas (1989) argues, exists now only as a promise. Party politics and the manipulation of the mass media have resulted in 'a "refeudalization" of the public sphere, where representation and appearances outweigh rational debate' (Holub, 1991) and where the rational–critical public is transformed into a mass, manipulated by persuasive authority. The public sphere has been undermined by, among other factors, class biases in criteria of admission, the expansion of an interventionist state, new techniques of opinion management and a loss of institutional meeting places.

'This refeudalization of the public sphere turns the latter into a theatre and turns politics into a managed show in which leaders and parties routinely seek the acclamatory assent of a depoliticized population' (Thompson, 1990). People have become suspicious of those who speak in the name, or interest, of the public (Robbins, 1990)–as indeed, they may have of all metanarratives (Lyotard, 1984). Kerala mediascape is not effective in activating the debates on any development interventions or grass roots movements,either at the macro or at the micro levels in the public sphere.

Chapter 7

Post-PPC: Democratising the Local Governance in Kerala

COVID-19 confined my space to the indoors of my flat in Mumbai, where I was happy with my family but extremely disturbed with the COVID-19 protocol. So when the Airlines restarted their schedules, we were one of the first to air-dash to Kerala. The security man of the housing complex in Mumbai asked me why I was taking the risk, since the number of reported COVID-19 cases in Kerala at that point of time was high, whereas the incidence of COVID-19 in Maharashtra was less. I had no convincing answer. My priority was to reach my home in those days of absolute uncertainty on all fronts.

The Pandemic didn't just turn our lives topsy-turvy; it threw our lives into a turbine that we lost our direction, didn't know whether we were moving forward or backward or getting pushed down or being pulled up. The virus ran wild. Death ventured into any place of its choice. Even death was shrouded in the COVID-19 protocol. Wrapped up bodies were dumped into pits since the dead didn't speak. With the society fragmented into containment zones, hot spots, and quarantine centres, and individual spaces redefined through social distancing, and individual identity camouflaged through masks, the social beings were forced to become floating islands in the ever threatening uncertainties of the pandemic. Most importantly, COVID-19 broke the social chain Kerala had painstakingly built through decades of progressive socializing, thanks to the reformation movements and the spread of Communist philosophy, though Kerala was and, to a great extent, is basically a society with the feudal moorings.

One of the factors that helped the Kerala society to inch through the unknown tracks, mired in death-traps, without doubt, was the effective functioning of the local self- governments having a dynamic interface with dedicated civil society and a committed bureaucracy. The timely intervention of the Kerala government—the first State in India to declare complete lockout—the active and functional local governance system, and the civil society engaging in social citizenship had begun their efforts to decelerate the pace of the growth of the pandemic, causing the curve to flatten, with more than two dozens of international media reporting the unbelievable success of Kerala in arresting the menace. Maharashtra, by that time, had become the hottest hot spot in India with the State government groping in the dark, mainly because the delivery system at the grassroots level was neither efficient nor effective .If it was the experience and expertise of the local governments, gathered through the decentralised governance that enabled them to make conspicuous and significant contributions to the service delivery mechanisms in Kerala, the credit, primarily, should go to People's Plan, which made a visible change in the decentralisation phase of Kerala and survived four regime changes, while remaining, essentially, intact.

In the international decentralisation literature, this fact alone sets the Kerala experience apart. The PPC created an environment that made it politically inexpedient to undermine decentralisation. As for the three great Fs of decentralisation—devolution of funds, functions, and functionaries— Kerala has not slid back. The total outlay for the Local Self Government Institutions in the Kerala Budget which had been Rs. 679 crore during 2015- 16 was enhanced to Rs. 12074 crore in 2020-21, increasing the outlay from 24% to 25.93% (Issaac, 2020).

The celebrated public health system in Kerala was in grave crisis by the 1990s due to decline in public health expenditure, resulting in marginalisation and inequitable infrastructure in the health sector and causing a hike in the infant mortality rate from 12 in 1997 to 15 in 2006. But an effective intervention of the local governance helped in reviving the public health system in Kerala. This is evident in the steep rise in the percentage of people using government medical facilities— from 34 % in the 71st round of NSSO to 48% in the 75th round of NSSO. Needless to say, it was the legacy of a deep rooted system of local governance, among other factors, that helped to arrest the spread of COVID-19 in Kerala.

The first social casualty of any pandemic is the loss of humane face. History is abound with such dreadful inhuman faces where the affected are left to struggle for life without medicine or care and thrown to burial pits before they are clinically dead till a Damien or a Florence Nightingale braved in and breathed in semblance of humaneness in the society, most of the time sacrificing her/ his life in the mission.

However, there was no need for one or two humanists to brave into the COVID-19 –stricken psyche of Kerala society. The well- oiled machinery of local governance, wrought by the multi-faceted interventions of People's Plan and the People Plan Campaign, took the challenge. While the migrant labourers in many states in India had to walk hundreds of kilometers, barefooted, with or without their nuclear family, including, in some cases, pregnant women or infants, to reach their home villages, the condition of migrant labourers in Kerala was different. There were agencies to make regular supply of essential commodities to the places where they were staying in groups, and when the Indian railway deployed rail service to their home lands, government agencies and voluntary groups supplied them food packets and drinking water to make them safe during the journey.

Despite being the first state in the country hit by COVID-19, right from the beginning the mortality rate of the pandemic was the lowest in Kerala. Before the COVID-19, Kerala witnessed two disasters- Nipah virus and the floods, both in 2018. The lived experiences of both these unexpected disasters helped Kerala to learn the system of contact tracing, which involves identification, isolation, and aggressive monitoring strategies. In both these disasters, active and responsive local governments enabled Kerala to proactively respond to the needy due to their proximity to the lives of people, which positioned them as efficient interlocutors of service delivery. These effective mitigation interventions of the local governments were duly recognised by the state government, and Kerala government initiated a community oriented disaster management plan in the annual plan budget of the local governance in 2020. LSGIs prepared the inventory list of the human resources at the local level, especially the survivors of the disasters, and their lived experiences were tapped in for the identification of the vulnerable communities and for delivery of the mitigation services. This prior experience of the inventorisation helped the local governance in furthering and expanding the document list with the health facilities like – ventilators, ICUs, X- ray machines- available at the local level. More than 800 out of the 1000 local governments have this information with them. Besides, emergency teams at the local level were also identified by the local governments with their contact details. The home quarantine activities of the State were monitored by the rapid response teams under the supervision of nearly 20,000 ward level committees of the local self-governments.

The spectacular intervention of Kudumbashree during the COVID-19 becomes politically and socially significant here. Kudumbashree, as discussed earlier in chapter four, is an offshoot of the PPC, and could be described as subaltern counter publics that facilitate gendered citizenship towards a deeper and fuller participation in governance issues. Kudumbashree started nearly 1.9 lakhs Whatsapp groups among nearly 3 lakhs NHGs for information dissemination of COVID-19-related issues. All the important decisions taken at the state/ local governance level regarding the pandemic interventions were disseminated to the households using the Whatsapp groups formed specifically for the mitigation interventions. Kudumbashree also effectively redesigned its thematic NHG groups – NHGs for the elderly, NHGs for the physically and mentally challenged, NHGs for the Destitutes— and incorporated specific interventions to address the needs and requirements of each group. Counseling sessions were given to the stressed; on line interactive and entertainment sessions/ competitions were planned for balasabahs (informal forum of children) that benefited children who are mostly affected by the house confinements, and regular visits and health check- up of the elderly were done by the trained health volunteers (santhwanam) of the Kudumbashree network. Kudumbashree through its network of local women resource persons present in all nooks and corners of the state responded to 1.54 lakh destitute families, worked with 1.14 lakh elderly people, the most vulnerable groups with co-morbidity during COVID-19. Kudumbashree designated 2,176 resource persons, who contacted the vulnerable communities once in five days and covered 95% of such vulnerable people in the State.

Another important intervention that still continues is providing cooked food to the needy through community kitchens (free food) and Janakeeya hotels/budget hotels (food at affordable rates) in rural and urban areas. These food chains of Kudumbashree are a remarkable way of institutionalising the food supply to the neediest in the COVID-19 times, especially to the migrant labourers and the destitute families in the State. It could be stated categorically that the interventions of Kudumbashree is one of the reasons for the Kerala state interventions to be acclaimed as effective with care and compassion in one of the most depressing times in history.

Kudumbashree as a CBO is working under the aegis of their respective units of local governance and this synergy with the LSGIs is one of its unique features, which brings back the active welfaristic role of the state in the development discourse. Thus Kudumbashree could be viewed both as a framework of analysis and methodology for assessing political changes with gendered lens in the post pandemic times. This phase of the care economy where Kudumbashree can take the leadership role can help it make the market speak about compassion and care, along with money, an unusual language but very apt for a state like Kerala, which was highly acclaimed for the public actions and social reforms that always tried to deconstruct the power centres.

Decentralisation has led to very tangible changes in infrastructure and institutional practice, setting conditions of possibility for expanding and deepening the democratic spaces towards that. It is true that the local governance could be pressed into service and the trained volunteers could spring to action during unforeseen contingencies and calamities, and the credit should definitely go to the PPC that churned the social psyche to be proactive. But when you consider the long standing, systematic, and systemic efficiency and functionality of People's Plan and the PPC in creating a sustainable, responsive, and deepening platform of decentralisation, devolution of power, and democratisation of power spaces, one cannot look askance at the much trumpeted achievements of the PPC.

In the consumerist world of Kerala, there are at least three visible processes that hamper the effective dissemination and implementation of the basic idea of the PPC. First of all, there is an emerging and a more encompassing consumerist ethics, where shopping, buying and consuming are the main ways of expressing oneself and one's identity. Moreover, the processes of globalisation and intensification of economic competition make people a-critical and a-reflexive, the norms best suited for the consumerist ethics (Stein, 1998). Equally important is the commodification and commercialisation of society. Individuals who are embedded in society in such a minimal way are unlikely to be politically active, engaging and socially responsible, the much needed requirements for decentralised and participative governance.

The second social process that threatens participation is the changing priorities of the media. Commercialisation process has penetrated the media, and the informative function is further undermined by the fact that emotions sell more. This *Diana-syndrome* where media dramatise and enlarge happenings in such a way that emotions like compassion, sadness, and joy become massified, the socially sensitive message of the PPC that lacked the emotional appeal and could not have been dramatised, did not hook the interest of either media or people.

The third is the mediasation of politics. Politicians are confronted with the consumerist ethics, commercialization, and a press hungry for superficial but hard selling news (Mazzoleni, 1999). Politicians adapt themselves to the media and its consumerist rules because they are partly dependent on votes. Form supersedes content, proving McLuhan right, where superficial and easy to apprehend messages become the norm of the day. Meaningful questioning of government actions by legislative members, serious debates on differences in developmental projects, and truthful accounts of ongoing political and development processes in panchayats did not fit into this flippant scheme.

Politics has become a drama and fun to look at; a soap series acted passionately, and consumed passively.

There is no magic formula for injecting participation into projects or communities. It must come from within. Power over implies understanding both the condign and conditioned power and thereby opening up access to the processes that lead the marginals to perceive themselves as 'capable' and entitled to occupy that decision-making space, and to exercise their agency in that 'democratic space' and so overlaps with the other categories of 'power to' and 'power from within'. To conclude, the social apparatuses created by the State during the process of decentralisation to devolve power, at the best, can be termed as the trappings of power in the lacings of devolution.

Embedded in a web of power relations and consumed by the anxieties about their own marginalities and the legacies of their past neglect, the marginals internalise the hegemonic values and pernicious norms into their cognitive, emotional and psychic systems and structures. Once embedded in their psyche, internalised hegemony conditions their desires. To maximise satisfaction of their desires, then, would be to collaborate in their own marginalisation. But the hegemony of power is such that even the counter-hegemonic desires are fashioned and designed by the hegemonic power. Most often this happens in an unconscious way as the hegemony of the power is strongly internalized by the marginals and paradoxically, the more completely they fulfill these desires, the worse off they become, a dangerous viciousness of the power.

I would like to end the book by quoting a powerful and insightful anecdote shared by a grassroots woman worker in Maharashtra during one of the programmes held by Manila Rajsatta Andolan (an NGO working with grassroots women on local governance)

*"We are the chosen few to ride the boat of decentralisation through the troubled waters of power politics to reach the island of power.It isa new boat with a forward-facing rowing facility.*The moment the great journey was declared inaugurated, we placed our oars in the oarlocks and pushed the water backward to take the boat forward. As the backwash created swashes, those on the land clapped and cheered us. It was a great moment of pride, joy, and confidence for us.

After days and months of rowing— we knew we had to go a long distance to reach the island of power— some of us pointed out that we had not moved an inch. It was unbelievable though, by this time, everyone was convinced what they had said was true. We didn't understand what went wrong? Was it our inexperience in rowing? Didn't we hold the oars correctly? A few of our friends dropped the oars in the water and jumped into the water and began to swim in their earnest attempt to reach the island of power. As we continued rowing without any progress, we saw some of our friends drowning and disappearing into the translucent layers of water. A few others were still swimming, braving the waves and oblivious of the undercurrents. Will they make it? Or will they too vanish into the blue? Did the dead see anything more than we had seen? Will those who are still swimming see anything more than the dead had seen? Who is better positioned; the dead, the struggling warriors, or we, who are on board?

We know the boat wouldn't move an inch. We know its keel is tied to the ground using an invisible chain we could never break. We are tired. Our sweat may, one day, flood the river. We are rowing…"

In the end, still it is the Power.

References

Achutha Warrier, S.: "Kerala Samsakaram", (Malayalam), Kerala Bhasha Institute, Kerala, 2008.

Ahlbäck, A.J.: "Mobilizing Rural People in Tanzania To Tree Planting - Why And How", Voluntary Paper Accepted For The XI World Forestry Conference, Antalya, Turkey, 1996.

Allen T. & A. Thomas (Ed.): "Poverty and Development In The 1990s, Oxford University Press, Oxford, 1992.

Altekar, A.S.: "State and Government In Ancient India", Motilal Banarasidass Publications, Banaras, 1955. Althusser, L: " Ideology and The State In Lenin And Philosophy", Verso, London, 1971.

Apte, V.M: "History and Culture of Indian People: The Vedic Age", Bombay, 1960.

Arnold, J.E.M.: "Community Forestry: Ten Years in Review", Community Forestry Note 7, Rome, FAO, Italy, 1992.

Aziz, A. and Arnold David (Ed): "Decentralised Governance in Asian Countries", Sage Publications, New Delhi, 1996.

Aziz A.: "Decentralised Planning: The Karnataka Experiment", Sage Publications, New Delhi, 1993.

Bagdikian, Ben H : "The Media Monopoly", Beacon Press, 1990.

Bardhan, Pranab And Dilip Mookherjee: "Capture And Governance at Local And National Levels", *American Economic Review*, 90 (2), 2002.

Baudrillard, Jean:" Simulacra and Simulation", University of Michigan Press, US, 1994.

Beauvoir De, Simone: "The Second Sex", Harmondsworth, Penguin, 1952.

Beauvoir, Simone De, Second Sex, Vintage Books, USA, 1949.

Berrigan, F.: "Access: Some Western Models of Community Media", UNESCO, Paris, 1977.

Berrigan, F.: "Community Communications: The Role of Community Media in Development", UNESCO, Paris, 1979.

Bharathy, Manjula: " Towards Globalisation of Television: Causes and Consequences", M.Phil. Thesis, J.N.U, 1992.

Bharathy, Manjula: "Voices from the Spiral of Silences", International Seminar on Democratic Decentralisation, Kerala, 2001.

Bharathy, Manjula: Decentralised Planning in Kerala, Unpublished Ph.D. Thesis, MCRC, New Delhi, 2002.

Bharathy, Manjula: "Thoray Report – Planning for A People Centered Future", Jamsetji Tata Trust, Bombay, 2007.

Bharathy, Manjula: "Feminisation of Invisibility and the Politics of Presence: Samatha SHGs in The People's Planning Campaign of Kerala", *The Indian Journal of Social Work*, Volume 71, Issue 4, 2010.

Bharathy, Manjula: "Negotiating the Politics of Presence: Engendering Governance in Maharashtra", Research Report, The Hunger Project, New Delhi, 2010.

Bharathy, Manjula: "From Objects to Subjects to Participants: Women and Gendered Governance in Kerala's participatory Democracy" in *Learning Citizenship by Practicing Democracy*, by Elizabeth Piinington and Daniel Schugurensky (eds.). Canada: Cambridge Scholars, 2010.

Bharathy, Manjula: "With and Against: Engendered Governance and Citizenship in Loal Democracy in Bihar, Rajasthan amd Karnataka", Research Report, Agaaz and Royal Norway Embassy Project, New Delhi, 2011

Bharathy, Manjula: " Intersubjectivity To Consensus: Engendering Local Governance in Bihar: in Traversing Bihar, (Ed) Manish Jha & Pushpendhara, Orient Blackswan, New Delhi, 2012.

Bhargava, B.S: "Grass-Root Leadership in Panchayati Raj Institutions", New Delhi, 1979

Bhatanagar, S: "Rural Local Government in India", Light and Life, New Delhi, 1978.

Biswas, Ajith: "Central Plan and its Regional Implications", Semianr Paper at Centre for Studies at Social Sciences, Culcutta, 1993.

Biswas, S. K.: "Forest Administration in India", Chugh Publications, Allahabad, 1988.

Blair, H: "Participation and Accountability at the Periphery: Democratic Local Governance in Six Countries", *World Development* 28 (1): 21–39, 2000.

Bodley, John: "Tribal Peoples and Development Issues: A Global Overview", Mayfield Publishing Company, California, 1988.

Bose, N. K.: "Integration and Secularism", In K. S. Singh (Ed), *The Tribal Situation in India*, Simla: The Institute of Advance Study, India, 1972.

Bose, N.K: "Selections from Gandhi", Navajeevan, Ahmedabad, 1948.

Bourdieau, P: "Outline of a Theory of Practice", Cambridge University Press, Cambridge, 1976.

Bradley, S.M.: "How People Use Pictures, An Annotated Bibliography and Review for Development Workers", IIED, London, 1995.

Brydon, L., and S. Chant: "Women in the Third World: Gender Issues in Rural And Urban Areas", Rutgers University Press, New Brunswick, 1989.

Butcher, Mellissa: "Transnational Television, Cutural Identity and Change:When STAR came to India", Sage Publications, New Delhi, 2003.

Casebiar Allen and Janet Casebiar: "Social Responsibilities of The Mass Media", University Press of America, Washington, 1992.

Cernea, Michael (Ed.): "Putting People First – Sociological Variables in Development Projects", Johns Hopkins Press, Baltimore, 1991.

Chakravarty: "A Note on The Structure of Multi-Level Planning For India" (Mimeographed) Planning Commission, New Delhi, 1972.

Channa, Subhadra: "Concept of the Mainstream", in Chaudhury, S. K. & Patnaik, S. M. (Ed) *Indian Tribes & Mainstreaming*, Rawat Publication, Jaipur, 2008.

Chathukulam, Jos And John M.S: "Five Years of Participatory Planning In Kerala: Rhetoric And Reality", *Economic And Political Weekly*, Vol. 37, No. 49, Kerala, 2002.

Chatterjee, Partha (Ed.): "Development, Plannning and the Indian State", Oxford University Press, 1997.

Chomsky, Noam: "Necessary Illusions: Thought Control in Democratic Societies". Pluto Press, 1989.

Collins Paul: "Decentralisation and Local Administration for Development In Tanzania", *Africa Today*, Vol. 21, pp. 15-25, Summer Issue, 1974.

Cooper, D.: "Power in Struggle: Feminism, Sexuality And The State", Open University Press, Buckingham, 1995.

Crook, R.C. And Manor J.: "Democracy And Decentralisation In South Asia And West Africa", Cambridge: Cambridge University Press, 1998.

Dahlerup, Drude. "Critical Perspectives on Gender and Politics: The Story of the Theory of Critical Mass.'' *Politics and Gender* 2, 511-521,2006.

Cruikshank, B.: "The Will to Empower: Democratic Subjects and Other Subjects', Cornell University Press, USA, 1999.

Danny Burns, Robert Humbleton and Paul Hogget: "The Politics of Decentralisation: Revitaliisng Local Democracy", The MacMillan Press Ltd, London, 1994.

Davis, A. : "Whither Mass Media and Power? Evidence for a Critical Elite Theory Alternative", Media, Culture and Society, 2003.

Dearing, James W and Rogers, Everett M.: "Agenda-Setting", Sage Publications Inc., New York, 1996.

Diaz Bordenave, J. (Ed.): "Participative Communication As A Part of Building The Participative Society", Sage, New Delhi, 1994.

Dube, R. H: "*Photoconductivity of Solids*", New York: Wiley, 1960.

Dubey, A. & S. Gangopadhyay: "Counting The Poor - Where Are The Poor In India?", Sarvekshana Analytical Report No. 1, Department Of Statistics, Government Of India, New Delhi, 1998.

Dubey, (Ed.) S.C.: Mass Media and National Development", University of Hawaii Press, Honolulu, 1976.

Dutta, B., M. Panda & W. Wadhwa: "Human Development in India - An Interstate Analysis", Mimeo, New Delhi, 1960.

Dutta, B., M. Panda & W. Wadhwa: "Human Development in India - An Interstate Analysis", Mimeo, New Delhi, 1960.

Escobar, Arthur: "Encountering Development: The Making And Unmaking of The Third World", Princeton University Press, Princeton, USA, 1995.

Fair, J.: "29 Years of Theory And Research on Media and Development: The Dominant Paradigm Impact", *Gazzette* 44,129-150, 1989.

Fairclough, N.: "Language and Power", Longman, London, 2001.

Ferguson, James: "The Anti-Politics Machine Development: Depoliticization, and Bureaucratic Power in Lesotho", Minneapolis, University Of Minnesota Press, 1994.

Feslar James W: "Centralisation and Decentralisation" In David L. Sills (Ed), 1968, *International Encyclopedia of The Social Sciences*, New York, Macmillan, p. 373, 1960.

Foucault, M.: "Governmentality" In Graham Burchell, Colin Gordon and Peter Miller (Eds.) in *the Foucault Effect: Studies In Governmentality*. Chicago, IL: University Of Chicago Press, 1991

Frank, Andre Gunder: "Capitalism and Underdevelopment in Latin America: Historically Studies of Chile and Brazil". New York: Monthly Review Press, 1969.

Freedman, M: "Martin Buber's Life and Work", Vols. I, II and III, New York: E. P. Dutton, 1983. Freire, Paulo.: "Pedagogy of Hope", Reliving Pedagogy of the Oppressed Continuum, Seaburg Press, New York, 1994.

Freire, Paulo.: "Pedagogy of The Oppressed", Seaburg Press, New York, 1983.

Freire, Paulo: "Cultural Action and Conscientisation", Harvard Educational Review, 1971.

Friedmann, J.: "Empowerment: The Politics of Alternative Development", Blackwell, Cambridge, 1992.

Gadgil, R.: "District Devlopment Planning", Gokhale Institute of Politics and Economics, 1967.

Galbraith, Kenneth: "Anatomy of Power", Houghton Mifflin Harcourt, Boston, USA, 1983

Gandhi, M. Das: "Harijan", November 1937.

Ganesh, K. N: " Kunjan Nambiar: Vakkum Samoohavum", (Malayalam), Sukapuram, Vallthol Vidyapeedam, Kerala, 1996.

Garnsey, E: "The Rediscovery of the Divisions of Labour. Theory and Society", (10): 337, 1981.

Ghai, D.: "Participatory Development: Some Perspectives from Grassroots Experience", United Nations Research Institute for Social Development, Discussion Paper 5, 1994.

Ghurye,G.S: "The Scheduled Tribes", Popular Prakashan, Bombay, India, 1963.

Giddens, A: "*Runaway World: How Globalization Is Reshaping Our Live*", Profile Books, London, 1999.

Gore, M.S.: "Some aspects of social development", Department of Social Work, University of Honkong, Honkong, 1973.

Gramsci, A.: "Selections from the Prison Notebooks", Lawrence and Wishart, London, 1971.

Guha, Ramachandra, and M. Gadgil: "State Forests and Social Conflicts in British India: Past and Present", A Journal of Historical Studies, 1989.

Guha, Ramachandra: "Adivasis, Naxalites and Indian Democracy", *Economic and Political Weekly* 42 (32) 3305–12, 2007.

Guha, Ramachandra: "India after Gandhi: The History of the World's Largest Democracy", Harper Collins, India, 2007.

Gulati, I.S.: "Panchayati Raj and Development", Thomas Nedumkallel Memorial Lecture, Nirmala College, 1994.

Habermas, Jurgen (Ed.): 'Struggles for Recognition in the Democratic Constitutional State' In Multiculturalism, Amy Gutman. Princeton: Princeton University Press, 1994.

Habermas, Jurgen: "Structural Transformation of the Public Sphere", Cambridge, Mass: MIT Press, 1989.

Hall, S. and Jacques, M. (Eds.): "New Times: The Changing Face of Politics in 1990s", London, 1989.

Harris John, Kristian Stokke, Olle Tornquist (Eds): "Politicising Democracy: Local Politics and Democratization in Developing Countries", Palgrave MacMillan, London, 2004.

Harris, John: "Depoliticizing Development: The World Bank and Social Capital", Left Word, New Delhi, 2001.

Harriss, John: Depoliticizing Development: The World Bank and Social Capital, Anthem Press, London, 2002.

Heller, P: "Reinventing Public Power in The Age Of Globalization: The Transformation Of Movement Politics In Kerala" in R. Ray, & M. Katzenstein (Eds.), *Social Movements in India: Poverty, Power and Politics*. New New York: Rowman and Littlefield Publishers Inc, 2005.

Heron, John And Reason, Peter: "A Participatory Inquiry Paradigm", *Qualitative Inquiry*, 3 (3), 1997.

Holub, C. Reobert: "Jurgen Habermas: Critic in the Public Sphere", Routledge, USA, 1991.

Iqbal Narain: "Panchayati Raj Administration: Old Controls And New Challenges", Indian Institute of Public Administration, New Delhi, 1970.

Isaac Thomas, T.M. & Richard Franke: "Local Democracy And Development: People's Planning For Decentralised Planning In Kerala", Left Word, New Delhi, 2000.

Isaac Thomas, T.M.: "People's Planning – Towards A Handbook", Paper Presented At The Workshop Organised By State Planning Board, Tripura, 2001.

Isaac Thomas, T.M: "People's Planning – Towards a Handbook", Trivandrum State Planning Board, 2000.

Isaac Thomas: "Celebrating 24 Years of People's Plan in Kerala", *The Indian Express*, July 23, Kerala, 2020.

Jahan, Rounaq: "The Elusive Agenda: Mainstreaming Women In Development", Zed Books, London, 1995.

Jain, Sugan Chand: "Community Development And Panchayati Raj In India", Allied Publishers, New Delhi, 1967.

Jankowski, N. : 'Reflection On The Origins And Meaning Of Media Access'. Kennedy, T. W.: "Beyond Advocacy: An Animative Approach to Public Participation", Dissertation, Cornell University, 1984.

Jayal, Niraja Gopal: 'Introduction: Local Governance in India: Decentralization and Beyond", by Pradeep Sharma, Niraja Gopal Jayal Amit Prakash. New Delhi: Oxford University Press, 2009

Jazairy, Idriss, Alamgir,Mohiuddin, and Panuccio,Theresa: "The State Of World Rural Poverty: An Inquiry Into Its Causes And Consequences", New York University Press, New York,1992.

Jeffrey, Robin: "India's Newspaper Revolution ", Oxford University Press, Delhi, 2002.

Jo Rowlands: "Empowerment Examined", Development and Social Diversity, Introduced By Mary B. Anderson A Development In Practice Reader, Oxfam (UK And Ireland), 1998.

Kabeer, Naila: "Reversed Realities: Gender Hierarchies in Development Thought", New York: Verso, 1994.

Khan, Joseph: "International Lenders' New Image: A Human Face". *The New York Times*, 2000.

Katzenstein, Mary Fainsod: "Comparing The Feminist Movements Of The United States And Western Europe: An Overview", In Mary Fainsod Katzenstein And Carol Mcclurg Mueller, Eds., *The Women's Movements of The United States And Western Europe: Consciousness, Political Opportunity And Public Policy*, Philadelphia, Temple University Press, 1987.

Keane, John: " The Media and Democracy", Polity Press, Cambridge, UK, 1991

Khan, Akhter Hamid: "Ten Decades of Rural Development: Lessons Learnt From India", Department of Agricultural Economics, Michigan State University, 1978.

Khushu, O.P.: "Satellite Communications in Asia, An Overview", *Media Asia*, Vol. 20, No.1, 1993.

Kuper, Adam: "The Invention of Primitive Society", Routledge, London, 1988.

Laclau, E. And Mouffe, C.: "Hegemony and Socialist Strategy", Verso, London, 1985.

Lewis, P. (Ed.): "Alternative Media: Linking Global and Local", UNESCO, 1993.

Lerner, D.: "The Passing of Traditional Society: Modernizing the Middle East", Free Press, New York, 1958.

Louw, E.: "Participative Media: Whose Agendas? Some Thoughts on The Practices of Funding Agencies And The Consequent Empowering of Factions", *PCR-Newsletter*, 1 (2), Fall, 1-3. 1993.

Luiz A.A.D: "Tribes of Kerala", Bharatiya Adimjati Sevak Sangh, New Delhi, 1962.

Lyotard, Jean-Francois: "The Postmodern Condition: A Report on Knowledge", Manchester University Press, Manchester, 1979.

Madathil, Sajitha: "Malayala Nadaka Sthree Charithram" (Malayalam), Kozhikode: Mathrubhumi Publishing House, Calicut, 2010.

Majumdar, D. N: "The Matrix of Indian Culture", Lucknow: Universal Publishers,1959.

Majumdar, D. N: "Races and Cultures of India", Bombay: Hindustan, India, 1958.

Majumdar, R.C.: "Corporate Life in Ancient India", Bharat Publications, Culcutta, 1918.

Malhan, P. and Uma Narula: "Communication Patterns In Slums", Indian Institute of Mass Communication, New Delhi, 1969.

Manaev, Oleg (Ed.): "The Alternative Press in A Transition Society In Peter Lewis Alternative Media, UNESCO, Paris, 1993

Manor, James: "Directions in Development: The Political Economy of Decentralisation", The World Bank, Washington DC, 1999.

Marshach and Marshach: " Centralisation and Decentraisation in Economic Organisations", *Econometrica*, 1959.

Mathew, G.: "Panchayati Raj: From Legislation to Movement", Concept Publishing Company, New Delhi, 1994.

Mathur, O.P.: "Planning For Districts: Some Problems in Developing A Conceptual Framework", *Prajnan*, Vol. II, No. 3, 1973.

Mathur, M.V. And Narain Iqbal (Ed.): "Panchayati Raj, Planning And Democracy, Asia Publishing House, Bombay, 1977.

Mattelart, Armand: "Mapping World Communication: War, Progress, Culture", Minneapolis: University of Minnesota Press, 2002.

Mazzoleni, Gianpieto And Schulz, Winfried: "Mediatization Of Politics: A Challenge For Democracy?", *Political Communication*, Volume 16, 1999.

Meenaskhi Sundaram, S.S: "Decentralisation in Developing Countries", Concept Publishing Co, New Delhi, 1999.

Melkote, S. :"Communication for Development in The Third World: Theory And Practice", Sage, New Delhi, 1991.

Menon-Sen, Kalyani: "The Problem: Towards Equality: A Symposium on Women, Feminism And Women's Movements". *Seminar* 505: 12-15, 2001.

Misra, B.B.: "District Administration And Rural Development In India", Oxford University Press, New Delhi, 1983.

Mohanty, B.B.: 'Development through People's Empowerment: Lessons from Rural Maharashtra, in Panchayati Raj Institutions and Rural Development", Lucknow, India, 1947.

Mohanty, Bidyut: "Women and Panchayats in India: Creating a New Space for Leadership in Asia, Rio de Janeiro, Brasil, UNESCO, 2005

Mohanty, Bidyut: "Women's Political Empowerment Day Celebrations on Panchayats", Women and Family Welfare, ISS, New Delhi, 1999

Molyneux, Maxine: "Mobilisation Without Emancipation? Women's Interests, The State and Revolution In Nicaragua". *Feminist Studies* 11, No. 2: 227-54, 1985.

Mookerjee, R.K.: "Local Government in Ancient India", Varanasi, 1958.

Moser, C.: "Gender Planning And Development: Theory, Practice And Training", Routledge, London, 1993.

Mowlana H And Wilson H: "Communication And Development: A Global Assessment Mulay, Sumati And Uma Narula: "Satiation In Family Planning Message Receptivity", UNESCO, Paris, 1987

Murdock, G: "Communications and the Constitution of Modernity", *Media, Culture and Society*. 15: 521 – 539, 1993.

Namboodhiripad, EMS: "Kerala Society and Politics", National Book Centre, New Delhi, 1984.

Narula, Uma And W.B. Pearce: "Development As Communication", Southern Illinois University Press, Illinois, 1986.

Nussbaum, Martha C: "Women And Human Development: The Capabilities Approach", Delhi: Kali For Women, University Press, Delhi, 2000.

Oates, W.E : "Fiscal Federalism", Harcourt Brace Jovanovich, New York, 1972.

Oommen, M.A.: "Reforms and the Kerala Model", Economic and Political Weekly, 43 (2), 2008.

Palit, S. (Ed.): "Indian Forest Departments In Transition, Village Voices, Forest Choices: Joint Forest Management In India", Oxford University Press, New Delhi, 1996.

Phillips, A.: "The Politics of Presence: The Political Representation of Gender, Ethnicity and Race", Clarendon Press, Oxford, 1995.

Pillai, Meena: "Gender And Development Report", Fourth International Congress on Kerala Studies, AKG Study And Research Centre, Kerala, India, 2016.

Pitkin, Hannah.: "The Concept Of Representation", Berkeley, .University of California Press,1967.

Poffenberger, M., B. Mcgean And A. Khare: "Communities Sustaining Indian's Forests in The Twenty-First Century, Village Voices, Forest Choices: Joint Forest Management In India. Oxford University Press, New Delhi, 1996.

Prasad, R.C.: "Democracy and Development: The Grass Root Experience in India, Rachna Prakashan, New Delhi, 1971.

Pyarelal: "Mahatma Gandhi: The Last Phase", Navajeevan, Ahmedabad, 1958.

Radha S &, Balu Roy Chowdhary, 'Women In Local Bodies', Discussion Paper No. 40, KRPLLD, CDS, Thiruvananthapuram, 2002.

Raghavan, G.N.S.: "Development Communication-Research Report," Indian Institute of Mass Communication, New Delhi, 1976.

Rai, Shirin: "Mainstraming Gender, Democratising the State? Institutional Mechanisms for Advancement of Women", Manchester, University Press, USA, 2003.

Raj, K.N: "Planning from Below with reference to District and State Planning", *Economic and Political Weekly*, Vol. 6, 1971.

Ramakrishnan, E.V: "Indigenous Imaginaries: Literature, Region, Modernity", Orient Blackswan, Hyderabad, 2017.

Ramanathan, Usha: "Public Purpose: Points for Discussion", In Walter Fernandes (Ed), *The Land Acquisition Amendment Bill 1998: For Liberalisation or for the Poor?,* New Delhi, ISI, 1999.

Rogers, E.M.: "Diffusion of Innovations", Free Press, New York, 1962.

Mehta, Ashoka: "Report of The Committee on Panchayat Raj Institutions, Ministry of Agricultrue and Irrigation, Government of India, New Delhi, 1978.

Rondinelli, D., McCullouch, J. S. and Johnson, R.W: "Analyzing Decentralization Policies in Developing Countries: A Political Economy Framework", *Development And Change* 20 (1): 57–87, 1989.

Lotherington; A.T., M. Haug, And A.B. Flemmen: "Implementation Of WID Policy", University of Oslo Center For Development And The Environment, Oslo, 1991.

Ruehl, S. (Ed.): "Sexual Theory And Practice: Another Double Standard", The Women's Press Limited, London, 1983.

Sahoo, A; "Global Indian Diaspora: History, Culture & Identity", Rawat Publications, New Delhi, 2008.

Santha, EK: "Local Self Government in Malabar, 1800-1960", ISS Working Paper Series OP-012, New Delhi, 1993.

Schramm, W.: "Mass Media and National Development", Stanford University Press, California, 1964.

Sreedhara Menon, A.: "Kerala Samskaram" (Malayalam), DC Books, Kottayam, Kerala, 2007 Sreedhara Menon. A "The legacy of Kerala", D C Books, Kottayam, Kerala, 2008.

Sreedhara Menon, A.: "Cultural Heritage of Kerala: An introduction Cochin: East - West, 1978.

Seemanthini, Niranjana: "Exploring Gender Inflections Within Panchayati Raj Institutions: Women's Politicization In Andhra Pradesh." *In The Violence Of Development: The Poltical Economy Of Gender*, By Karin Kapadia, 352-392. London, UK: Zed Books, 2003.

Seidman, S: "Contested Knowledge: Social Theory in the Postmodern Era", Blackwell, USA, 1994.

Sen, Amartya: "More Than 100 Million Women Are Missing." *New York Review of Books* 37 (December 20): 20, 1990.

Sen, Amartya: "*Social Exclusion: Concept, Application, and Scrutiny*", Social Development Papers No. 1, Office of Environment And Social Development, Asian Development Bank, 2000.

Shah, A., Thompson, T. And H. Zou: "The Impact of Decentralisation on Service Delivery, Corruption, Fiscal Management and Growth in Developing and Emerging Market Economies: A Synthesis of Empirical Evidence", CESIFO DICE Report Journal for Institutional Comparisons 2 (1): 10-14, 2004.

Shah, S. A.: "Status of Indian Forestry", Wasteland News, 1996.

Sherwood Frank P.: "Devolution As A Problem of Organisation Strategy", In R.T. Daland (Ed) *Comparative Urban Research*, Beverly Hills, Sage, 1969.

Singh, K. S: "The Scheduled Tribes", Vol. III, Anthropological Survey of India and Oxford University Press, Delhi, India, 1994.

Smith,B.C: " Bureaucracy And Social Power", Martins, New York, 1985.

Stein, Laura: "Democratic Talk, Access Television and Participatory Political Communication", Javnost - The Public, Volume 5, No 2, 1998.

Stiglitz, Joseph: "The Future of Global Goverannce", Oxford University Press, New York, 2008.

Tehranian, M. (Ed): "Development Theory and Communication Policy, The Changing Paradigm", in Progress In Communication Sciences, Norwood, Ablex, 1979.

Tehranian, M.: "Communication and National Development", London, 1978.

Thompson, J: " Ideology and Modern Culture: Cultural Social Theory in the Era of Mass Communication", Stanford University Press, USA, 1990.

Thomas, M.V.: " Madhyamangalum – Malayala Sahityavum",(Malayalam), Cultural Publications Department, Kerala, 2004.

UNDP Human Development Report, 2005.

Varis, T.: "Global Traffic in Television", *Journal of Communication*, Vol. 24 (1), 1974.

Varis, T: "The International Flow of Television Programs", *Journal of Communication*, Vol. 34 (1), 1984.

Verrier, Elwin: "Loss of Nerve: A Comparative Study of the Contact of Peoples in the Aboriginal Areas of the Bastar State and the Central Provinces of India, Bombay, 1941.

Vijayan, A and J. Sandhya: "Gender And Decentralised Planning in Kerala", Sakhi Women's Resource Centre, Thiruvananthapuram, 2004.

Visalakshi, N.R.: "Administration of Village Panchayats in Kerala", Trivandrum, 1967.

Wang, G. And W. Dissanayake: "Culture, Development, and Change: Some Explorative Observations", Ablex, New Jersey, 1994.

White, Peter B: "Online Services and 'Transactional Space': Emerging Strategies for Power and Control in the New Media", *Telecommunications Policy*, Volume 21, No 6, 1997.

White, R:"Contradictions in Contemporary Policies for Democratic Communication", Paper IAMCR Conference, Paris, 1982.

Woolf, Virginia: "A Room of One's Own", Hogarth Press, London, 1929.

World Bank: "Overview of Rural Decentralization In India. Volume III: Background Papers": World Bank, 2000.

William, Tordoff: "Decentralization: Comparative Experience in Commonwealth Africa", in *Journal of Modern African Studies*, Vol. 32, No. 4, 1985.

Index